Fine payable for Late Return:

D1080275

THE INSTITUTIONAL TRANSITION OF CHINA'S TOWNSHIP AND VILLAGE ENTERPRISES

To my husband Ximin Sun,
who understands, encourages, and supports. Always.

And to my beloved daughter
Xin

The Institutional Transition of China's Township and Village Enterprises

Market liberalization, contractual form innovation and privatization

HONGYI CHEN
California State University, Fullerton, USA

Ashgate

Aldershot • Brookfield USA • Singapore • Sydney

Published by
Ashgate Publishing Ltd
Gower House
Croft Road
Aldershot
Hants GU11 3HR
England

Ashgate Publishing Company
Old Post Road
Brookfield
Vermont 05036
USA

Ashgate website: http://www.ashgate.com

British Library Cataloguing in Publication Data
Chen, Hongyi
    The institutional transition of China's township and village
    enterprises: market liberalization, contractual form
    innovation and privatization. - (Ashgate studies on the
    economic reform of China)
    1. Producer cooperatives - China 2. China - Economic
    conditions - 1976-
    I. Title
    334.6'0951

1005303343

Library of Congress Catalog Card Number: 99-75453

ISBN 0 7546 1050 0

Printed and bound by Athenaeum Press, Ltd.,
Gateshead, Tyne & Wear.

Contents

List of Figures

List of Tables

Preface

1

The day I finished revising the manuscript of this book, I went to a nearby Chinese restaurant for a little celebration. When I opened the 'fortune cookie' after dinner, a small piece of paper fell out. It read: 'always keep old memories and young hopes.'

Always keep old memories and young hopes!

How many old memories do I have? How many young hopes do I hope? Tears came to my eyes.

I was born in Shanghai, China. When I was a teenager, I believed that the socialist system was the best economic system in the world, just as every Chinese teenager then believed. I had many, many beautiful dreams, just as every teenager has in this world. However, the 'Cultural Revolution' brought all my beautiful dreams down. I was sent to a small village in northeast China on the border between Russia and China. After eight years of living and working as an ordinary farm girl in that village, I learned what was 'rural China'. Hungry all year round, because the limited food supply was never sufficient to support a growing body; chilled to the bone in snowy and icy winter, because fuel was always scarce; sitting up all night in stormy summer, because our cabin (I could hardly call it a 'house') leaked…. A big question gradually took shape in my mind: can we call a system 'the best system' if it cannot provide the people living under it with a decent life?

With this big question in mind, I selected 'Economics' instead of 'Chinese Literature' (which I had loved since I was a little girl) to be my major when I finally got the opportunity to return to Shanghai and enter Fudan University after the 'Cultural Revolution'. I was eager to find out what was wrong with the centrally planned socialist system, and to learn what we should do to improve the life of a billion ordinary rural Chinese people, among whom I was now a member. After two years of boring and frustrating studies on socialist economic doctrines, however, I decided to skip the remaining undergraduate program. I passed nationwide exams and was admitted to be a graduate student majoring in 'Modern Western Economics'. (I am always grateful to the then Economics Department chair of Fudan University, Professor Xunhua Zhang. He not only allowed, but actually also encouraged

xi

me to make this decision.) Modern economics opened my eyes in searching for the answer to my question. I learned how private property rights and the free market system allocate resources to their most efficient usage, and how this system has substantially improved people's lives in the past century. I came to the conclusion that China needed an economic reform and, very fortunately, it was at that time that China did start her new era of economic reform.

After graduation, I became an instructor, teaching modern economics at Fudan University. For some years, I had believed this would be the best way to contribute to China's ongoing economic reform, but then I began to be unsure. In many cases, the orthodox economic theories seemed inapplicable to the phenomena observed in transitional China. They did not provide satisfactory solutions to problems facing the reform. My new search led me to the Ph.D. program of the University of California at Berkeley. It was at the Berkeley campus that I had the opportunity to take courses and to attend seminars and workshops offered by outstanding scholars like Professor Irma Adelman, Sherman Robinson, Pranab Bardhan, and Oliver Williamson, to mention a few. I gradually acquired knowledge in Development Economics and Institutional Economics, which made it possible for me to observe and understand China's economic reform at another level and from a new angle. When I reached the final stage of the Ph.D. program, I selected China's economic reform as my degree dissertation topic, which was fully backed by my dissertation advisor Professor Brian Wright and the dissertation committee members Professor Irma Adelman and Professor Thomas Gold. This present book, which is completed on the basis of that dissertation, is the fruit of my search in the past decades. I hope it will also serve as a new step in my contribution to the progressing economic reform in my beloved motherland – China. It is my hope that the hardworking Chinese people will at long last rid themselves of poverty and enjoy a much deserved prosperity as a result of this reform.

2

Despite the fabulous performance in economic development during her two decades of economic reform, China's economic achievements were often overshadowed by her slow movement in the political system reform. Interestingly, in the western academic world, literatures of transitional economics ignored China's experiences. It is probably because China had ignored the typical reform strategy of an early and rapid privatization suggested by western advisors. However, during the 1990s, China's transitional economy became a subject of broad interest for many economists, policy-makers, and international organizations, and led to debates well beyond the community of China research specialists. This interest is enhanced by China's obvious success in her sustained economic growth, as well as in her accomplishment in the move toward a free market system and property rights reform. Since China did not follow the 'sure path' to economic reform suggested by western advisors, her experiences raised a flood of questions. Why has China's transitional economy performed so differently from those of Eastern European countries and the former Soviet Union? What special condition(s) did China have that made it possible for her to adopt a seemingly unpromising strategy to result in a surprising achievement? What are the implications of China's success for policy and economic analysis regarding the transitional economies of Eastern Europe? This book is one among many efforts made by economists, sociologists, political scientists, and policy-makers to answer these questions.

China's economic reform began by decentralizing administrative control of micro-management institution and allowing micro-units to share part of the newly created profits so as to improve the micro-incentive mechanism as well as the productive efficiency. Subsequently, the resources allocation mechanism was reformed to meet the demands of the micro-units for a fair and more competitive operation environment. Free markets gradually emerged. What characterized China's reform differently from her Eastern European counterparts is that the reform of the macro-policy environment, especially the reform in property rights institutions lagged behind for a prolonged period. The central government of China had been hesitant to privatize property rights, private rights being one of the principle taboos in socialist ideology. It was at the grass-roots level, however, that property rights reform was initiated. The decentralized decision-making process and the increased autonomy of the micro-units resulted in changes in managerial organization of firms. Development of the market system meanwhile enhanced the organizational changes, which in turn accumulated into a fundamental reform in the property rights structure. Therefore, the property rights reform in transitional China is a bottom-up process driven by endogenous forces, rather than a top-down process imposed by exogenous policy design. It is this unique feature that has made China's grass roots agents the solid support and catalyst of property rights reform. The economic reform arising from and supported by the overwhelming majority of the population is irreversible.

   Taking China's township and village enterprises (TVEs) as example, this book provides an illustration of the realization of property rights reform through firm contractual form innovation. My whole research is based on a field investigation conducted in rural China in 1994, and a follow-up investigation conducted in the winter of 1998. The book begins with a brief description of the development of China's TVE sector in Chapter 1. It then turns to a discussion on China's rural organization and the property rights structure of collective TVEs in Chapter 2. The chapter also explains why community public ownership of collective TVEs was superior to both state-public ownership and private ownership in a transitional economy. Chapter 3 of the book documents the contractual forms that have been implemented in the TVE sector, their evolution and variations in the past decade. In Chapters 4 and 5, a theoretical analysis is applied in order to search for the factors that determine selection of contractual forms and evolution of contractual structure. Model simulations and hypothesis tests demonstrate that the development of the market system and the firm technical structure are crucial in determining and innovating contractual structure in the firms. The last chapter describes the model of endogenous economic reform. In this model, firm contractual form innovation plays a critical role in transforming the central government's partial reform efforts in market liberalization into a fundamental reform in property rights. The latter reform is completing the move from a centrally planned system toward a market system in China.

   While revising the manuscript, I considered omitting a large section of Chapter 2, which describes the community organization of rural China and the property rights structure of collective TVEs. This was because it is not directly related to the topic of the book – firm contractual form innovation. However, I retained this part after consulting my dissertation advisor Professor Brian Wright. As he pointed out, the readers of this book, western researchers in particular, may not be familiar with China's rural organization. This part will serve as a background description to help the readers to understand the institutional environment within which China's economic reform takes place.

3

I am greatly indebted to Professor Scott Rozelle of the University of California at Davis. It is he who has inspired me and helped me with his research expertise from the beginning to the end of my work. Without his generous and attentive advice in research topic selection, field investigation, analysis method design, and material tailoring, it would have been impossible for this book to be written.

I have profited immensely from the arduous, yet very inspiring Ph.D. program of the University of California at Berkeley. I learned a great deal from the distinguished faculty at the Department of Agricultural and Resources Economics. In particular Professor Irma Adelman, Brian Wright, Sylvia Lane, George Judge, David Zilberman, Alain de Janvry, Elisabeth Sadoulet. Their constant encouragement, comments, and suggestions have been invaluable toward the completion of this research.

I also benefited from the comments, criticisms, and suggestions I received at a number of academic conferences and seminars where I presented my research work, and from members of other institutions. My special thanks go to Margaret Maurer-Fazio, Yingyi Qian, Jiahua Che, Jean Oi, Albert Park, Michel Oksenberg, Kejiro Otsuka, Hehui Jin, Nobuhiko Fuwa, Jinhua Zhao, Susan Whiting, Vernon Ruttan, Bruce Reynolds, Cheng Hsiao, Justin Yifu Lin, James Guanzhong Wen, and Stewart Long.

I am grateful to Professor Gary Jefferson of Brandeis University. He reviewed the draft of my dissertation, encouraged me to revise it for publication, and recommended the manuscript to Ashgate Publishing. His suggestions helped me to successfully conduct a follow-up field investigation that effectively updated the information included in this book. My friend Dora Chen edited the book to make it more fluent and readable. My deep appreciation goes to her. The staff at Ashgate Publishing were superb in developing my manuscript into a publishable copy. I would like to thank Peter Nielsen, Anne Keirby, and Claire Annals for their very thoughtful and patient assistance. As always, the author is solely responsible for the views expressed and any mistakes contained in this book.

My very special thanks to two of my Chinese advisors, Professor Chengxian Song and Professor Pei-Kang Chang, who guided me to the study of Modern Economics in an academic environment where Socialist Economics dominated exclusively, and encouraged me to take rural development as my research field. I cannot describe the depth of my sorrow when Professor Song passed away early this year. He did not live long enough to see the publication of this book. I want also to thank the government officials and firm managers who gave their cooperation enthusiastically during my field investigation in rural China.

The scholarship of CEERC (Committee on Economics Education and Research in China)/Ford Foundation and the scholarship of the World Bank that enabled me to participate in the prestigious Ph.D. program at University of California at Berkeley are also acknowledged.

Series Editor's Preface

GARY JEFFERSON

With the publication of Professor Hongyi Chen's manuscript, *The Institutional Transition of China's Township and Village Enterprises*, Ashgate and I are delighted to introduce the new Ashgate Series on China's Economic Reform. This volume is an excellent starting point.

By now, we are all aware of the dramatic, albeit somewhat surprising, success enjoyed by China's rural township and village enterprises, at least through the first two decades of China's economic reform. Among China's major categories of enterprise ownership, township and village enterprises (TVEs) now account for the largest share of China's industrial output, surpassing the contributions of the once-dominant state sector and the fast-rising foreign-invested and domestic-private sectors

Most believe that the robust expansion of township and village ownership resulted from the decentralized nature of property rights that determine the governance structure of TVEs. Few, however, understand the actual details of the contractual arrangements that shape the incentives of local officials and managers whose behavior drives the performance of these rural enterprises. Through an refreshing and effective mix of theory, extensive on-site interviews, mathematical modeling, and econometrics, Professor Chen provides us with a clear account of the forces that are shaping the contracts used to specify the distribution of property rights between local government officials and TVE managers.

Using a transactions cost approach, Professor Chen models the bilateral negotiations that establish the distribution of property rights between local government officials, whose comparative advantage lies in managing the external environment of enterprises, and firm managers, who specialize in managing matters internal to the firm. External conditions, notably the completeness of various types of markets, alter the optimal distribution of property rights between managers and officials. As they evolve across localities and time, changing market structures are motivating revisions in basic contract forms. Building on prior literature, the model provides a more complete story about the processes of 'endogenous reform' and 'induced privatization' within China's economy.

As China enters its third decade of economic reform, the restructuring of China's enterprise system, including its heretofore-robust TVE sector, stands as one of the focal points. Professor Chen's analysis of the evolution of China's township and village enterprises belongs on the short list of material to be read and digested by anyone with a serious interest in the subject.

1 Introduction

'Township and Village Enterprises' (known as TVEs) is a new, but already familiar term in the research in recent years on China's economic reform and rural development. The prosperity of China's economy during the reform era, its swift and long sustained growth rate (about 10 percent per year for the past 20 years), and the substantial improvement in the living standards of more than one billion people, have made China's achievements spectacular. The achievements have been referred as the 'China miracle' by some authors. Such achievements cannot be ignored. Likewise, no one should ignore the TVE sector and its incredible contribution to China's rapid growth.

Growing out of rural grassroots communities like wild vegetables sprouting after spring rain, the TVE sector was not designed, and was certainly not supported in its early years, by the Chinese central government. The central government at first attempted to restrict the development of TVEs, suspecting them to be rivals who might compete against the state-owned sector for input resources and output markets. After recognizing the TVEs' role in absorbing rural surplus labor, the central government became supportive, but with significant reservations. Up until the late 1980s, the central government was not fully aware that TVEs had become the most dynamic and rapid growing part of China's economy. When Deng Xiaoping said in 1987[1] '......The most fabulous result that was completely out of our expectation is the development of township and village enterprises', he admitted that the astonishing achievement of the TVE sector which had not been launched by the central government was beyond the government's wildest expectations.

Very few observers could really understand the TVEs because of their extremely intricate ownership structure and organizational forms. The 'mystery' to many researchers was how an economic sector, which had neither clearly defined property rights nor strong support from government

---

[1] Cited from Gao, Yinuo's article on *Economic Daily*, Beijing, China, June 13, 1993.

development strategy, could have played such an increasingly important role in a reforming economy. Economists, political scientists, and sociologists have exerted intensive efforts to explore ways and means to solve this 'mystery'. This book attempts to provide a comprehensive and consistent answer to explicate the why's and how's of TVEs' organizational structure leading this sector to become the driving force in China's economic growth.

As an introduction, this short chapter is divided into four parts. The first section briefly traces the fast development of the TVE sector and its role in China's economic growth. Section 2 presents an overview of the research focus of this book, which illustrates how the core concepts of institutional economics can be used to explain the structure of the TVEs contractual form and its evolution and variations. Section 3 describes the research design. The sources and methodologies used to accomplish the goals are demonstrated. The last section provides a short outline of the book as a whole.

1. TVE Sector and Its Role in China's Economic Growth

The TVE sector comprises four types of enterprises: township enterprises (Xiangban Qiye), village enterprises (Cunban Qiye), enterprises owned by joint rural households (Lianhu Qiye), and enterprises owned by single rural households or individuals (Geti Qiye).[2] It is a sector which has been growing at over 30 percent annually for the past 18 years and over 45 percent per year from 1990 to 1994.[3] In 1995, this sector had 22.03 million enterprises, hired 128.61 million employees, produced 6.9 trillion yuan of

---

[2] Some researchers refer to 'TVEs' only as collectively-owned township enterprises and village enterprises, *i.e.*, the first two categories of rural enterprises. However, according to China's Statistical Bureau, the four categories of enterprises are all included in the 'TVE sector'. So for a wider definition, TVEs include all rural non-agricultural enterprises; while a narrower definition of TVEs, which refers to the first two categories only, is also used very often. In this book, most of the time 'TVEs' stands for its general definition. I will use 'collective TVEs' to define the first two categories of rural enterprises.

[3] Calculation is based upon price-adjusted data of Gross Output Value from ZGXZQYNJ (China TVE Yearbook), China Agricultural Press, 1991, 1992, 1993, 1994, 1995.

gross output value.[4] Its gross output value of industry reached 5.1 trillion yuan, which accounted for 56 percent of national gross output value of industry.[5]

The TVE sector is not only the most rapidly growing sector in China's economy, it is also a sector that plays an increasingly important role in China's economic growth. As shown by Table 1.1, in 1978, this sector hired only 9.2 percent of rural labor and provided 7.0 percent of nationwide employment. However, in 1995, these figures rose to 28.6 percent and 18.9 percent respectively. Its gross output value of industry in 1978 accounted for less than 10 percent of the national gross output value of industry. After only 17 years, it produced 56 percent of national industry output in 1995. In a similar manner, this sector contributed only 4.2 percent of the total tax revenues in 1978, but this contribution reached 21.6 percent in 1995.

Since 1978, when rural economic reform began, the income of rural Chinese people has had a dramatic increase. This incredible income increase is not only the result of the replacement of household responsibility farming system to commune system, it is also due to the rapid spread of non-agricultural rural economic activities, particularly the development of rural enterprises. As reported by the Chinese Ministry of Agriculture (ZGXZQYNJ, 1994), in 1993, 64 percent of rural per capita net income increase was contributed by TVEs. Table 1.2 presents the income sources of rural households. In 1978, an average rural resident earned only 3 yuan of labor income from enterprises, which accounted for 3.4 percent of his total labor reward and 2.3 percent of his net income. By contrast, in 1996, an average rural resident earned 311.51 yuan of labor income from enterprises, which was 69.1 percent of his total labor reward and 16.2 percent of his net income. If we view rural households' non-agricultural business as enterprises' type income sources, then, the share of the combined income of household non-agricultural business and the labor income from enterprises in total net income increased from 6.1 percent in 1978 to 28.6 percent in 1996. Neither the significant contribution in output, employment, and tax revenue made to China's economy, nor the contribution made to the improvement of rural income by the TVE sector can be ignored. Without central government's initiation or encouragement, the TVE sector took only 8 years to increase its gross output value from 100 billion yuan to 1.1 trillion yuan, compared to the 31 years the state-owned sector took to arrive

---

[4] *China Statistical Yearbook,* China Statistical Press, 1996, page 387-391. In 1995, 1 US$ = 8.37 yuan.

[5] *China Statistical Yearbook,* China Statistical Press, 1996, page 389 and 403.

at the same increase.[6] According to the prediction of the National Conference on Township and Village Enterprises (Quanguo Xiangzhen Qiye Huiyi) held in September 1993, by the year 2000, the gross output value of TVEs will reach 7.6 trillion yuan, tax payment 750 billion yuan, and labor employment 150 million people. If this projection actually comes true, 50 percent of GNP will be contributed and 60 percent of non-agricultural labor will be hired by the TVE sector.

Rural enterprises that have grown out of rural grassroots units and residents become the most active part in a nation's economy as well as the key impetus of a nation's economic growth is a unique experience in the history of world economic development. In China's post-Maoist development, the export-oriented growth strategy seemed to be of less importance than her development of the TVE sector. In 1995, China's share of world trade was 2.6 percent.[7] Considering that China has a population of nearly one fifth of the world's population, this is not such a spectacular share, though its volume of trade has been increasing rapidly since the early years of the reform era. In this sense, China has been unique among her surrounding Asian nations too. Lack of capital investment and human resources might have been the major obstacle that prevents an agricultural economy from industrialization. This is particularly true in a large, poor, and densely populated country like China, where more than 80 percent of its population lived in rural areas and concentrated on agricultural production. The small urban industrial sector was unable to absorb rural surplus labor, which was rapidly released due to the rural economic reform. A high rural unemployment rate could not only have constricted the country's economic growth to below its potential, but also led to social chaos. Under such circumstances, TVEs have efficiently utilized local resources to provide employment opportunities to rural surplus laborers. In this way, they turn seemingly unlimited rural labor at a cost barely above survival line into valuable outputs, supplement the state-owned industrial sector in the supply of domestic as well as world markets, and most importantly, increase rural incomes. The increase of rural income stimulates consumption demand, and greatly enlarges domestic markets. These are undoubtedly the major sources for fast economic growth.

---

[6] *Economic Daily*, Beijing, China, January 4, 1992.
[7] OECD: *Economic Outlook* (60), December 1996, page 127.

Table 1.1 Development of TVEs in China, 1978-1995

	1978	1980	1985	1990	1995
Number of TVEs (million)	1.5	1.4	12.2	18.5	22.0
Employees (million)	28.3	30.0	69.8	92.7	128.6
Employees/rural Labor (%)	9.2	9.4	18.8	22.1	28.6
Employees/national Employment (%)	7.0	7.1	14.0	16.3	18.9
Gross Value of Output (billion yuan)	49.5	66.5	275.5	958.1	6891.5
Gross Output Value of Industry (billion yuan)	38.5[*]	50.9[*]	182.7	605.0	5125.9
GOVI/national GOVI (%)	9.1	9.9	18.8	25.3	55.8
Taxes Paid (billion yuan)	2.2	2.6	13.7	39.2	130.2
Tax Payment of TVEs/Total Tax Revenue (%)	4.2	4.5	6.7	13.9	21.6

* Figures for township enterprises and village enterprises only.

Sources: ZGTJNJ (China Statistical Yearbook), 1990, 1991, 1992, 1993, 1994,
        1995,1996.
        ZGXZQYNJ (China TVE Yearbook), 1991, 1992, 1993, 1994, 1995, 1996.
        Ma, R. et al. eds. *Investigation on China's TVEs in 1990s,* Oxford
        University Press, 1994, p.7.

Table 1.2 Annual Per Capita Net Income and Its Constitution of Rural Households, 1978-1996 (yuan)

	1978	1980	1985	1990	1996
Per Capita Net Income	133.6	191.3	397.6	686.3	1926.1
Net Income by Sources					
Reward of Labor	88.3	106.4	72.2	138.8	450.8
From Enterprises	3.0	5.9	27.7	54.1	311.5
Household Business	35.8	62.6	296.0	518.6	1362.5
Agricultural[a]	30.6	53.4	255.7	445.2	1122.4
Non-agricultural[b]	5.2	9.1	40.3	73.4	240.0
Transfer and Property Income	9.5	22.4	29.9	29.0	112.8
Share of Enterprises Income in Labor Reward (%)	3.4	5.6	38.4	38.9	69.1
Share of Enterprises Income in Net Income (%)	2.3	3.1	7.0	7.9	16.2
Share of Enterprises Income and Household Non-agricultural Business Income in Net Income (%)	6.1	7.9	17.1	18.6	28.6

a. Agricultural Income includes incomes from Farming, Forestry, Animal Husbandry, Fishery, Gathering and Hunting.
b. Non-agricultural Income includes incomes from Industry, Handicraft, Construction, Transportation, Commerce, Food Services, Services Trade and Other.

Source: ZGTJNJ (China Statistical Yearbook), 1996, p.301; 1997, p.313.

2. TVEs' Organization and the Focus of the Research

The fact that the TVE sector has played an undeniable role in China's economic reform and growth poses questions regarding TVEs' organizational mechanisms such as: how are TVEs organized? Why are they growing so fast? What are the special characteristics Chinese rural communities have that make the swift proliferation of rural enterprises possible? Many researchers were puzzled when analyzing the organization of TVEs to discover that this sector was actually predominated by collectively owned enterprises rather than private enterprises.

As mentioned above, the TVE sector consists of four types of enterprises: township enterprises, village enterprises, joint-household enterprises, and private enterprises. The history of township enterprises and village enterprises can be traced back to the years of communization. They were born with the People's Commune as commune enterprises or brigade enterprises for the purpose of promoting agricultural mechanization, particularly following the 'Great Leap Forward' in the early 1960s. After the commune system was abolished by the rural economic reform in 1978, communes were replaced by townships and brigades by villages. Commune enterprises and brigade enterprises have since then been known as township enterprises and village enterprises. They are collective enterprises owned by all residents of the township or of the village, at least so *de jure*. The joint-household enterprises are owned by a group of rural residents, which can be viewed as semi-collective enterprises. Only the fourth type of enterprises is owned by private owners.[8] As we can see from Table 1.3, although private enterprises accounted for the majority in the number of enterprises in the TVE sector, they hired less employees than collective enterprises did, and produced less than 30 percent of the sector's output, *i.e.,* they were less important players in this sector.[9]

---

[8] There are various kinds of joint-ventures, such as township-foreign, village-foreign, private-foreign, collective-state owned, private-state owned, collective-other collective. etc., in this sector too. However, the officially published data does not include a special category for these enterprises. They are classified according to the status of the owner who owns the majority of the assets.

[9] However, this situation has changed, especially after 1994. In 1996, private TVEs accounted for 89.2 percent in enterprise number (only about 2 percent increase from 1994), but they hired 48.6 percent of TVEs' employees, which was a 7 percent increase from 1994. The gross output value data is not available after 1994. See ZGXZQYNJ (China TVE Yearbook) 1997.

Table 1.3 Constitution of TVEs, 1984-1994 (%)

	Township	Village	Joint-household	Private
Number of Firms				
1984	6.6	24.1	15.0	54.3
1987	2.4	6.6	6.8	84.2
1990	2.1	5.8	5.3	86.8
1994	2.3	6.5	4.2	87.0
Employees				
1984	36.1	40.4	10.0	13.5
1987	27.2	26.4	10.5	35.9
1990	25.2	24.4	8.8	41.6
1994	26.1	25.9	6.4	41.5
Gross Output Value				
1984	47.6	38.0	7.5	6.9
1987	38.4	29.5	9.0	23.1
1990	35.8	29.5	7.6	27.1
1994	35.0	32.6	5.8	26.7

Source: ZGXZQYNJ (China TVE Yearbook), 1993, 1994, 1995.

Researchers who view the property rights of township enterprises and village enterprises not clearly defined wonder why collective enterprises have better business performance and faster growth records than their private counterparts in this sector (Weitzman and Xu, 1994). It is believed in modern economics that a clear assignment of entitlement to productive resources and a well-forced rule of contract is the precondition of an effective market system. Failure in property rights assignment may damage a firm's efficiency and result in a lower growth rate. Therefore, in an economy where the reform effort has been made to replace centrally planning system with market system, one would reasonably expect private enterprises to outperform their collective counterparts rather than the opposite.

The seemingly anomalous performance of collective TVEs becomes a subject of intense research interest among economists (Che and Qian, 1998; Jefferson and Rawski, 1994b; Mckinnon, 1992; Putterman, 1994; Rawski,

1994; Sachs and Woo, 1994; Weitzman and Xu, 1994), political scientists (Cui, 1994; Oi, 1992, 1996; Pan, 1996), and sociologists (Nee, 1992; Peng, 1992; Walder, 1994, 1995a; and Whiting, 1995) in recent years. These researchers have predominantly directed their research efforts to explicate the nature of ownership of the collective TVEs. They hope that such explication would offer valid explanations that may relate collective TVEs' superior performance to their ownership structure. Some authors using an all-embracing term have begun to refer to all collective enterprises (whether located in urban or rural areas) and private enterprises as the 'non-state sector' (Sachs and Woo, 1994), and view collective enterprises as 'semiprivate' or 'hidden private' firms (Liu, 1992; Peng, 1992). This is to explain their economic behavior that differs from that of firms with state ownership. Some others confirm that collective TVEs are public firms with public ownership, but emphasize the effect of the government's reform policies on firm performance. They argue, when the economy is under reform, the government's partial reform efforts in market liberalization (especially product markets) have exposed firms to market competition, and the competition should give firms incentives to improve their efficiency (Jefferson and Rawski, 1994b; McMillan, 1994; Naughton, 1994b). Another factor they argue is the government's reform efforts in taxation system, which has led to government officials' entrepreneurial behavior. It is believed that such behavior is inspired by revenue incentives and has resulted in improved performance of the firms (Byrd and Lin, 1990; Oi, 1992, 1996; Whiting, 1995).

While these explanations contain elements of truth about the changing incentives and constraints facing firms and governments that may improve firms' performance, they may also be misleading in some dimensions. The first argument ignored the essential fact that though community public ownership does differ from state ownership, however, it is still public ownership, and not in any way private ownership. However, the two types of ownership are not identical. The competition argument implied that the property rights of the firm were not as important in explaining the firm's performance as the market competition. If this is true, then the firm's performance must be explained in a more consistent way. The observations have revealed that TVEs were still outperforming state-owned enterprises and private enterprises in the 1990s, even though all three kinds of enterprises were undergoing very much the same market competitive pressures during this period.

The most recent research work done by Walder (1995a) and Che and Qian (1998) have provided a coherent and internally consistent explanation regarding the rise of TVEs when the researchers recognize the *de facto* ownership of local community governments with respect to collective TVEs.[10] They confirmed that collective TVEs '*are under a form of public ownership no different from the large urban state sector, except that government has clearer incentives and a greater ability to monitor firms and enforce their interest as owners*' (Walder, 1995a, p.266). They view the local community government as a 'public entrepreneur', which has clearly defined property rights, hard budget constraints, and strong incentives to enforce improvement in efficiency in collective TVEs. In the meantime TVEs are treated as separate divisions, branches, or subsidiaries of a 'community corporation'. With such an organizational arrangement, the problem of weakened incentives, soft budget constraints, and inaccurate monitoring of information inhered in public ownership can be effectively reduced to an extent that will not severely damage firm efficiency.

As much as I agree with their arguments, I still do not feel the 'mystery' has been entirely solved. Walder, Che and Qian have not explicitly addressed the relationship between the community government leaders -- the *de facto* owner (or the principal) of the firm, and the firm managers (or the agents of the principal) who are in charge of the daily operation of the firm. Two problems remain unresolved. One is that the mechanism through which the community government as the *de facto* owner enforces the efficiency improvement of the firm is not clearly addressed. Even though one has sufficient reason to believe that community government leaders have incentives as well as abilities to enforce efficiency improvement, we still have to know *how* they do it. The second problem is closely related to the first one. In their arguments, community government property rights have been treated as a static structure, without an explicit explanation about how this structure adapts to the changing environment. In a transitional economy under economic reform, substantial alterations take place in the institutional environment within which economic entities operate. The existing property rights of a firm have to make certain responses to such environmental alterations in order to achieve desirable performance records or even just to survive. Therefore, I have narrowed my research from the ownership structure of collective TVEs to the contractual form structure of

---

[10] Also see Liu, Z et al. 1995. *Property Rights, Markets, and Development,* Jiangsu People's Press, China.

collective TVEs, *i.e.*, I turn my study focus from the commonly asked question of how the properties of the collective TVEs are owned to the question of how property rights in the collective TVEs are assigned. To my knowledge, no comprehensive research work has yet been done on this question.

My research, based upon an intensive field investigation conducted in rural China in 1994, is aimed at providing a general framework to explain the contractual structure of property rights and the evolutionary pattern of the organizational mechanisms of collective TVEs. I argue that when we view rural (township and village) community governments as public agents of local residents in their control of the operation of firms, the property rights of collective TVEs are unequivocally defined. Local government leaders under the pressure of institutional reform have strong incentives to launch and promote the development of TVEs (Oi, 1996; Whiting, 1995). At the same time, because of the dual role they play in rural community organization, they also have significant comparative advantage over private entrepreneurs to do so (Byrd and Lin, 1990; Naughton, 1996; Ody, 1992).

When both market and government are imperfect in a transitional economy, local community public ownership of collective TVEs is an organizational form superior to state public ownership as well as private ownership for a number reasons. This form is better than state public ownership, because it not only provides stronger incentives and harder budget constraints to firms, even more importantly, it enables the *de jure* owners of the firms to more effectively monitor the behavior of the agents who possess control rights over the firms. Local community public ownership is also better than private ownership. This is because when market is either absent or underdeveloped, the community governments' ability in securing property rights, gaining access to resources, and absorbing risks may effectively substitute or supplement market forces to support firms growth. In this sense, the superiority of local community public ownership comes from the fact that this form is able to combine local leaders' incentives with their comparative advantage to promote the growth of enterprises in their communities.

When markets gradually replace the central planning as a result of the government's partial reform efforts in market liberalization, the institutional environment changes. Such changes lead to institutional innovation, *i.e.*, the evolution in firm's managerial contractual form in the TVE sector. Firstly, local government leaders, as the *de facto* owners of collective TVEs, must find *their* agents to take over the daily management responsibilities previously assumed by themselves. The emergence of independent, professional, and efficiency-pursuing firm managers is the result of such a change. After the community government leaders delegate a significant part of control rights over the firms to professional firm managers, the organization of collective TVEs becomes a two-tier principal-agent system (local residents -- community government -- firm managers). Secondly, such a two-tier principal-agent system is not a static arrangement but, rather, an evolving one. With the progress of economic reform, the institutional environment is changing. The firms' organizational form must adapt to the alteration in the environment to pursue efficiency improvement. Therefore, the contractual form governing the relationship between local government leaders and firm managers has been innovated continuously since the early years of the TVEs' development. As found in my field investigation, it has followed a unique evolutionary path to evolve from a fixed-wage form to a profit-sharing form, then to a fixed-payment form. The general trend of such an evolution is that firm managers become more independent and responsible in the decision-making processes to run the firms. For their increased responsibilities, they are rewarded with an increasing share in the claim of residual profit. In the meantime, local leaders gradually withdraw themselves from the process and become sheer rent collectors of the collective properties. A new class of rural entrepreneurs has taken shape and the ultimate implication of such an organizational evolution is an 'induced privatization' in this sector. However, such contractual form innovation is neither an instantaneous, nor a homogeneous process, but a gradual and divergent one. As observed in the field investigation, firms in a given area are apt to operate with different contractual arrangements. The contractual structure also varies substantially from region to region. A thorough understanding of TVEs' organizational mechanism requires a consistent explanation of the changing scenario and the exploration of the driving force(s) of the contractual form innovation.

The solid foundation for establishing a contractual relation is a bilateral interdependence between the contracting parties. Each must bring something valuable to the contract to make the contractual relation mutually beneficial. Community government leaders grant control rights to firm managers through certain contractual arrangement, because they must rely on the firm managers' ability to manage the firms' daily operation. Likewise, firm managers deliver profit to the community government as the contract specifies, because they are reliant on community government leaders to a greater or lesser extent to assume their managerial responsibilities, which is the source of their personal income. What both parties bring to the contractual relation in the TVEs' organization, I maintain, are the non-marketed inputs necessary to the firms' operation: internal and external management. In a transitional economy with imperfections, community government leaders have comparative advantage in external management, and firm managers have comparative advantage in internal management. The community public ownership and the contractual arrangements between community government leaders and firm managers of collective TVEs become a desirable organizational form for combining the comparative advantage each party possesses to provide more efficient managerial inputs. Consequently, the focal point of the study becomes: what is the determinant factor that affects the contracting parties' decisions in choosing a specific contractual form, or in innovating an existing contractual form for a certain firm in a given period?

The contracting parties select among various available contractual forms based upon their cost-benefit calculations associated with each contractual form. The prevailing contractual form is the one that minimizes the transaction costs of contracting. Any factor that affects contracting parties' cost-benefit calculations or their relative bargain power can lead to innovation in the contractual form on the condition that the factor has a strong enough effect to change both parties' incentive sets. In TVEs' case, market liberalization and development, as the result of central government's reform efforts, reduce the comparative advantage of community government leaders in firms' external management, while raising their agent monitoring and contract enforcing costs. In contrast, market forces strengthen firm managers' ability in external management and make them less dependent on local leaders for completing managerial tasks. This is the key force that stimulates community governments and firm managers to take action in moving from a more leader-dominant to a more manager-dominant contractual arrangement. This evolution in the organizational form of TVEs is an induced institutional innovation, which stems from the rational response of local government leaders and firm managers to the changing institutional environment. However, such privatization-oriented innovation may be discouraged by the central government since the costs and the benefits brought about by such innovation are different for the central government from those for its local functionaries.

Moreover, firms with different technical structures require different combination of internal and external management inputs corresponding to their diversified technical attributes. This fact gives different weights to community government leaders' input and firm managers' input, which results in deviated decisions in the contractual form selection for technically diversified firms. At the same time, the economic setting of a locality also influences the contractual structure of local collective TVEs, for it determines the opportunity cost correlated to each contractual arrangement. The community government in a richer area with a sizable and profitable TVE sector is more willing to play a less dominant role in the operation of any individual firm than its counterparts in a less developed community.

Government intervention is usually viewed as contradictory to efficient functioning of markets in a developed free market economy, therefore it should be limited to the minimum necessary level. However, as explicated in this research work, it is possible that the administrative functions of government may supplement the function of markets in promoting a firm's development. This is particularly true in a transitional economy where markets are underdeveloped and the replacement of a market system for the centrally planning system is a gradual process, which may be prolonged. China's experiences in the development of the TVE sector may have provided an example of how government administrative functions and market functions may supplement each other to stimulate economic growth. It can also be seen how a bottom-up gradual and induced privatization rather than a top-down instantaneous privatization in firms' property rights takes place to prevent the economy from drastic decline and to avoid social chaos.

3. The Sources and the Methodology

This research work is basically an empirical study. In order to reveal the underlying forces that have propelled TVEs to rapid expansion, some important factors must be examined. Such factors feature the macroeconomic environment within which TVEs are operating as well as characterize the microeconomic structure of firms that defines a firm's objective and constraint sets. The study is designed to take advantage of spatial and dynamic variations in examining the empirical relationship among variables of interest. Two types of information are thus targeted: one is cross units (firm and region) data that demonstrates the divergence of firms in a given time period. The second is time-series data that captures the evolutionary trend of all firms over time. However, one simple descriptive statement could fall far short of providing a systematic and consistent research to identify the most crucial factors among relevant concerns. Therefore, the study is also designed to take advantage of the prolific contributions of institutional economics and other economic theories in developing models to capture the characterizing factors from the descriptive statistics. Such a theoretical analysis is designed in the attempt to generate general hypotheses and predictions through model simulations, which can be further tested in a more rigorous way.

Different localities of rural China differ greatly in their geographical features, resources endowments, wealth accumulations, infrastructure development, and even culture and tradition. Without a doubt, this kind of differences will have immense impact on the local economic situation. This is particularly true after nearly two decades of reform. As reported by some researchers (Lin, Cai and Li, 1996; Rozelle, 1994; Zhou, 1993), the cross-regional disparities in local economic settings, development levels, and reform progress have significantly increased during the reform era. Therefore, field study results from a few of the firms located in one county, or even in one province, may be too idiosyncratic to describe the whole picture of the TVE sector. On the other hand, however, an extensive field investigation covering many localities demands huge inputs of financial as well as human resources, which was far beyond my ability as a single researcher (especially as a graduate student when the field investigation was conducted). In an attempt to be as comprehensive, intensive, and convincing as possible in my research scope, I have mainly relied upon first hand sources -- my own field investigations and conference participation, as well as secondary materials from a number of sources.

My fieldwork was conducted in the second half of 1994. In the summer of that year, I participated in an international conference held in Hangzhou, Zhejiang Province of China, which was on the property rights reform in China's TVE sector. Before the conference, I joined with a group of scholars undertaking a research trip in Zhejiang Province. During the well-organized trip, I had the opportunity to visit enterprises in four counties and one city (Wenzhou); interview local government officials, communist party cadres, firm managers, private owners, and rural enterprise workers; and exchange views with scholars and researchers from both China and the United States. After that conference, I participated in another conference on a similar topic held in Shanghai, China. Then, I visited two townships in south Jiangsu Province. The preliminary fieldwork was extremely conducive to my understanding in the general structure of China's TVE sector and the evolutionary pattern of firm organizational forms in this sector. It also helped me to make a selection of field research sites and design the field investigation surveys.

I selected Jiangsu and Zhejiang, two coastal provinces, and Jiangxi and Hubei, two inland Yangtze Delta provinces, as my research sites. Jiangsu and Zhejiang are relatively developed areas, especially in their vigorous TVE sectors. Moreover, Jiangsu was famous in its collective style of TVE development, while Zhejiang was well known for the rapid development of private TVEs. Jiangxi and Hubei were less developed, but not backward, provinces in TVE development. They were selected as comparative sites to explore the causes of cross-regional disparities in firm organizational form evolution. I did not select more remote and less developed areas as my field investigation sites due to the limited number of TVEs and a lack of well-maintained statistical records.

Since it is impossible to obtain an existing comprehensive data set characterizing TVEs at the micro-level, most data used in this research were collected in my field investigation taken in four townships, one from each of the above mentioned provinces. The small sample of townships and enterprises investigated for this research work is not intended to be representative of rural China as a whole, or to make generalized conclusions. Rather, the research is made in the hope that the information provided by the research sample may be helpful to establish a solid foundation in understanding the detailed organizational characteristics of TVEs. Such an understanding, I believe, will lead to a clarification of the mechanisms through which TVEs innovate in response to the varying environment and translate incentives into superior performance.

Interviews with the sample township government leaders (the secretary of the Communist Party township committee or the township director) and the township government officials who were in charge of local TVE affairs took place before enterprises investigation started. Such interviews presented me with the general picture of local TVEs' history of development, ownership structure, organizational structure, and the progress of reforms in TVEs' property rights in the township. In most cases, a township government official who knew the local TVEs and their managers well accompanied me to visit villages and enterprises to undertake firm and firm manager investigations. All these interviews, whether with government leaders or with others (firm managers, staff, or workers) were very unreservedly open and turned out to be fruitful. Besides the designed investigation survey forms, ample valuable information was acquired through such interviews. All interviews and case studies cited in this book, unless indicated otherwise, were conducted either in the four investigation sites, or during my preliminary fieldwork. Whenever such a citation is made, I will indicate the information source with 'L' denoting government leaders or officials, 'M' denoting firm managers, and 'W' firm workers.

Statistical yearbooks, either national or local whenever appropriate, academic journals, newspapers, journalistic reports, books published in China, central or local government's documents, conference papers, and other printed materials collected by myself are the main sources of secondary materials. Although the reliability of the data regarding TVEs published by the Chinese government is sometimes suspect, I believe it has been a relatively consistent data source when compared with other available sources. I try to introduce macro-level data from secondary materials whenever necessary, so as to put a particular finding in a larger perspective and to explore the general implications of such findings.

Unlike many researchers in this field, who mainly depend on officially published data to analyze the macroeconomic performance of TVEs as a sector, my research is basically at the microeconomic level. I view the collection of macro variables as the given institutional environment, or 'shift parameter', which specifies the opportunity sets for economic players such as local government leaders, firm managers, and TVEs workers. My research focus is on the institutional innovation at the firm's level, *i.e.,* firm's contractual form innovation. In other words, my research objective is an exploration into how the firm organization, or its contractual form, adapts to the reforming institutional environment; what principle forces motivate or restrict such adaptation; and what such adaptation implicates in the firm's property rights reform. To meet the research objective, I apply modern institutional economics to my research with emphasis on understanding the interactions among three main groups of economic factors, *i.e.,* the firm's organization (contractual form); the behavioral attributes of individuals (local government leaders and firm managers); and the institutional environment (the extent of market development and the economic setting of a locality). The information collected in the field investigation was analyzed using a number of different techniques. Due to the highly diversified economic and political features that characterize firms and localities, descriptive statistics and case studies are important to an understanding in the essential facts regarding TVEs' property rights constitution. They are also important for explaining the temporal evolutionary pattern and the spatial variation of the structure of the firms' organizational form. More sophisticated principle components analyses are performed to capture the underlying factors that motivated such evolution.

On the basis of microeconomic theory of agrarian institutions, a principal-agent model is developed to describe the decision-making behavior of rural government leaders and of firm managers, and to explain how a particular contractual form is selected for a given enterprise. Several predictions are derived from the simulations of the model. These predictions predict how a firm's contractual form adapts to the changing institutional environment as a rational response of the principal and of the agent, and how such an adaptive process varies depending on the firm's technical structure and the economic setting of a locality within which the firm is operating.

The empirical observations are used to examine the predictive power of the theoretical model. Econometric methodology is also applied to test the hypothesis drawn from the model, and the estimated results are used to determine the relative importance of each factor in its influence on the firm's contractual form selection and innovation.

4. The Organization of the Book

The arguments of this research work are presented in six chapters. Chapter 2 lays out the foundation for subsequent chapters by illustrating the property rights structure of collective TVEs as a two-tier principal-agent relation in rural China. Specifically, it examines local community government leaders' incentives to promote rural enterprise development. It also shows that such incentives stem from the dual role local leaders have to play in rural community organization. On the basis of the property rights theories, it explains how the community public property ownership takes advantage of assigning control rights in collective TVEs to the community government and thus bringing about superior performance of collective TVEs over both state-owned enterprises and private enterprises. Then it turns to illustrate the second-tier principal-agent relations between local community government leaders and firm managers, which directly leads to the major argument of the research work -- the contractual structure innovation of collective TVEs.

Chapter 3 focuses on TVE contractual forms. It documents seven different contractual forms that have been implemented in collective TVEs, and demonstrates the essential characteristics of each form by detailed description and case studies. These contractual forms are then classified into three categories: fixed-wage, profit-sharing, and fixed-payment. The observations show that they coexist in a given area, evolve over time, and vary across regions.

In order to explain the co-existence, evolution and the variation of TVE contractual forms, Chapter 4 extends the descriptive discussion of property rights by developing a theoretical framework to systematically analyze various factors that may have had influence on firm contractual form determination. It provides a brief review of institutional economics and the theory of induced innovation. A principal-agent model is then formulated to show the behavioral features of local community government leaders and firm managers. The model simulations generate a number of predictions in explaining how the contractual form evolution and variation is substantially attributable to the reforming environment and the firm technical structure. It argues that the development of the market system in a transitional economy may lead to innovations in firm governance institutions, though such innovations may be subject to constraints in firm technical attributes and local economic settings.

Chapter 5 is an extension of Chapter 4. It tests the predictive power of the theoretical model developed in Chapter 4 by empirical analyses. Descriptive statistics are presented to examine whether or not the model predicted factors actually explain the observed contractual structure of collective TVEs and its evolution and variations. A more rigorous econometric analysis is also performed to explore the relative importance of model predicted forces in determining firm contractual structure. This empirical analysis confirms the predictive power of the model. It also reveals that, among other factors, market development and firm technical structure may be the most crucial forces that affect the decisions on the contractual form by which the firm is run.

The book concludes with the last chapter, Chapter 6. This chapter examines the feedback effect of contractual form innovation of collective TVEs in several dimensions. The feedback effects support the 'endogenous reform' model that views China's reform as a gradual and cumulative process characterized by 'induced privatization'. It argues, insofar as the process of induced firm contractual structure innovation is explicitly illustrated by this research, the completed chain of 'induced privatization' can be deduced. The whole mechanism through which the government's partial reform efforts in market liberalization have been translated into a more fundamental and profound reform practice in property rights structure is now clarified.

2 Local Government Leaders, Firm Managers, and the Two-tier Property Rights Structure of Collective TVEs

Two groups of actors participate in decisions that have led to the expansion of TVEs in rural China: local government leaders and the firm managers who have been hired by leaders to run the firm. In China's TVE movement, one of the most intriguing aspects is the role and importance of leadership in the TVEs of local officials. Local leaders in China have generally been the catalyst to China's modernization drive, but in other transitional counties, this group of individuals tends more to be barriers to growth (Brada, 1996; Oi, 1992; Winiecki, 1990). This unique aspect of China's rural industrialization has led many authors into trying to explain the role of local leaders in the process (Byrd and Lin, 1990; Che and Qian, 1998; Oi, 1992, 1996; Pan, 1996). Due to the multiple responsibilities, which extend far beyond the operation of TVEs that local leaders must assume (Byrd and Lin, 1990; Rozelle, 1994), necessarily more and more of their work overflow onto the shoulders of another group of individuals, *i.e.*, firm managers. However, literature contains little about the role of firm managers in TVEs' development, or the relationship between firm managers and local leaders in spite of the fact that at the very least, this class of individuals has been charged with producing the vast volume of output accredited to the TVEs. There are some researchers who provided a more coherent and internally consistent explanation of the rise of TVEs by recognizing the leadership of the local community controls and drawing a parallel between TVEs' organization and the structure of modern corporations (Che and Qian, 1998; Walder, 1995). Although even they appeared to be less aware of the mechanism that governs the relationship between the community governments and the firm managers. They simply viewed such relationships as analogous to that between the general managers and the division chiefs or plant heads within a corporate. And since firm managers have thus been virtually treated as a subordinate, rather than an independent group of participants in the TVE movement, their relations with another group of participants can hardly be the focus in any comprehensive TVE studies.

We may conveniently describe the property rights and the governance of collective TVEs as two-tier principal-agent proxy relations as shown by Figure 2.1.

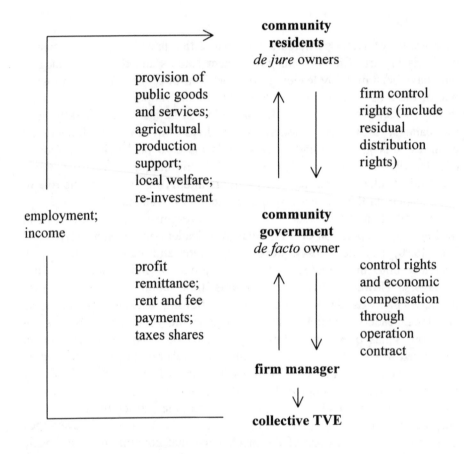

Figure 2.1 The Two-tier Principal-agent Relations in Collective TVEs

The community residents, as the nominal, or *de jure,* owners of a collective TVE, delegate the control rights (including the residual distribution rights) in the firm to the community government, who serves as the *de facto* owner of the firm. In return, the community government assumes responsibility in the provision of public goods and services, agricultural production support, local welfare, and capital re-investment for the community residents. This completes the first-tier of principal-agent relations.

The community government, as the principal, re-delegates at least part of the control rights in the firm to the firm manager. In return, the firm manager receives certain economic compensation through an operation contractual arrangement. The firm manager thus has the obligation to remit profit, pay rents and fees to the community government. The community government through the fiscal system will share the taxes paid by the firm to the state as well. This illustrates the second-tier of principal-agent relations in collective TVEs' organization.

The community residents enjoy the employment opportunities and income increase provided by the firm.

The overall purpose and the focus of this research is to provide a general framework in explaining the structure of the second tier of principal-agent relations. To date, it has almost been a virgin field in TVEs research. However, before I can go directly to the second tier principal-agent relations a number of questions may arise if I leave the first tier principal-agent relations unexplained. For example, people may doubt over the necessity of the first-tier proxy, *i.e.,* the necessity of having the community government involved in the governance of the firm: why do the *de jure* owners not exercise their control rights by themselves? Or, why do the community residents delegate the control rights to the community government to begin with rather than to the firm manager directly, even though such delegation can be proved necessary? Doubts such as these are apprehensible due to the widespread skepticism of government ownership in transitional economies. This is because the agent costs associated with control rights delegation are higher in a two-tier proxy than in a one-tier proxy. Therefore, in this chapter I will attempt to give a general sketch of the first tier principal-agent relations, heavily based on the work of many other researchers as well as on my own observations. I shall then turn to the second tier relations in the following chapters.

The focus of this chapter is to provide a convincing explanation of why such a two-tier principal-agent organizational form has been shaped in

TVEs' governance, and why such an organizational form seems more vigorous than other forms. I start the chapter in Section 1 by briefly discussing the dual role that local community government leaders have been playing in China's rural organization. Section 2 describes the objectives and incentives of local leaders in their enthusiastic commitment to the TVE movement. I argue that such objectives and incentives are directly derived from the dual role they have to play. Section 3 provides a theoretical explanation to the reason why community public ownership of collective TVEs is superior to state public ownership according to property rights theories. Section 4 illustrates the comparative advantage of having community governments as the *de facto* owners of collective TVEs as compared with privately owned TVEs. I will argue that such comparative advantage only exists in response to the imperfections of both market and government institutions in a transitional economy. Hence, it will not perpetuate when a healthy and vigorous market system finally replaces the centrally planning system. The last section, Section 5, describes the re-delegation of the control rights from the community government to the firm manager, and the constitution of TVE managers as a newly emerging class in rural China. The basic mechanism of the governance of collective TVEs will be summarized at the end of the chapter, which will also serve as the introduction to the following chapters.

1. The Dual Role of Local Leaders in Rural Organization

Compared with other transitional economies, the community governments functioning as the catalyst rather than barriers is one of the most distinctive features in China's reform practice. Their active and powerful role in rural enterprise development and modernization is probably a unique experience among many developing countries. This experience will bring about a profound influence on China's long-run development. The inherent cause of such a distinctive feature may be traced back to the dual role the various community governments played in China's rural organization, and their objectives and incentives in playing that role. The basic organizational structure in current rural China may be simplified as shown by Figure 2.2 (Li, K. 1992). In 1996, China had a rural population of 864.39 million belonging to 234.37 million rural households, 740,128 (administrative) villages, and 45,484 townships.[1] Before the economic reform, rural China was organized by a commune-brigade-production team system. A county usually consisted of eight to fifteen communes. After the nationwide implementation of the household responsibility farming system in the early 1980s, the economy of the production team collapsed. After that, in 1984 communes and brigades were terminated and replaced by townships and villages that were supposed to be mainly administrative bodies instead of economic organizations. A township is usually smaller than a commune in area as well as in population. The smaller size is desirable because it is more effective in serving individual farming households. In north China, an administrative village often coincides with a large natural village. However, in densely populated south China, an administrative village is often an artificial grouping of a number of small natural villages close to each other. Unless indicated otherwise, 'village' in this book refers to the administrative village rather than the natural village.

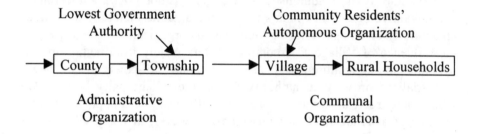

Figure 2.2 The Organizational Structure in Rural China

Township government is the lowest government authority in China's formal bureaucratic hierarchy. It performs government administrative functions through various apparatuses, such as Fiscal Department (Caizheng Suo), Tax Department (Shuiwu Suo), Department of Industrial and Commercial Management (Gongshang Guanli Suo), Public Security Station (Gongan Paichu Suo), etc. It also administers public facilities such as schools, hospitals, broadcast stations, in its jurisdiction. Two kinds of officials are in the power nucleus in a township. One is the township

---

[1] ZGTJNJ (China Statistical Yearbook), 1997, p.363.

director and deputy directors. These officials are popularly elected government executives, and supposed to be in charge of all the administrative affairs of the government. The second kind of officials are the cadres of the Communist Party. The real control of a township actually rests in the hands of the township party secretary instead of the township directors. This is because most township directors are township party committee members under the leadership of the party secretary. They are elected in most cases because of the nomination of the township party committee. Township party secretaries are usually appointed by higher level authorities. They are drawn either from the local cadres' pool, or from other government apparatuses or areas. The appointment of township government branch chiefs and the recruitment of government staff is mainly controlled by the township party committee. Township government officials receive formal salary payments from government payrolls.

According to the Law of Villagers' Committee Organization (Cunmin Weiyuanhui Zuzhifa) of November 1987, the Villagers' Committee is the formal authority of an administrative village. It is not a *de jure* government administrative branch in China's formal bureaucratic hierarchy but, rather, an authority of village residents' autonomous organization. The power and the influence of Villagers' Committee differs widely from being virtually invisible in agriculture-based areas to being all-powerful in newly industrialized areas. Real authority lies in the village party branch. The village party secretary generally has more influence than a popularly elected director of a Villagers' Committee does. However, in many villages, the two major positions are held by one person, though there is a trend in recent years to split it to reflect a compromise among multiple power centers (Pan, 1996). Unlike township government officials, village leaders are indigenous village residents and keep their status as 'peasants' instead of 'cadres' in almost all cases. They receive no formal salaries from the government payrolls. They may receive some subsidies either from the township government or from the Villagers' Committee, the amount of subsidies depending greatly on the budget of the township government or the village revenues, which come from village enterprises and residents' payments. Village leaders may be promoted to township government positions and thus change their status to formal 'state cadres' (Guojia Ganbu). It is interesting, however, to note that township government officias hardly ever return to the village to assume a village position.

It is obvious that townships define state, or administrative organization, while villages define society, or communal organization. They comprise the primary organizational framework of rural China.[2] The state-society boundary is blurred at the township-village level. Township government leaders and village leaders are rural authorities with the most direct and decisive influence in almost every aspect of local political and economic activities, down to the daily life of local residents.

Rural leaders have long been pictured as 'dual agents' of state and community. They serve simultaneously as agents of the central government and representatives of local residents (Pan, 1996; Whiting, 1995). They play the role of state government agents, for they are obligated to perform the administrative functions in implementing central government policies, designing local development strategies, collecting taxes, maintaining public order, investing in public goods, etc. Even the village leaders, who are not *de jure* agents of the bureaucratic hierarchy in the administrative organization, must perform at least part of the state agent's role. Under the vigilante guidance of township governments, they have to fulfill certain tasks assigned by township governments from levying collections to overseeing birth control compliance. Therefore, it is not surprising that they are regarded by local residents as the representatives of the central government.

However, local leaders have to play the role of local communities' agents as well. Whenever a local community is in conflict with other communities or higher authorities, local leaders must represent community interests and negotiate with the other party to solve the problem, sometimes through compromise. When the reform awarded more and more economic autonomies to local authorities, many local leaders became actively involved in the initiation and the development of township and village enterprises. Soon, their personal interests became inseparable from community interests with the result that the local authorities are vigorously motivated to protect local interests against any invasion from outside. In the case that such an invasion is from higher authorities, they may manipulate by legal or even illegal methods to ensure the interests of the community (Ma et al., 1994). In this sense, they have become veritable representatives of local benefits and less likely to serve as state agents. At least they would only play the role of state agents less conscientiously and enthusiastically.

---

[2] Kang Li described in every very detail the rural organizational framework in his book *Rural Community Development in Transitional China: An Investigation and Analysis Toward Rural Community in Taoyuan.* China Scientific and Technology Press, 1992.

2. The Objectives and Incentives of Local Leaders

Although townships and villages are defined as administrative rather than economic organizations, township and village leaders must assume multiple responsibilities, both economic and non-economic, in their executive routines. These responsibilities are directly derived from the dual role they play.[3] The 'dual agents' role local leaders have to play formulates the incentives and constraints for them, and determines their behavior in a way that coincides with the development of rural enterprises.

2.1 The Objectives

To achieve designed growth objectives in the years of reform, governments at different levels assign growth targets to lower authorities within their jurisdiction. Since township and village leaders are the lowest authorities in rural China, they have the obligation to fulfill such assigned targets to build up their political image and ensure promotion. Many local leaders whom I personally interviewed said they were under great pressure to meet the assigned growth targets for fears of being removed from their current positions and relegated to lower ones. They could also be transferred to a remote and/or less developed area if they were unable to achieve those targets. They would 'lose face and lose future' if such situation applied to them.[4] Assigned targets range from overall production value to per capita rural income, sometimes even including growth rate in firm profit or exports (Whiting, 1995). Besides the economic targets there is a category of non-economic objectives to be brought about by the local leaders (Li, K. 1992; Rozelle, 1994; Whiting, 1995). Though the concrete objectives vary from

---

[3] This phenomenon has been known as 'failure to separate party, government administration, and economic management' (Dangzheng Bufen, Zhengqi Bufen), and regarded as one of the major problems centrally planning economy. The design of two sets of rural authorities -- communist party committee and executive directors in township and communist party branch and director of Villagers' Committee in village -- is the effort made to separate party from the government. The establishment of Industrial Corporation (Gongye Gongsi), Industrial Office (Gongye Ban), or Economic Management Office (Jinguanzhan) at the township level in early 1990s is in an effort to separate government from economic management, though these are still government apparatus under the direct guidance of township government.

[4] Informant L6, L14.

place to place, they generally include three kinds of tasks: political control and social issues such as party-building and crime rate control; cultural and public development such as completion rate for compulsory education and local infrastructure construction; and family planning compliance. The accomplishment of these tasks may weigh as much as achievements in economic objectives. These non-economic responsibilities exert just as much pressure on the local leaders. Nevertheless, local leaders often give priority to economic achievements against non-economic fulfillment in recognition that the carrying out of the non-economic objectives is apt to drain resources. 'You need money to do things,' they argued, 'economic growth is a solid target, all the others, such as spirit civilization development (Jingshen Wenming Jianshe), are vain targets'.[5] Understandably local leaders view economic achievements as the 'hard criterion' and non-economic fulfillment 'soft criterion' in measuring a leader's success as a state agent. Seeing how the setting up of rural enterprises directly leads to economic growth more than any other single means, *e.g.*, the expansion of agricultural production, local leaders tend to exert themselves in the development of TVEs in order to meet the 'hard criterion' and to provide financial support to fulfill non-economic objectives and meet the 'soft criterion'. They are highly motivated to achieve economic objectives and view such achievement as a necessary method to achieve non-economic objectives.

Township and village leaders have been playing another role at the same time -- as community agents. This role has put them in a position to face more directly the pressure of providing employment opportunities to rural laborers. They must also improve rural living conditions than any other level of authorities in China's bureaucratic hierarchy. Before the economic reform was launched, eighty percent of the Chinese population, *i.e.*, nearly one billion people were farmers living in rural areas. More than 40 million of rural laborers worked on 1.5 billion mu[6] of arable land, averaging less than 4 mu per laborer. The strict residence registration system and the commune system had been effective barriers to prevent rural laborers from migrating to urban areas, helped to reduce employment pressure and maintain social stability. However, under such a system, the rural population was deprived of their rights to search for other employment opportunities and had been generally excluded from the industrial sector

---

[5] Informant L10, L17.

[6] 15 mu = 1 hectare; or 1 mu = 0.165 acre.

and urban areas. After the abolishment of the commune system, family farming replaced the collective agricultural production in rural China. This reform gave more freedom to rural households in production related decision-making and output disposal. Rural households were fueled by strong incentives to work harder and produce more, which effectively increased the agricultural outputs to a great extent (Lin, Cai, and Li, 1996; Pan, 1996). However, this reform has brought about some by-product -- severe unemployment in rural China. Previously disguised rural unemployment had manifested itself almost everywhere. Tens of thousands of rural surplus laborers were hunting for employment opportunities but rejected by the urban industrial sector due to the discriminative residence registration system, and the limited ability of state-owned sectors in absorbing rural surplus labor at a large enough scale and fast enough speed. It is estimated that around one third, *i.e.*, more than 13 million rural laborers are surplus even under the agricultural productivity in the late 1980s (Ma et al., 1994, p.438). It is reported by the Research Institute of Sector Economy of the Shanghai Academy of Social Sciences that, of the 2.44 million rural laborers in the suburban counties of Shanghai, only 0.5 million were estimated to be needed to meet the demand of agricultural production. This is to say that about 80 percent of the rural labor force must find non-agricultural employment opportunities (Xie and Lin, 1994). To ease the unemployment pressure, which was threatening public order and might lead to social chaos, township and village leaders needed a miracle to create employment opportunities for rural surplus labor. They did find such a miracle – township and village enterprises.

Despite the fact that TVEs were discriminated against and discouraged by the central government in their early stages for their 'competition with state-owned sectors for raw materials and markets',[7] this sector was expanding rapidly under the enthusiastic promotion of local leaders. Shortly after, the Chinese central government realized that the setting up of rural enterprises to absorb rural surplus labor is a much better and easier way to solve the rural unemployment problem than allowing rural labor to search for employment opportunities in urban areas, thus putting pressure on the reform in the residence registration system and the state-owned sectors. It turned around to affirm that the TVE sector is 'an important part in our national economy', and 'contributes to deter large scale migration of rural

---

[7] China TVE Yearbook: 1978-1987, Beijing, Agriculture Press, 1989, p.1.

population into urban areas'[8] in the 1984 Number 1 and Number 4 Document of the Central Committee of Chinese Communist Party. These documents led to a drastic development of TVE sector in 1980s.

If the initial motivation for local leaders to launch township and village enterprises is to deal with the unemployment problem (Byrd and Lin, 1990; Ma et al., 1994), this objective has been gradually replaced by another one. This new purpose is to increase local incomes and improve local living conditions.[9] Whenever leaders of a township or village observed that their neighboring townships or villages had increased income brought about by newly established enterprises, they simply launched enterprises of their own to catch up with such income increase. A Villagers' Committee director in Jiangsu expressed such a feeling during my interview: 'when I saw many residents in our neighboring village had built new houses, I was really ashamed. My fellow villagers elected me as the director, hence, it is incumbent upon me to improve their life. I then made my mind and promised to set up more and better enterprises in our village than our neighbor's.' And that was exactly what he did.[10] The awareness of local leaders of their responsibility to stimulate community income increase has led to their active involvement in, and commitment to, the development of TVEs. A tremendous portion of TVEs, particularly village enterprises, are actually initiated by local leaders and reliant on local leaders to a great extent in their development process. Not surprisingly, many local leaders view the township enterprises or the village enterprises as their 'own enterprises', for those firms are 'our creatures as our children'.[11]

Ordinary rural residents who had no experience in starting their own non-agricultural business have very naturally turned to local leaders for leadership in launching community enterprises. It is not unusual to hear rural residents blaming their leaders for inability or unwillingness to set up collective enterprises in their communities. In my Jiangxi investigation site, I interviewed a group of village enterprise workers, who were outside workers from another county. They complained that their village leaders were selfish and stupid, had no interest in establishing village enterprises to bring prosperity to their village. Under leaders without initiative many

---

[8] China TVE Yearbook: 1978-1987, Beijing, Agriculture Press, 1989, p.422-427.

[9] Zhibiao Liu found in his field investigation that increasing local income was ranked first motive by rural community leaders to launch TVEs, providing employment opportunity the second, and increasing government's revenue the third.

[10] Informant L1. Also see Case Study 1 in Chapter 3.

[11] Informant L9.

villagers were forced to leave their home village to look for jobs in other areas. They wished they could be rid of the old leader and elect someone, who could lead them in building their own village enterprises, so that they would have jobs and prosperity at home.[12]

2.2 The Incentives

Local leaders were directly impelled by a number of factors to enthusiastically promote the development of rural enterprises. Among which, the fiscal system reform,[13] the cadre evaluation system,[14] and leaders' personal benefit in the reform era played the most prominent role.

The Revenue Incentives: After the abolishment of the commune system, the township became the lowest level authority organ of the Chinese government, and the rural household the unit of production and accounting. Local leaders, especially at the village and to a lesser extent at the township level, lost their legitimate access to all income from agriculture, except for a share of the agricultural tax paid by rural households. The incentive structure confronting township officials was shaped by the sources of funds on which they depend in order to function and to meet the performance criteria set by the cadre evaluation system. '*The imperative of self-financing combined with the overwhelming township government reliance on rural industry as a revenue source created an incentive for township cadres vigorously to promote the development of rural firms*' (Whiting, 1995, p.31). Under the reformed fiscal system, the 'unified income and expenditure system' (Tongshou Tongzhi)[15] was replaced by the self-financing and revenue sharing system. This new system made each sub-national level of government primarily responsible for its own revenues and expenditures. The township government must negotiate a multi-year fiscal contract with the county government (the next higher level in the

---

[12] Informant W64, W65.

[13] Oi (1992) and Whiting (1995) conducted comprehensive research on the reform of the fiscal system and its consequent impacts on local leaders' incentive in rural industrialization.

[14] See Whiting (1995), and K. Li (1992).

[15] Under the 'unified income and expenditure' system, each level of government turned over virtually all tax receipts as well as the profit from state-owned firms to the central government; the lower levels then looked to the central government for budgetary allocation to finance local government expenditures.

administrative hierarchy). According to such fiscal contract, the township government as an agent of the central government collected taxes from the enterprises and other entities under its jurisdiction and received a share of the tax revenues it collected. In general, the contract sets a specific base level of the tax revenue the township government must submit to the upper level government in the base year, and a certain percentage of increase thereafter in the following years. At the same time, the contract guaranteed that a certain portion of this remitted revenue would be returned to the township, and the county would also grant an annual budgetary fund to the township for expenditures. The returned revenues and county government granted funds constituted the 'budgetary revenue' (Yusuan Nei Shouru) of a township government. As observed by Susan Whiting in her field investigation (Whiting, 1995), the lion's share of township government's budgetary revenue came from the return of above-target tax remittances. Clearly, the more TVEs a township had as its tax revenue source, the more budgetary revenue the township government would receive via the revenue-sharing fiscal contract.

The other two sources of a township government's revenue, the non-budgetary revenues, are 'extra-budgetary revenue' (Yusuan Wai Shouru) and 'self-raised funds' (Zichou Zijin). The self-raised funds derived almost exclusively from rural enterprises. The sources of these funds were divided into two main categories: profit remittances and fees. Township-owned enterprises turned their profit over to township government, whereas the profit generated by village-owned enterprises was mainly disposable by the Villagers' Committee. Rural enterprises, no matter township-owned, village-owned, or privately owned, also paid a number of officially mandated fees, which accrued to local governments as self-raised funds. After 1992, when leasing became a popular organizational form of collective TVEs in some areas, the rent paid by leasing firms was added as an important source of self-raised funds of the township governments.

Distinct from self-raised funds, extra-budgetary revenues derived primarily from income of so called 'public institutions' (Shiye Danwei) were generally not subject to direct or indirect taxes. The 'social welfare factories' that mainly employed handicapped workers, and the 'school-run factories' that were affiliated with some town schools, constituted the major part of this category.

Since the early 1990s, the non-budgetary revenues comprised an increasing share of the township government's total revenue. Whiting reported that in four of her investigation sample townships, the self-raised funds accounted for 31 percent to 58 percent of townships' total revenue in 1991 (Whiting, 1995, p.46). The rough data I acquired during the field investigation also shows that, except for Huazhuang Township of Jiangsu, the township government's revenue from TVEs (including direct profit remittance, fees, and rents) surpassed government's revenue from county governments' grants in all of the other three sample townships as in Table 2.1.

Table 2.1 Sample Township Government's Revenue and Its Sources, 1993 (million yuan)

	Total	Fiscal Grant from Higher Government	TVEs' Payments
Doumen, Zhejiang	13.00	2.58	3.36
Guohe, Hubei	0.36	0.08	0.12
Qingyunpu, Jiangxi	1.32	0.31	0.44
Huazhuang, Jiangsu	11.47	NA*	3.77

* Huazhuang Township did not provide this data.

Source: Author's Survey, 1994.

Village enterprises are the most important source of village revenues (Ma et al., 1994). They paid various fees, whether a firm was profitable or not, and remitted a certain percentage of their after-tax profit to the village to cover its routine expenditures such as village leaders' subsidies and public relation expenses. They were also frequently drawn from to cover the costs for the provision of public projects of the village.

A township government requires a minimum amount of revenues to perform its essential administrative functions. For instance, all the township leaders and government staff are on government payroll, which is backed up by government revenues. Office supplies and transportation are necessities too. Local leaders are desirous of extra funds, beyond the basic expenditure, to perform other functions. Under the current cadre evaluation system in China (see the following section for detailed description), local leaders' repute and likelihood for political promotion are determined by their career achievements. In turn their achievements are evaluated in most cases by the availability of disposable funds for the performance of various 'visible' functions. The functions, such as the launching of local infrastructure projects, supporting agricultural production, improving local cultural or welfare facilities, to what extent and to what degree of perfection are reliant on that government's ability to generate revenues. A superior ability in government revenue generation generally led to rapid and remarkable community development. For example, the total agricultural investment during the seventh 'five-year plan' was 2.8 billion yuan in Shanghai, from which, 51.8 percent, *i.e.*, 1.41 billion yuan was provided by TVEs (Xie and Lin, 1994). Luoshe Township in Wuxi County of Jiangsu is a 'star Chinese township' (Zhongguo Xiangzhen Zhixing). It had 282 TVEs in 1991, which generated 157 million yuan of pre-tax profit for the township. The township government reported that they spent 40 million yuan to build a hospital, a theater, a bridge etc., in the town between 1987 and 1991. All of its 22 villages had built their own kindergarten, primary school, and health clinic. These facilities were generally financed by revenues from TVEs.[16] A village in Wu County of Jiangsu also reported that in 1994 a new village chemical factory provided 1 million yuan in total to build another village factory, install a running water system for the whole village, and buy a Volkswagen sedan for the Villagers' Committee.[17] While some township governments were struggling for the funds for daily operation, some other townships were able to put large scale projects in practice. Table 2.2 provides a startling example to show how far apart two townships may be in their governments' expenditures.

---

[16] *The Report from Luoshe Township,* Chinese Communist Party Committee of Luoshe Township, Jiangsu Province, November 1992.
[17] Informant L1.

Table 2.2 Sample Township Government's Expenditures, 1993

	Huazhuang, Jiangsu		Guohe, Hubei	
	Amount (10,000 yuan)	Share (%)	Amount (10,000 yuan)	Share (%)
Total Expenditure	1143	100	35.3	100
Government Staff Salary	35.0	3.1	12.5	35.4
Government Staff Bonus	10.0	0.9	3.4	9.6
Local Infrastructure Development	420.0	36.7	7.2	20.4
Agricultural support	183.0	16.0	1.0	2.8
Local Welfare	48.0	4.2	0	0
Other	447.0	39.1	11.2	31.7

Source: Author's Survey, 1994.

Guohe township had 0.35 million yuan of total expenditure in 1993, that was about 3 percent of Huazhuang Township's total expenditure in the same year. From this expenditure, 45 percent went to government staff's pockets to fuel the government's operation. Only a tiny amount, though nearly one fourth of its total expenditure, was committed to local development. In contrast, Huazhuang spent only 4 percent of its expenditure to cover staff costs, while the dominant share was devoted to community development and welfare. As we look back to Table 2.1, comparing these two township governments' revenue from TVEs, it is not difficult to understand how important the revenue from TVEs to a township government is for performing its functions, and why local leaders were impelled to actively commit themselves to TVEs' development.

The Cadre Evaluation System: To supervise and encourage local leaders' effort, so as to ensure the achievement of the objectives desired by higher level authorities, a cadre evaluation system was designed to make local leaders responsible for the performance of the community in economic as well as in social and political terms. As Whiting's research shows:

> *In most cases, performance criteria (Kaohe Zhibiao) were set by the county Office of Management and Administration. The criteria did not exhaust the full range of functions performed by township leaders; rather, they reflected the priorities of county leaders and were the means of conveying these priorities to township officials -- and through them to village leaders. This approach facilitated cadre management at the county level by reducing the complex issues of township development to a few key indicators. Such a system also allowed county officials to compare the performance of township leaders across locales and helped identify the most competent cadres for promotion* (Whiting, 1995, p.60).

The cadre evaluation system had a powerful and independent influence on local leaders' behavior and created incentives for them to maximize the revenue under their control by promoting the growth of rural enterprises. Township leaders were extremely sensitive to the criteria by which they were evaluated. Because their performance on these criteria determined their level of remuneration, influenced their tenure in office, and opportunity for promotion. As argued by Whiting (1995), township leaders' major objective was to seek the maintenance of their positions of power.

Table 2.3 reproduces the performance criteria for Qingyunpu Township government in 1993. The information acquired in fieldwork shows that other sample townships had similar evaluation criteria as this one, though they differed slightly in concrete items and the weight given to each item. The city government (Qingyunpu belongs to Nanchang City) specified the targeted growth rate or objective of each item. Achieving the targeted objectives would ensure full credit for the evaluated cadre. Certain points would be added for each percent above the targeted achievement and deducted for each percent below the targeted achievement.

Table 2.3 Performance Criteria for Township Leaders
(Qingyunpu Township, Jiangxi Province), 1993

	Points
Economic Development	
Increase of TVEs' Gross Value of Output	15
Increase in Gross Value of Industrial Output	15
Increase of Industrial Profit	10
Increase in Gross Value of Agricultural Output	10
Increase of Grain Output	10
Grain Sales to the State	5
Increase in Per Capita Net Income of Rural Residents	10
Township Fiscal Revenue	10
Accomplishment of Agricultural Capital Investment	5
Other (Totaled)	10
Total Points	100
Spirit Civilization	
Cadre Management and Supervision	20
Political Propaganda	10
Public Order (Crime and Conflict Control)	20
Education (Completion Rate for Compulsory Education and Fund Dedicated to Education)	15
Family Planning (Birth Control)	15
Other (totaled)	20
Total Points	100

Source: Author's Survey, 1994.

The overall performance of a township leader is reflected by her/his total points awarded. Township leaders received a base salary from the state payroll. Their evaluated performance affected only their bonuses. However, the bonuses usually accounted for the largest single share of their income (Li, K., 1992; Whiting, 1995). In practice, the development of TVEs was the single most direct and critical determinant of township leaders' performance. Yet, the provision of public goods, such as education, public order, and agricultural capital construction, was also important in evaluating overall performance. However, the performances in most of the other criteria were closely correlated with revenue generation, which was in turn determined by the development of local TVEs. Thus, the cadre evaluation system reinforced the incentives created by the fiscal reform to promote TVEs development. Performance on the full range of indicators would be recorded in official personnel files and therefore could affect their promotion prospects.

Village leaders were differently motivated by the evaluation system than township leaders. Since they are not formal officials of the government, do not receive salaries from township government, the evaluation criteria designed by the township government would mainly influence their incomes rather than their political promotion. They have incentives to achieve the goals structured by the evaluation criteria, particularly economic goals, because superior performance in the criteria would result in higher subsidies and bonuses. The evaluation criteria set for village leaders differed from that for township leaders in that they included more detailed items, especially for 'Spirit Civilization' category. Generally, the Economic Development category included gross output value of agriculture and industry, per capita income of village residents, TVEs industrial output and profit, grain output and sales to the state, collection of taxes and government levies, etc.; the Spirit Civilization category included family planning (out of planning birth control), illegal activities control, school participation of school-age children, and party training participation of village leaders and party members. The total points awarded were determined by the village leaders' achievement in each criterion, and referred to the village leader's overall performance.

As described by Kang Li (Li, K. 1992, p.5-12), township governments usually set very detailed, sometimes too meticulous, targeted objectives to measure and calculate village leaders' achievements. The total subsidy funds (Butie Jijin) for village leaders in a village must be approved by the township government with reference to the economic achievement of the village in the respective year. A certain portion of this fund was dedicated to village leaders' salary-kind 'basic subsidy' (Jiben Butie), which was determined depending on the size of the village and the position of the leader. The remainder of the fund was 'bonus fund' (Jiangli Jijin) to reward better performance. Village leaders who received less than 80 percent of the total designed points would lose the entire bonus, while over 100 percent satisfactory performance might receive extra bonus from the township government. The total subsidy funds were mainly from two sources: profit generated by village enterprises and various levies imposed on village residents. Therefore, the more profitable the village enterprises are, the more subsidy funds are available to the village leaders, and the less conflict between village leaders and villagers. It is particularly true that when local leaders control only agricultural economy, few options are left with them but to levy *ad hoc* surcharges and various fees and penalties on villagers as the main source of revenue. This state of affairs is often referred to by the Chinese press as 'increasing the peasants' burden'. When one considers that 'increasing the burden on the peasants' results in grievance from the residents that may threaten village leaders' power or positions, it is not difficult to understand why village leaders associate subsidy funds and bonuses directly to the development of village enterprises. They also associate indirectly the availability of funds that are needed to support non-economic achievements to the development of village enterprises. Both are in the purpose of improving village leaders' overall performance evaluation.[18]

In some cases, superior performance might lead to promotion to positions in township government, so that the village leaders might change their status into formal government officials and get the so-called 'iron bowl' (TiefanWan). However, many of the village leaders I interviewed, particularly the younger ones, were not enthusiastic in competing for such promotion. They preferred to be real leaders with decisive power in a smaller area instead of being a minor staff member in a larger area.[19] They also expected to acquire more actual economic interests when retaining their village positions than what they might gain in a minor position in the township government.[20] However, elderly village leaders tended to prefer the 'iron bowl', due to less pressure and competition.[21]

Under such a cadre evaluation system, a local leader's remuneration was contingent upon the performance of other township or village leaders, thus pitting local leaders in competition against each other. Strong performance in one township or village tended to drive up targeted levels for others. This characteristic of the evaluation system encouraged local leaders to innovate in order to improve their performance relative to others. However, it also gave incentives to local leaders to manipulate statistical records and overstate their achievements, which is the main cause of unreliable official

---

[18] Also see Ma et al. eds. 1994, pp. 234-235.

[19] Informant L1.

[20] Informant L9, L12.

[21] Informant L7.

statistical data. When I asked local leaders whether it was difficult for them to meet all of the evaluation criteria, they laughed and told me: 'we could always meet the targeted levels of the criteria, might exceed a little bit, but not too much. It's really up to us.' They asked me not to release their names and positions in my publications for fear of exposure of false reports.[22]

Local Leaders' Personal Benefits: As described above, the remuneration of local leaders was determined by the development of local TVEs to a great extent. However, this is only the basic and formal part of local leaders' income. There are various side-payments and personal benefits for local leaders that became possible as a result of local TVEs development.

The number one category of such benefit is the privileged welfare program for local leaders funded by local governments' revenue. For example, a township in Jiangsu had built a number of townhouses at the cost of 140 thousand yuan each, exclusive of land costs. These townhouses were sold to the major township leaders at the price of 20 thousand yuan each in 1994.[23] Another perk was travels. Many of the local leaders I interviewed had traveled all over the country, even abroad, at the expense of the township governments or villages. Those travels were in name of business trips, training trips, or research visits. Actually, they were mostly recreation trips. A township party committee secretary told me that he had been to the United States twice, both in the name of business negotiation, but actually 'I knew nothing about the project negotiated. I just enjoyed the travel, seeing a lot of things I'd never seen before'.[24]

Another category is the possession of consumer goods produced by local TVEs. Two furniture producing factories in the Hubei investigation site reported that about 10 percent of their output was taken by local leaders, either from their own township and neighbor townships, or from the city which is the direct higher authority of the township, at below cost price.[25] Other products like clothes, shoes, foods, cosmetics, were taken as 'free samples'.

Yet another category that incurs the most criticism is the side payment in the form of free dinners and valuable personal presents, usage of luxury

---

[22] Informant L6, L9, L10.
[23] Informant L1.
[24] Informant L6.
[25] Informant M87, M88.

goods 'borrowed' from TVEs or TVE managers,[26] or even direct cash payments to the local leaders in exchange for favored tax treatment, land or credit allocation privileges, raw-materials or energy provisions to the enterprises. An extreme example is a private enterprise owner spending 200 thousand yuan to host a wedding party for a major township leader's daughter.[27]

Obviously, the ability of a local government to sponsor an official welfare program for its leaders is constrained by its available revenues. More TVEs, particularly profitable TVEs, in a locality means more sources of government revenues, as well as personal benefits, either through legitimate or illegitimate methods. These personal benefits also reinforced local leaders' incentive in promoting TVEs development.

3. The Property Rights Structure of Collective TVEs

The extraordinary performance of the TVE sector is one of the recent 'hot' subjects among researchers. Many of them attributed the success of TVEs to the strong incentives of local government leaders in TVEs' development. However, any incentive must have some kind of organizational structure so as to be translated into actual economic growth. Observations on TVEs' organizational structure have revealed that the collective TVEs, which account for the majority of this sector, are nominally owned by local community citizens, and under the direct control of local community government leaders. This phenomenon has led to debates on the true property rights of collective TVEs: are the property rights of collective TVEs clearly defined and secured? Are they public firms, or actual private firms under the title of 'collective firms', or a mixed or hybrid kind of firms? Should they be referred to as 'non-state sector' firms to distinguish them from state-owned public firms? Furthermore, what is the critical feature in the property rights structure of collective TVEs that has made the

---

[26] In most cases, luxury cars. Due to the regulation of the central government, local governments are prohibited to buy luxury cars for cadre use. This rule dose not apply to enterprise managers. Hence, some local leaders 'borrow' such luxury cars from firm managers on a long-term basis. I observed the use of a Mercedes-Benz, a Cadillac, and a Lincoln-TownCar, etc., by local leaders, and was told they were 'borrowed' from TVE managers.

[27] Informant M79.

collective TVEs outperform both state-owned enterprises (SOEs) and private enterprises?

Answers to these questions are extremely important, because it is a widely held belief in economics that markets require a clear assignment of initial entitlement to most resources and well-enforced rules of contract. The clarity of property rights is the prerequisite condition for a well-functioning market system, and thus economic prosperity. 'Getting property rights right' in transitional and developing economies is thus considered crucial to the success of reform and development. To quite a number of economists and policy makers, a rapid privatization is a necessary first step for institutional transition from a centrally planning economy to a decentralized free market economy. Public ownership or vaguely defined property rights are undoubtedly contradictory to the reform strategy of the government that intends fostering a market system. Therefore, researchers who argue that collective TVEs are public enterprises, or that the property rights of collective TVEs are vaguely defined, must explain how the seemingly anomalous performance of collective TVEs related to their property rights structure. They also have to explain why the current property rights structure of collective TVEs is vigorous in the development of this sector.

3.1 Property Rights Theory

Despite the lack of a single universally accepted statement of property rights theory that can readily be cited, well-defined property rights can typically be viewed as a set of exclusive but not unrestricted rights governing the ownership and control of assets.[28] These rights include three basic elements:

(1) To every property is assigned a well-defined owner or owners with exclusive rights of ownership;

(2) To the owner of the property goes the residual income accruing to the assets;

(3) The owner has the right to control or determine use of the existing assets, to restructure the property, and to alienate (sell, lease, or destroy) the property.

---

[28] Alchian and Demsetz (1972); Demsetz, (1967); Furubotn and Pejovich (1974); and Williamson (1985).

In other words, property rights include rights of ownership, rights of control, and rights of residual claim toward an existing asset.

Though these rights entitle a given person, or a group of people, to own, control, and earn income from an asset, they *'do not refer to relations between men and things but, rather, to the sanctioned behavioral relations among men that arise from the existence of things and pertain to their use. Property rights assignments specify the norms of behavior with respect to things that each and every person must observe in his interactions with other persons, or bear the cost for nonobservance. The prevailing system of property rights in the community can be described, then, as the set of economic and social relations define the position of each individual with respect to the utilization of scarce resources'.*[29] Therefore, the crucial point of the property rights is the exclusive entitlement of the assets, which set the norms of inter-personal behavior in a society.

North and Weingast pointed to the importance of secure property rights for economic development,[30] though their discussion has been limited to a large extent to market economies and private ownership. Since well-defined and secure private property rights will entitle the owner of the property to enjoy exclusively the benefit generated by the property, hence giving the owner the strongest incentive to use his property efficiently. The private owners, who are uniquely positioned by having the proper rights and the incentive, will tend to allocate his resources to the highest valued use, and make sure these resources will be used as efficiently as possible to increase the profitability of his property, given that profit maximization is the rational objective of the property owner. Such rational behavior will undoubtedly lead to rapid economic growth as observed in world economic history. Without well-defined private property rights, a firm will tend to operate relatively inefficiently, and an economy will tend to perform in a relatively inferior manner (Alchian and Demsetz, 1972).

However, this set of rights does not have to be always held by one person or one group of people in order to refer to 'well-defined'. One of the important features of the property rights is the 'separability of the rights'.

---

[29] See Eirik Furubotn and Svetozar Pejovich, 1972, 'Property Rights and Economic Theory: A Survey of Recent Literature', *Journal of Economic Literature,* 10(4):1139.

[30] Douglass North and Barry Weingast, 1989, 'Constitutions and Commitment: The Evolution of Institutions Governing Public Choice in Seventeenth Century England', *Journal of Economic History,* 49 (December).

As pointed out by Alchian and Demsetz,[31] this set or 'bundle' of rights is divisible in that one party may hold some of these rights while delegate other rights to another party. This may happen when an asset is 'publicly' owned, *i.e.*, it is owned by an extremely sizable group of individuals. While each of these individuals owns a certain share of the asset and hence has the corresponding rights in the residual claim, it becomes impossible for each of them to directly control the use of the asset. When the property rights theory is applied to the Theory of the Firm, then the asset is a firm and the individual owner will be unable to control the operation of the firm directly. In this case, the owners of the firm must find a much smaller party as their 'agent', and delegate the rights of control in the firm to the agent in the cost of sharing part of the profit generated by the firm with the agent. This is the typical property rights structure of a modern corporation in free market economies.

The advantage of such a structure is to combine the available resources owned by a group of people (the shareholders, or the 'principal') with the entrepreneurship embodied by another group of people (the management, or the 'agent') to promote economic growth. However, such a structure may lead to the attenuation of owners' property rights in the firm. This trend is caused by the fact that the dispersion of shareholding combined with management's advantages in proxy fight have led to a rise in the power of managers and have reduced their dependence on the owners (Berla and Means, 1968). The managers are able to deviate from the profit maximization position that represents the owners' desideratum, to pursue their own goals within certain limits. This attenuation of shareholders' rights in the modern corporation takes the form of a reduced ability of the principal to control the deviating decision-making behavior of the agent. However, this attenuation results not from legal restraints on private property rights, but from the costs to the owners of detecting and policing managerial decisions and enforcing profit or wealth maximization (Larner, 1966; Samuelson, 1966). The greater the dispersion of stock ownership in the firm, the higher will be the costs to shareholders of reassigning decision-making authority, and the easier it will be for management to substitute other objectives for the goal of profit or wealth maximization. Hence, in a modern corporation structure, the agent costs that are positively correlated to the division of the property rights may lead to the attenuation of the

---

[31] Alchian and Demsetz, 1973. 'The Property Rights Paradigm', *Journal of Economic History*, 33(1), p.18.

principal's property rights, to the deviation of the agent from the profit maximization objective, and to the damage of the firm's efficiency.

As pointed out by Furubotn and Pejovich (1972, pp.1150-1151), however, the agent's abuse of power and deviating behavior may be constrained by three factors in a free market system: market valuation of the firm, managerial rewards, and competition in manager market. In other words, the institutional arrangements of the free market system have provided effective restrictions on the agent's behavior to protect the interests of the principal. The deviation from the profit maximization objective is thus constrained to a tolerable extent in the principal's cost-benefit calculation, and the modern corporation structure is vigorous in a free market institutional setting and consistent with economic growth.

In summary, the property rights theory defines a set of rights -- ownership rights, control rights, and residual claim rights -- to an asset, and argues that only under well-defined private property rights an economy will operate efficiently and realize rapid economic growth. This set of rights is divisible. In a modern corporation structure, the ownership rights are separated from the control rights. The agent costs related to the rights delegation may lead to the attenuation of the principal's property rights and the deviation from the profit maximization objective. However, the institution of free market system will effectively restrict such deviation and ensure the consistence between the firm property rights structure and economic growth.

3.2 The Property Rights Structure in Socialist Public Enterprises

The conventional economic analyses frequently attribute the inefficiency of socialist public enterprises to their ill-defined property rights. Since the ownership rights of a socialist public firm are assigned to every citizen in the society, it is therefore as if 'assigned to nobody'. As a consequence, such property rights structure impoverishes economic incentives and undermines the vigor of the economy. However, it is arguable why ownership rights that have been assigned to an extraordinary sizable group of individuals, say, all the citizens in a given society, must be viewed as not clearly defined. As argued by Oi (Oi, 1992, p.100), '....there is no inherent reason why secure property rights will be an effective incentive only if they are assigned to individuals'.

If we agree that property rights do not refer to relations between men and things, but to relations among men, then we must agree that so long as the current property rights structure assigns these rights *explicitly* and *exclusively* to a certain group of individuals, no matter how massive this group is defined, we may still view the property rights as clearly defined. Even though the socialist system assigns the ownership of a state-owned firm to the citizens of the whole country, we know this ownership is entitled to this certain group of individuals and exclusive of all the other individuals who are not included in this group. The property rights are therefore clearly defined.

As discussed by the theory of modern corporation, it is impossible for owners to operate a firm directly with such a widely spread ownership. They must delegate their control rights to some agent. In the case of a socialist public firm, owners delegate their control rights to the government -- the first-tier principal-agent delegation, the government then delegates the rights to the firm managers -- the second-tier principal-agent delegation. In other words, the owners in this two-tier principal-agent structure delegate their control rights directly to the government, and indirectly to the firm managers. I will focus on the first tier delegation in this chapter and leave the second tier delegation to the following chapters.

Up to this point, I would argue such property rights structure of socialist public enterprises is significantly analogous to that of modern corporations in its dispersion of ownership rights and the division of ownership rights and control rights. The problem of the socialist property rights structure is perhaps derived from the owners' ability to control the agent's decisions, which is in turn dependent on the cost-benefit calculation of the owners. As the administrative executive, the government has strong incentives to deviate from the profit maximization objective to pursue its own goals, such as employment provision, material balance in input-output, trade promotion, political control and stabilization, etc., at the cost of firm efficiency. Under such a highly dispersed ownership, the owners' costs in detecting, policing and enforcing agent's decision-making behavior may increase to an incredibly high level, incidentally reducing the owners' ability to control the agent's decisions to the minimum. The government as the agent has plenty of freedom to deviate from the owners' objective to pursue its own goals. The problem becomes particularly severe because the institutional arrangements of the socialist system do not provide effective constraints over the deviating behavior of the government to protect the owners' interests.

The crucial point, as pointed out by Weitzman and Xu (1994) and Chang and Wang (1994), is that the participation of the ownership in a socialist public firm is not a voluntary decision independently made by the *de jure* owners of the firm but, rather, an automatic acquisition of the rights through citizenship. In the same sense, the owners have no way to terminate their participation in the ownership so long as they want to keep their citizenship in society. The owners have thus lost their most powerful means to restrict the agent's behavior, *i.e.*, the termination of the rights delegation.

Access to information regarding the performance of a public firm, which is usually out of the reachable scope for most owners, could be either unavailable or extremely costly to any individual owner. In the case that a single owner is unsatisfied with the decisions of the agent and decides to take action, then he must challenge the entire system, for the system is under the control of the current government. The cost of taking such action could be fatal to a single citizen, even though he has the legal right to do so as an owner. Compared with the negligible share of any possible benefit an owner may enjoy from the improvement in the efficiency of a firm, it is really questionable whether any single owner would have a strong enough incentive to actually claim their rights to challenge the agent's decisions. In this sense, the *de jure* owners of socialist public enterprises have been deprived of their rights to terminate the delegation of the control rights in the firm to the agent, and have very limited ability to control the decisions made by the agent. Though the government as the agent may argue that all the material benefit generated by the public firms are dedicated to the improvement of the welfare of the citizens who are nominal owners of the public firms, the *de jure* owners in a socialist economy are at best the passive beneficiaries of the public enterprises, instead of independent entities with property rights entitlement over those firms. Therefore, the inefficiency of the socialist public property rights structure is not caused by its widely dispersed ownership but, rather, by the high cost and low ability of the owners in controlling their agent, and the lack of institutional arrangements that provide effective restrictions on the government's behavior to protect citizens' rights. This may be attributed to the institutional environment of the socialist system and seems beyond the scope of this book.

3.3 The Property Rights of Collective TVEs

As I argued in the above section, the inefficiency problem of the socialist public enterprises may be attributed to the low ability of the owners in controlling the agent's decisions and the lack in the institutional arrangement that can restrict the agent's behavior. Supposing that, there exists some institutional arrangement that may provide the agent with a strong incentive not to deviate from the principal's profit maximization objective, or change the cost-benefit calculation of the principal in monitoring the agent's decisions, hence increasing the principal's ability in agent behavior control, the problem could then be solved. Such an arrangement will make it possible to reduce the agent's deviation tendency to a tolerable extent and make the socialist public property rights structure consistent with economic growth, at least to certain degree. The property rights structure of collective TVEs may have provided such a practical experience.

As indicated by 'The Regulation on Township and Village Collective Enterprises of the People's Republic of China'[32] issued by the Chinese State Council in June 1990,

> *Township and village collective enterprises are the component of the socialist public economy in our country* (Article 3, Chapter 1). *Assets (of a collective TVE) are owned collectively by the whole of rural residents of the township or village which runs the enterprise; the ownership rights over the enterprise assets should be exercised by the rural residents' meeting (or congress) or a collective economic organization that represents the whole of rural residents of the township or village. The ownership rights of the enterprise assets will not change when the enterprise is under a managerial contract responsibility system, leasing, or joint operation with enterprises of other types of ownership* (Article 18, Chapter 3).

> *The owner of a TVE, according to the law, determines the direction and formats of its business operations, selects managers or determines the method of such selection, determines the specific distribution ratio of after-tax profit between the owner and the enterprise, and has the rights over the enterprise concerning its spin-off, merger, relocation, stop-operation, close-down, application for bankruptcy, etc.* (Article 19, Chapter 3).

Obviously, the property rights -- including ownership rights, control rights, and residual rights -- of a collective TVE are clearly assigned to the whole of the legal residents in a community that runs the firm. This entitlement is exclusive against all the 'outsiders', even though they live or work in the

---

[32] The Regulation on Township and Village Collective Enterprises of The People's Republic of China, See Yu, Z., Zhan, Y., and Sun, W. eds. 1995. Rural Cooperative Economy and Its Management, People's Press, Beijing, China.

same community.[33] TVEs' assets legally belong to the residents of the township or the village, neither to the government of the township, village, or any higher level authorities, nor exclusively to enterprise employees as in a producer-managed firm. Because of this widely dispersed ownership right, collective TVEs can not be operated under the direct control of every *de jure* owner of the firm. The control rights are therefore delegated to another party -- township government in a township enterprise case, or the village leaders in a village enterprise case. Through such delegation, local government leaders, as the agents of local residents, acquired the control rights over collective TVEs and became the *de facto* owners of those enterprises as argued by many observers and researchers (Chang and Wang, 1994; Che and Qian, 1998; Jefferson and Rawski, 1994; Oi, 1992, 1995; Tian, 1995; Walder, 1995a; Whiting, 1995). The property rights structure of collective TVEs is hence analogous to that of state-owned public enterprises in two features: the public dispersion of ownership rights and the control rights delegation to the government. It has another significant similarity with the state-owned firms -- the involuntary participation of the ownership. The *de jure* owners have no freedom to choose the agent and terminate the control rights delegation in their will. In this sense, collective TVEs *are* public firms (Jefferson and Rawski, 1994; Naughton, 1994; Oi, 1992; Walder, 1995) with deprived rights of *de jure* owners.

However, the property rights structure of collective TVEs differs from that of state-owned public enterprises in two ways, which have made collective TVEs a more vigorous organizational form than state-owned public enterprises in a transitional economy like China. The first is that the local government leaders instead of the central government have been positioned as the public agents to take over the control rights over the enterprises. Generally speaking local leaders have less non-profit-maximizing goals than the central government. For example, local leaders do not have the material balance objective. They are less responsible for the

---

[33] Most collective TVEs in my investigation sites excluded non-resident workers from firm welfare programs such as medical care, paid sick-leave, pensions, etc. Non-resident workers and their family members were also excluded from local community facilities like schools. Quite a number of managers and local leaders called non-resident workers 'our hired laborers', and thought it was fair to pay non-resident workers less, assign them heavier and dirtier jobs, and exclude them from managerial positions. The only reason for such discriminative treatments is 'they are not local residents, they have no rights over *our* firms'.

political order and ideological control than the central government is. Even in the case of provision of employment opportunities, though the local leaders face more direct pressure from the residents, this pressure is limited to a much smaller scope. Local government is obligated only to the laborers within its jurisdiction, not to the whole population of the country. This is particularly true to the relatively developed coastal areas. With the development of local TVEs, all the surplus rural labor has been absorbed by non-agricultural sectors. These localities have reached full employment, or have been in shortage of labor in recent years. Local leaders face completely zero pressure in rural employment.[34] Whereas in the same period, the central government is confronting a severe problem in the provision of employment opportunities not only to rural labor but also to urban surplus labor. Therefore, local community government as public agents have fewer incentives to deviate from the owners' profit-maximizing objective. Furthermore, as described in Section 2, in addition to local leaders' personal benefits, the revenue incentives of the local leaders facing the reforming fiscal system, and profit and income criteria directly specified by the cadre evaluation system have resulted in the coincidence between owners' objectives and agent's objectives. As the *de facto* owner of the 'community corporation', local leaders are meeting with hard budget constraints (Che and Qian, 1998; Walder, 1995a). They are impelled to improve the efficiency and profitability of collective TVEs under their control, which is in the interests of the owners.

The second is that ownership rights are dispersed to a much smaller group of individuals. The community governments are positioned under the direct supervision and regulation of higher authorities. Their performance is also observable directly by the owners. This institutional arrangement provides to some extent effective means to the owners in disciplining local leaders' behavior when deviating from the profit-maximizing objective. The development of local TVEs is the most important single criterion to evaluate the performance of a local leader, which ensures local leaders giving priority to improvement in collective TVEs' efficiency among other objectives. At the same time, regulations from higher authorities have prevented the local leaders from abusing their power in the profit distribution of collective TVEs. As stipulated by 'The Regulation on

---

[34] Two out of four townships in my investigation sites (Huazhuang Township of Jiangsu and Doumen Township of Zhejiang) reached full employment. A number of villages I visited there had more than 90 percent of rural laborers working in TVEs. They even hired laborers from other areas in both agricultural and TVEs production.

Township and Village Collective Enterprises of the People's Republic of China',

> ....*The part (of after-tax profit) retained by the enterprise should be no less than 60 percent of the total and should be arranged to under the enterprise's autonomous decision. The retained after-tax profit for the enterprise should be mainly used for the increase of the funds for production development in technological transformation and expansion of reproduction'*, and '*also for the appropriate increase of welfare funds and bonus funds,* and *the part remitted to the owner of the enterprise should be used mainly for the svpport of construction of agricultural infrastructures, agricultural technology services, rural public welfare, renewal and transformation of enterprises, or development of new enterprises'* (Article 32, Chapter 5).

This regulation restricts the rights of using collective TVEs' revenues by community residents as single individuals, *i.e.*, it deprives the firm *de jure* owner's rights in direct residual claim. More importantly, however, it also restricts the rights of using this revenue by the local community governments to pursue their goals other than the development of local economy and the improvement of local welfare, so as to secure most of the benefit from collective TVEs toward their *de jure* owners.

On the other hand, collective TVEs are usually located within the community that runs them, and most township and village leaders are residents of the same community. A township, especially a village, is a small community. Unlike state-owned enterprises, the performance of both the firm and the local leaders are relatively easy to be observed by local residents. In other words, the *de jure* owners, or the principal of the collective TVEs, have relatively lower costs in detecting agent behavior of the local leaders. They are relatively more sensitive to and concerned with the performance of the collective TVEs in the community, for their interests are more directly and closely related to the performance of those enterprises. For example, the expansion of old enterprises or the development of new enterprises may provide local residents with more and better opportunities of employment; they may acquire more agricultural subsidies or enjoy more welfare or public projects that are made possible by the improvement of the community collective TVEs' profitability.

Although in the absence of formal voting or election, local residents may not directly exercise their control and regulate the behavior of the community government leaders. Nor can they change the decisions made by local leaders. However, local residents may 'voice out' when they are unsatisfied with the performance of the community TVEs or local leaders. Such repeated 'voice' could severely damage the reputation of local leaders, project a bad impression of local leaders to higher authorities. Furthermore, it could cost the local leaders future promotion or even current positions. During my field investigation, I heard several similar stories of how the 'voice' of local residents led to the removal of village heads from their positions. In one village, I was told, the village director decided to lease a profitable village enterprise to his brother-in-law, resulting in the closedown of the firm due to wrong decisions made by the leaseholder. The massive taking-away of the firm properties by the village residents led to a fight. As a consequence the township leaders decided to remove the director away from his position.[35] Another story is that a village party branch secretary was involved in a fake joint-venture swindle. He was invited to Hong Kong for a 'business trip', then paid a huge amount of money to import some machinery equipment to establish a village 'joint-venture'. The imported equipment was later found to be useless second-hand garbage. The 'partner' had never put in any investment as was previously agreed after they sold the 'equipment'. The village residents driven by anger reported the sad affair to the township and county governments, and finally had him removed from the position.[36]

Compared with the *de jure* owners of state-owned enterprises, the *de jure* owners of collective TVEs obviously have stronger incentives and greater ability to discipline the decisions made by their agents -- the governments at different levels -- due to the different cost-benefit calculations of these two categories of owners.

The rural community organization and the property rights structure of collective TVEs have positioned the local leaders between two tiers of supervision. The one is from above, the higher authorities; the other from below, the community residents. Such arrangements exerted constraints on the decision-making behavior of local leaders in favor of local residents' benefit, and are consistent with the economic growth in a locality. We, at this point, present an inherent explanation as to why the collective TVEs, as community public firms, are more vigorous than and have superior performance over state-owned public enterprises in the economic development of a transitional economy.

---

[35] Informant L1.
[36] Informant M4.

4. The Advantage of Local Leaders as *de facto* Owner of Collective TVEs

The discussion in Section 3 provides a possible explanation as to why the property rights structure of collective TVEs -- community public ownership with local government as *de facto* owner to hold the control rights -- is dynamic and outperforming state-owned public firms in economic growth. However, this discussion very naturally leads to another question: why private enterprises failed to outperform collective TVEs at least until the early 1990s, in spite of the fact that they enjoyed clearly defined private property rights. Nor did they have the disadvantage of a separation of ownership rights and control rights, which might attenuate the owner's rights and damage the firm's efficiency and economic growth.

Many researchers have pointed out that the local government leaders have made critical contribution to the development of local TVEs (Byrd and Lin, 1990; Chang and Wang, 1994; Ma et al., 1994; Nee, 1992; Oi, 1992; Whiting, 1995). Such contributions ranged from securing property rights, mobilizing and providing access to resources, absorbing risks, to interfacing with outsiders. I will discuss these contributions in turn.

4.1 Securing Property Rights

The contribution of local leaders in securing the property rights of collective TVEs seems quite straightforward. China is a country with a long tradition of authoritarian government. This tradition is developed to an unprecedented extreme under the rule of the communist party. To ensure 'comprehensive proletarian dictatorship', Mao devised a political system that gives the communist party the right to intervene in every aspect of society. Private property and personal economic incentives were regarded as bourgeois, and capitalism evil. People who undertook non-public or non-collective productive activities were at risk of 'taking the capitalist road', and capitalist-road-takers would have to 'cut the capitalist tail'. Under such a political environment, private property rights are insecure, or at least inferior ideologically. Besides long-standing political and administrative obstacles against the free establishment of firms by individuals, private enterprises were discriminated against by most units in society as late as the 1980s (Lin, 1990, in Byrd and Lin, ed. 1990). On the other hand, local community governments are part of the large government institution with broad powers given by the fundamentals of the political system. The title 'collective enterprises' effectively protects firms against political discrimination, while the involvement and support of local community government would provide additional credit to a firm, and confidence to the business partners of the firm. The property rights of a collective TVE with the community government as the *de facto* owner are secure in three ways. Firstly, the collective ownership rights can not be deprived whether by law or by socialist ideology. Secondly, in case the properties owned by a collective TVE face the threat of encroachment, either from higher authorities or other parties, (say, the taking over of the firm by a higher level government, forced merger with firms in other communities, or forced transfer of machinery to outside firms, etc.), the community government leaders would enthusiastically take action to resist such encroachment, for they are the *de facto* owners and joint-beneficiaries of the enterprise[37] (Ma et al., 1994). The third, when a collective TVE is in conflict with outsiders, the community government as the local administrative executive can more effectively and easily negotiate with the other party than any private individuals to reach a favorable agreement to protect the firm's interests.

Needless to say, security in the property rights is a precondition for a firm's long-run development. This is a main reason why so many private enterprises chose to disguise themselves as collective firms though actually 'hidden' private firms (Liu, 1992; Peng, 1992). The community government did not only tolerate but sometimes also helped the private enterprises in disguise. For example, there are four firms in my field investigation sample that were actually private firms under the title of 'collective village enterprises'.[38] All of these four firms are in Qingyunpu Township of Jiangxi Province. In 1994, Qingyunpu township government implemented a new policy -- leasing 'collective enterprise' title to local private enterprises. The overall purpose of such a policy was to help local private enterprises to overcome the frustration in their business caused by discrimination in society. As indicated by the township leader,[39] 'our collective enterprises

---

[37] The central government does not have such incentive as long as the transferred assets are still publicly or collectively owned, and within the boundary of the country. Sometimes such encroachment of local properties is actually desired by the central government.

[38] They were randomly selected as the sample firms because they were on the list of collective TVEs provided by the township government. I did not recognize that they were actually private firms until I interviewed with their managers (owners) and acquired the detailed information from the firms.

[39] Informant L6.

sector is not as strong as in coastal areas, and the township government doesn't have the money to establish more collective TVEs. We must support private enterprises to develop local economy. However, private enterprises have been discriminated against in many aspects by government policies and by society. Not only are they discriminated against by state-owned or collective enterprises, even other private enterprises themselves do not trust them or each other. They prefer to do business with non-private firms rather than private firms. As a township government, we do not have the ability to change the political and economic environment, but we can help to eliminate or reduce such discrimination by letting private firms use the title of "collective enterprise"'. He admitted that government revenue increase was also within the scope of this policy consideration.

In practice, township government, especially Villagers' Committees, signed 'leasing' contract with private owners. The typical 'leasing' contract consisted of three parts: collective enterprise operation license leasing, land leasing, and electric transformer leasing.[40] As specified by the leasing contract designed by the Villagers' Committee of Huangxi Village of Qingyunpu Township, the village (party A) leased the Collective Enterprise Operation License to the private firm (party B) during the period of firm's business operation for a fee of 2,400 yuan per year. Party A then assumed the responsibility to protect the lawful interests of party B, and coordinate with other parties on behalf of party B's benefit. At the same time, party B had the responsibility to follow any applicable laws and regulations of the government, operate within the license permitted business field, and accept the supervision of the Villagers' Committee. Party B assumed complete obligation for financial loss or debts in case it had business losses or if such losses further led to a closedown of the firm. Obviously, private enterprises, which obtained the title of 'collective enterprise' through such leasing contracts, had not changed their property rights in substance, but gained some degree of protection from the community government against discrimination in society. To what extent might such protection be effective in securing the property rights of private enterprises is unclear. However, the fact that most private enterprises in that township had signed such a

---

[40] The electric power supply facilities in rural China are usually owned by village. Private enterprises must get the permission from the Villagers' Committee to use the electricity through the transformers. According to the contract, the village had the obligation to put additional transformer(s) when more electricity was demanded by the firms, while firms had to pay the 'leasing fee' that was contingent upon the wattage they used.

contract[41] implies there are advantages, at least psychologically, for private owners.

As a contrast, community governments in some other areas adopted different methods to 'secure' local collective enterprises' rights. They limited the issue of certain kinds of operation license to private applicants in order to protect local collective TVEs from competition from private enterprises in similar industries. This kind of policy gave local monopoly to collective TVEs by setting entry barriers to private firms (Ma et al., 1994).

4.2 Access to Resources

Local government leaders were more effective at launching new enterprises than private entrepreneurs, especially during the early part of the reforms when underdeveloped markets did not allocate resources or distribute products efficiently (Byrd and Lin, 1990; Ody, 1992; Oi, 1996; Wong, 1992). Many have described how local leaders could, by using their political, social, and personal connections, more consistently find sources of capital (Che and Qian, 1998), mobilize labor (Meng, 1990), allocate land (Ma et al., 1994; Naughton, 1994), etc., to support local collective TVEs. In other words, local leaders' comparative advantage over private entrepreneurs in gaining access to resources stemmed from the imperfection of markets. With the rapid development of product markets, local leaders' role in output distribution has been apparently reduced. Their role in labor mobilization became negligible due to the existence of a numerous pool of rural surplus labor and the reform in rural labor market. However, their role in gaining access to many resources necessary for firm operation was still extremely vital, because the markets for resources had not been fully developed. These resources might include land, financial capital, technology and human capital, and other resources such as certain types of raw materials and energy.

Land: Land is a collectively owned resource in China. There did not exist a formal or officially approved land market up to the early 1990s. However, although only the rights to the use of land were entitled to rural communities, the rights to transfer and dispose of land were not, any allocation of farmland lies in the hands of local community governments. Any units in society, public or individual, who needs land must obtain

---

[41] Informant L6, L7, L8.

permission to the right of land usage from local community governments (Kirsch, Worz, and Engel, 1994; Lin, Q., 1990).

Village leaders have the easiest access to land because land is under their direct control. When a Villagers' Committee decides to launch a new village enterprise, it simply assigns a piece of land within the boundary of the village farmland to this proposed enterprise. The peasant household that was previously cultivating the land would be moved to other piece(s) of land, generally without much ado. The village may provide the household employment opportunities in the firm as compensation. Very few financial exchanges would be involved in such land acquisition.

When the higher levels of governments have their eye on land that is out of their direct control (such as land that does not belong to the township but belong to a nearby village) to set up collective enterprises, they must negotiate with the community that has the rights over the land. In most cases, the community leaders can not refuse such requisition, but would bargain for more favorable compensation. In the early years of collective TVEs, land requisition from a village by the township government might be compensated by the provision of certain agreed amount of employment positions in the proposed factory depending on the area of the land to be taken (Tudi Dailao, usually 1 to 3 persons per mu of land), without or with only nominal financial compensation (several hundred yuan per mu) to the village.[42] Since the late 1980s, land occupation by the township government is usually associated with financial as well as employment compensations toward the village. However, the amount of the financial compensation is not determined by the market price of the land but, rather, by the negotiation power each party had. It could range from several thousand to several tens of thousand yuan per mu.[43]

On the other hand, private entrepreneurs would face much more restricted access to land. Since they could not gain the rights of land usage at the market-determined price, it became entirely a personal relationship problem between the private entrepreneur and the local leaders. Sometimes it could be a very frustrating process for the private entrepreneurs if they were not relatives or friends of local leaders. They could spend anything from several months to several years running from one official department to another. They might have to give sizable side payments to local leaders to acquire the land use permission.[44]

---

[42] See Ma et al. eds. 1994, p.177, 209, 213, 257

[43] See note 42.

[44] Informant M32.

Financial Capital: In countries all over the world, new firms have great difficulty in obtaining capital to start and to expand. This is particularly true in developing countries. The lack of wealth of the entrepreneurs to invest directly, and the difficulty to acquire loans restrict capital formation and industrialization in rural areas. In the absence of formal capital markets and credit markets in a transitional economy, access to financial capital becomes a critical factor for the success of a firm. However, local community governments in rural China have successfully managed to mobilize sizable financial resources that enabled them to engage in rapid capital formation and firm development, despite the rudimentary financial market and underdeveloped banking institutions. Local government leaders have prominent comparative advantage over private entrepreneurs in obtaining such access in several ways: their direct control of collective properties; their influence on local credit suppliers; and their ability to help firms evade taxes.

During the commune era, the initial investment of commune or brigade enterprises were collectively owned resources such as land, buildings, equipment and tools (Ma et al., 1994), and financial funds extracted from the Collective Accumulation Funds (Gongji Jin)[45] (Wang, X., 1990). These were collective properties directly controlled by local leaders. The usage of such collective properties as private capital investment was illicit and almost impossible. After the replacement of the commune system by the household responsibility system, the collective properties of the communes or the brigades were transferred to the townships or the villages, but still under the control of local leaders. Local leaders have the decisive power to determine the allocation of these properties, *i.e.*, they have direct access to the existing capital that was accumulated in the commune era. Such access was denied to private entrepreneurs.

However, the rapid development of TVEs led to a tremendous increase in financial capital demand that was far beyond the available existing collective properties and financial resources. Many enterprises were reliant to a great extent on loans from banks and Rural Credit Cooperatives (RCCs) for establishment and even for daily operations. As reported by the rural

---

[45] The Collective Accumulation Funds were the retained collective incomes that were not distributed to individual commune members. These funds were the major source of collective investment in re-production and productive expansion, local infrastructure, or public facilities.

investigation team of the State Statistical Bureau,[46] their field investigation conducted in ten Chinese provinces in 1986 revealed that, from the total initial establishment capital investment of sample TVEs, the collective accumulation of the communes and the brigades accounted for 23.6 percent, state granted fund 4.2 percent, fund raised from enterprises' employees and local residents 6.5 percent, while the loans from different sources amounted to 44 percent. This survey report shows that as early as in the first half of 1980s, loans constituted the lion's share of the financial capital sources of TVEs.

Table 2.4 summarizes the investment sources of my sample TVEs from the year 1989 to 1993. We may find from the table that both the overall investment and the average size of firm investment had been increasing. However, the share of the investment directly provided by the community governments stayed small, never exceeding 10 percent. Two major sources of firms' investment were the firms' own retained revenues and loans. The latter surpassed the former throughout the five years.

As described by other researchers (Liu et al., 1995; Ma et al., 1994; Oi, 1992; Putterman, 1994; Whiting, 1995), local community governments have considerable influence on the loan allocation decisions of local credit organizations. These credit organizations (bank branches and RCCs branches), though not government apparatuses, have a close relationship with community governments and local leaders. They are operating within the jurisdiction of the community governments, and under the general leadership of local party committees. They thus have to consider the preference of the community governments in their loan allocations. On the other hand, leaders of local credit organizations are usually former colleagues or current friends of local government leaders with combined interests. Interviews confirmed that this kind of personal relations makes it very difficult for credit organization leaders to refuse a loan request placed by community government leaders. As described by a township leader[47]: 'I can't order the bank (branch) or RCC to loan money to a firm, but I can "talk" with their head persons to persuade them to do so. We are friends and familiar with each other. They won't turn down my request for they themselves frequently ask me to help them in dealing with various things, in

---

[46] See Zhou, Qiren and Hu, Zhuangjun, 1987, 'Assets Formation, Operational Features, and Macroeconomic Impact of TVEs: An Analysis of A Sample Survey of Large Township Enterprises in Ten Provinces', *China Social Science*, 87-6.
[47] Informant L6.

fact much more than I ask them. If they turn down my request, I can turn down theirs.'

Table 2.4 Sample Firms' Investment and Sources, 1989-1993*

	1989	1990	1991	1992	1993
Total Investment (million yuan)	23.31	32.87	47.97	96.29	294.99
Per Firm Investment (million yuan)	0.42	0.60	0.87	1.75	5.36
From Which (%)					
Firm	25.6	21.8	31.0	29.0	18.7
Government	9.1	7.0	5.1	5.9	7.3
Loan	51.2	56.3	54.2	37.3	40.6
Fund Raising	7.0	6.9	4.4	5.2	4.1
Foreign	0	0	0	14.7	14.3
Other	7.1	7.9	4.7	7.7	15.0

* Data covers the total investment made by 64 sample TVEs in the corresponding year. Sources of Investment are defined as following: Firm -- firm retained revenues; Government -- community government's direct investment; Loan -- loans from bank or RCCs; Fund Raising -- fund raised from local residents, firm employees, or personal borrowing; Foreign -- investment from foreigners; Other -- other sources such as state-owned or collective joint-venture partners' investment.

Source: Author's Survey, 1994

Besides the organizational and personal relations between local credit organization leaders and community government leaders, the credit organizations have other reasons to favor collective TVEs in their loan decisions. In the reform practice of the credit system, local state bank branches and RCCs are at least partially responsible for the repayment of previous loans. To prevent credit default, the credit organizations might ask for formal or informal guarantors and/or collateral from the loan applicant to secure repayment. Evidently, it is relatively easier for collective TVEs to obtain loans than private enterprises under such rules, since collective TVEs have the community government backing them up. As the *de facto* owner of collective TVEs, local community governments are more than willing to serve as loan guarantors for the collective TVEs. This is because they hold the control rights over more than one firm that could be regarded as reliable loan collateral. They also have the ability to order other profitable collective firms to repay a collective-firm borrowed loan, which turned out to be a bad loan due to investment failure (Byrd, 1990; Ma et al., 1994; Ody, 1992). This would effectively reduce the default rate for the credit organization.

However, things are different for private enterprises. Limited resources for sizable loan collateral and unreliable guarantor handicap private entrepreneurs in rural China from obtaining loans, especially large loans to start or expand their businesses.[48] As reported by Lin (Lin,Q., 1990): *'They have the most difficulty in obtaining bank loans, and when the state decides to tighten credit, loans to private enterprises are the first to be cut. Thus they may be forced to get loans at much higher rates from informal credit organizations.'*

We may find from Table 2.4 that investment funds from 'other' sources, mainly from the joint-venture partners of state-owned enterprises or other collective enterprises and from foreign investors, had increasing importance in TVEs' investment in 1990s. The fund raised from individuals as firm employees and local residents, or from personal borrowings, also accounted for a stable portion in firms' investment.[49] However, the panel data collected in my investigation revealed that, the difference in firms' ownership might significantly affect the constitutions of financial capital sources of the firm.[50] In 1993, the average per firm investment of private

---

[48] Che and Qian (1998) cited a field sample investigation survey by Zhang and Ronnas, it reported that the mean size of loans extended to township enterprises, village enterprises, and private enterprises in 1989 was, respectively, 299,649 yuan, 218,873 yuan, and 58,996 yuan.

[49] The official statistical data has shown the same trend. In 1994, the nation-wide TVEs' investment was constituted by 3.7 percent of government granted funds, 28.2 percent of loans, 31.6 percent of firms' own retained revenues, 9.4 percent of fund raising, 9.0 percent of foreign investment, and 18 percent of other sources fund. See *China TVE Yearbook*, 1995, p.227.

[50] Also see Byrd, 1990, 'Entrepreneurship, Capital, and Ownership', and Wang, X. 1990, 'Capital Formation and Utilization', both in Byrd and Lin ed. *China's Rural*

sample TVEs was 0.34 million yuan, of which fund-raising accounted for 44.8 percent and the firm retained profit accounted for 23.2 percent of this small scaled investment. No investment from community government, foreigners, or investors of other non-private sectors has been observed. In comparison, another group of sample TVEs -- the joint ventures between collective TVEs and state-owned, other collective, or foreign enterprises -- has a much larger investment scale and different constitutions of investment sources. The average per firm investment of this group of TVEs was 19.22 million yuan, nearly sixty times as that of the first group. From this investment, 27.1 percent was from foreign investors; while 23.0 percent was from non-private joint-venture partners. These two accounted for half of the total investment. The community government also contributed 13.5 percent of the investment, while fund raised from private investors accounted for 1.4 percent only. This observation implies that the 'outsiders' (state-owned enterprises, other collective enterprises, and foreign investors) had significant preference in favor of collective TVEs in selecting joint-venture partners and making capital investments, probably because of their securer property rights and larger existing operation scales. Therefore, collective TVEs have vaster sources of financial capital than their private counterparts. The later must depend heavily on restricted private sources in capital provision.

I was at first confused during my field studies by the reported 'state supporting funds' (Guojia Fuchi Jijin) included in TVEs' sources of capital investment. I was then told such 'supporting fund' were not actual financial investment granted by the central government but, rather, the fund generated by a tax exemption or reduction that was the result of preferential policies of the central government. This part of funds accounted for about 1 percent of TVEs total fixed capital investment in 1994 as the official statistical data reported,[51] however, it is reasonable to expect the actual percentage to be much higher than 1 percent.

Whiting (1995) found in her field studies that more than 75 percent of her sample collective TVEs had been involved in alternative tax evasion practices. Furthermore, local government leaders driven by revenue incentives not only tolerated, but also colluded, in such tax evasions *'in order to shift revenues from shared budgetary (tax) channels to non-*

Industry, Oxford University Press, 1990. Whiting, 1995, *The Micro-foundation of Institutional Change in Reform China: Property Rights and Revenue Extraction in the Rural Industrial Sector,* Ph.D. Dissertation, University of Michigan, Ann Arbor.
[51] China TVE Yearbook, 1995, P.227.

budgetary channels that the township alone controlled.[52] Although the central government, who mandated preferential tax policies to benefit rural collective enterprises, sought to control the application of preferential policies to prevent substantial tax revenue erosion, it was a general trend that such preferential policies were abused by local government leaders to favor community benefits. My investigation confirms Whiting's finding that local government leaders were actively involved in the collusion of tax evasion. Some kinds of tax evasion were in fact under the direct inspiration and guidance of local leaders, or by their manipulation. Otherwise it would have been impossible. For example, one workshop of a collective enterprise would be separated and registered as a new enterprise under the design of the community government for acquiring eligibility for a multi-year tax exemption or reduction. I was told in a township, three enterprises had been former workshops of a fourth one and registered as independent firms in the last five years.[53] In another village, I observed two factory signs on the same gate. The village leader told me, there was only one firm. 'They are two workshops of the same factory. We registered one workshop as a new firm last year when it started producing a new product. We have thus got the preferential treatment of tax exemption for the new firm as well as for the new product.'[54] In both cases, the township government and the village leaders were the decision-makers of tax evasion through firm separation. Registering a collective enterprise as a welfare or school-run enterprise for complete tax-exemption status was also a tempting target for local leaders in their tax evasion tactics through firm registration manipulation (Whiting, 1995).

Manipulation in firm accounting records is another commonly used means to evade taxes. The collusion between the community government leaders and the firm could be done in a variety of ways. As described by Wang et al.,[55] not a few rural collective TVEs had three different sets of accounting records: the 'true' records for the firm's own operation, the 'approved' records (Renke Baobiao) dealing with financial affairs between the firm and the community government, and the 'reporting' records (Shangbao Baobiao) for the calculation of tax payments as the report to higher authorities. The 'reporting' records generally stated lower pre-tax

---

[52] Whiting, 1995, p.202.
[53] Informant L3.
[54] Informant L8.
[55] See Wang, H. et al. 1994, 'The Investigation on J Township Telecommunication Cable Factory', in Ma, et al. 1994.

profit than the 'approved' records. The difference between these two records, or so-called 'profit adjustment', reflected the concealed taxable revenue of the firm that was known to and approved by the community government. The evaded tax payment was shared by the firm and the community government, or left to the firm for capital investment. Under reporting sales or output value, and/or inflating production costs were the most pervasively used methods to lower the pre-tax profit, thus reducing the taxable revenue of the firm. A firm might conceal its sales by increasing its reported inventories (Ma et al., 1994), or pad the wage rolls with fictitious names (Whiting, 1995). In many cases, such tax-evading behavior was indeed encouraged by the community government leaders so long as it was not perceived as concealment by local leaders. Local government leaders even allowed the firm to deduct loan repayment or extract 'enterprise funds' as costs from the pre-tax profit, on the condition that the firm apply the extracted 'enterprise funds' to its capital investment in the following years (Ma et al., 1994).

To summarize, the community government leaders have been taking advantage of their direct control over collectively accumulated capital properties, their influence on local credit organizations, their relationship with potential outside investors, and their power and ability in tax evasion to help the collective TVEs in gaining access to financial capital. Private entrepreneurs were excluded from such access when facing an imperfect financial system and rudimentary credit market.

Technology and Human Capital: Fewer researchers to my knowledge have discussed in detail the role local government leaders have played in the acquisition of technology and human capital for collective TVEs. Needless to say, technology and human capital are scarce resources in rural development of developing countries. This is particularly true in a centrally planning economy. In pre-reform China, research and development institutes and higher education institutions were clustered in state-owned sectors and urban areas. State-owned sectors were monopolist employers of almost all scientific researchers and experts, engineers, designers, technicians, even skilled industrial workers. There did not exist any kind of technology or human resources markets that might mobilize technologies or human capital responsive to market demand rather than to central government's plan. Since the very beginning of the TVE movement through early 1990s, shortage in applicable technologies and product designs, and lack of experienced engineers, technicians, and managerial staff had been a significant obstacle to TVEs' development.[56] Therefore, the availability of technologies and human capital became a major factor influencing a region's development of TVEs (Yang, D., 1990; Jin, H. and Du, Z.). Rural areas near large cities with strong state-owned sectors have been developed more rapidly in TVEs, especially in industrial enterprises (such as Yangtze River Delta and Pearl River Delta), than remote inland areas far from industrialized large cities. Simply because of the former has easier access to the technologies and human capital endowed by state-owned sectors.

Many TVEs have acquired necessary technologies and/or product designs from state-owned sectors through three ways, two are formal while the third is informal. One way for a TVE to obtain the technology or product design from the state-owned sector is to subcontract with a state-owned enterprise, producing assembly components or spare parts for it (Naughton, 1994a). The subcontracting between state-owned enterprises and TVEs is often bridged by community governments. Community governments seek information about appropriate partners, make connections with state-owned enterprises, provide services for enforcing contracts concerning quality and delivery problems, as well as serve as a mechanism for conflict and dispute resolution (Che and Qian, 1998). Several joint-ventures between the state-owned enterprises and the township or village enterprises among my sample TVEs were initiated by such subcontracting arrangement.

The second formal method is to establish various forms of economic and technical cooperative arrangements by TVEs with state-owned industrial enterprises, research units, and higher educational institutions (Jefferson and Rawski, 1994; Zhou, S. and Liu, J. et al., 1993). As Yu (Yu, C., 1994) observed, a village enterprise in Shandong Province established a cooperative relationship with a technical school in a nearby city, and became a 'training factory' of the school. It acquired capital investment, product design, technical consulting and technician services thereby, in exchange for the acceptance of the school students to have their training practice in the factory, (plus some cash side payment to school leaders). In most cases, local community governments are the most enthusiastic initiators and supporters, as well as powerful intermediates of such cooperative arrangements due to their comparative advantage in better access to information, wider organizational contacts and personal relations,

---

[56] Among from fourteen listed 'most difficult aspects in firm's operation', shortage of applicable technologies and product designs was second, lack of technicians was sixth, ranked by 64 sample TVE managers in my field investigation. Shortage of capital funds was ranked first.

and political reputation. In the absence of formal technology market, technologies were transferred from state-owned sectors to TVEs without explicitly set prices. TVEs might provide some 'kickback' cash payment or products to the state-owned units as exchange. However, the real costs of the technologies were relatively low. Collective TVEs thus had cost advantage in technology acquisition over private entrepreneurs (Yang, M., 1994).

The third, or the informal way, *i.e.*, acquiring technologies, product designs, and/or technical consulting services from state-owned units through personal connections, is in fact the most frequently and commonly used way by TVEs in their acquisition of technologies and human capital. Almost all of the case studies conducted by the Sociology and Anthropology Institute of Beijing University report the practices of such personal channeled acquisition (Ma et al., 1994). However, even though personal relations are the main channels of technology acquisition, local community government leaders still have the comparative advantage over private entrepreneurs for the same reasons indicated above.

As described by Lin (Lin, Q., 1990), in TVEs development practices, in many cases whether enterprises prosper depends less on technology than on the availability of managerial and technical talent. Success depends on such 'capable persons' even more than on funds, land, labor, and other factors of production. Local community governments are better endowed with human capital than private entrepreneurs in two senses. The first is that local government leaders are usually better educated or trained, capable, and experienced individuals than ordinary rural people (Chang and Wang, 1994). They are thus more sensitive to political or policy changes, outside information, and business opportunities, which make them more qualified potential candidates for economic organizers or entrepreneurs.

The second is that local community governments have the comparative advantage in attracting and recruiting talent, and fostering their own experts. A state-owned sector employee working part time for collective TVEs might be regarded compatible with the regular duties of his position, if such moonlighting did not interfere with his duties. Such behavior was thus tolerable, if not supported, by his state employer. However, if the same person worked for a private TVE on the side, such behavior would be mostly considered incompatible with his regular duties and prohibited by his employer. This would substantially restrict the source of part-time technical services provided by state-owned sector employees to private enterprises, and force private TVEs to pay much higher salaries to recruit technical personnel in competition with collective TVEs (Lin, Q., 1990). Collective TVEs may attract more employees with various talents because they can provide them with better economic compensations and other favorable treatments. Such treatments not only gave the recruited personnel more satisfaction than they might have in state-owned units, but were often beyond the ability of a private firm (Liu, X., 1994; Yang, M., 1994). For instance, when employment was strictly controlled by the central government's plan and migration was restricted by the residency registration system, private enterprises had almost no hope for recruitment of expert in demand from state-owned units or other regions. However, when such an expert was demanded by a collective TVE, the firm could negotiate with that expert's employer with the community government involved as the intermediate. In case such negotiation failed, it was still possible for the collective TVE to recruit the expert, for the community government might simply register him as a local resident without the migrating permission issued by his employer and legal residency region. Several experts or managers I interviewed were cases in point. Some of them were university graduates allocated by the government to remote provinces many years ago. Local governments let their whole families (as large as five or six in some cases) move back to their hometowns in coastal areas, registered them as local residents, and provided housing for them.[57]

Sending local young cadres and employees to full time or part time educational or training programs is a frequently adopted method to foster indigenous experts. Due to the high costs and relatively long-term absence of the trainees, private enterprises have weaker incentives to join such a program. However, community governments, especially those in relatively rich areas with many collective TVEs, have much stronger incentives to do so. Because they can team these trainees together to establish local 'Cooperative of Scientific and Technical Services' to provide technical services to all collective TVEs in the community, and the costs and the services would be shared efficiently by many firms.[58]

Other Resources: Besides land, financial capital, and technology, a lot of other resources, such as certain kinds of raw materials and energy, were out of the reach of rural enterprises as well. At the beginning of the reform, both collective and private TVEs were disadvantaged in their access to

---

[57] Informant L3, L11, M49, M66.
[58] Informant L2, L12.

planned productive material inputs by virtue of their position outside of state plan networks. They depended on market as well as informal non-market arrangements to gain access to material inputs. For the inputs that were supplied under the central planning allocation system with lowest prices (for example, steel, copper, aluminum, cement, etc.), the quantities allocated to rural areas were severely restricted. Very few rural enterprises, except for those who were producing for the central plan, were able to enter the formal supply channels of such central allocated inputs (Oi, 1992). Collective TVEs were more successful at gaining more formal access to planned resources via their joint-venture relationship with state-owned enterprises. For example, an industrial battery producing village enterprise in Qingyunpu Township had hundred percent of demanded silicon steel and rubber supplied by its state-owned joint-venture partner at the low plan prices. Another township enterprise in Huazhuang Township that manufactured electrical wires also reported getting nearly all copper inputs before 1992 from the central planning channels at the plan price through its joint-venture partner -- Shanghai Telecommunication Bureau. The Shanghai Agricultural Committee estimated that in the early 1990s, about 20 to 30 percent of the steel and about 10 percent of the coal needed by collective TVEs was controlled by plan via state-collective joint-ventures (Whiting, 1995, p.158). The role local community governments played in helping collective TVEs to gain access to such planned material inputs may be best embodied by mediation in the relationship between collective TVEs and state-owned enterprises.

However, the number of inputs allocated by the plan has declined markedly since 1988. Many state-owned enterprises must rely on market for the supply of their material inputs themselves, and hence stopped or reduced the supply to their rural joint-venture partners (Whiting, 1995). Consequently, the problem TVEs must solve was not the access to inputs that were allocated by the central government planning, but the access to inputs that were simply scarce. Firms competed for the opportunity of purchasing the best of the available items at the market prices. For instance, supply of electricity, fuel oil, gas was usually at a shortage. Certain kinds of raw materials might also be scarce on the markets. Under such circumstances, it is incumbent on the community governments to give favorable treatment to local collective TVEs. This means privileged access to the resources within community government's reachable scope, say, being able to buy raw materials, fuel oil, or coal that the local Material Supply Bureau was able to procure at favorable market prices; to hook up to a special electric generator the community had installed to provide uninterrupted power; or to get sufficient water or gas supply from local suppliers. The more important a collective enterprise was in the community government's revenue generation, the more privileged access it might obtain (Ma et al., 1994; Oi, 1992). As late as 1994 when I conducted my field investigation, 85 percent of the electricity in Huazhuang and 60 percent in Guohe township were allocated by the township government with the focus to ensure supply to 'key' collective TVEs. Due to their insignificant contribution to the government's revenues, most private TVEs would be excluded from such privileged access provided by the community governments. Many of them had to allocate substantial financial resources not simply to the purchase of material inputs but to the development of relationships that would facilitate their access to scarce resources (Lin, Q., 1990; Whiting, 1995). Whenever the supply of scarce resources was in the control of the community governments, private enterprises always suffered the first cut when facing local supply shortage (Lin, Q., 1990).

4.3 Uncertainty and Risk Absorption

In TVEs' development, especially private TVEs' development, one fundamental constraint is the uncertainty and risk underlying the venture of capital investment and firm operations. The uncertainty and risk may exist in political as well as economic environments within which the TVEs are operating. The entrepreneurial activities in the creation of a new firm, as defined by Byrd (Byrd, 1990), involving certain scales of capital investment are inherently risky. The risk must be borne or absorbed by the entities involved in these activities.

Political Uncertainty: The political uncertainty and risk in the creation of a new firm are mainly embodied by the insecure property rights in a transitional economy. In the early years of TVE movement, the arbitrary expropriation of private capital by the government was the major concern and the most apparent obstacle for private entrepreneurs to launch new firms or new projects. Together with the difficulty in obtaining the access to financial capital or loans, such concern resulted in an extremely small scale of private enterprises. This is because uncertain future curbed private enterprises' desire to reinvest and made them very shortsighted in their operations. Private entrepreneurs preferred to spend their earnings on consumption rather than undertaking long-term investment to expand their production. Their small scale of production[59] is viewed by researchers as the obvious reason for their low efficiency in comparison with collective enterprises. For the same reason, their capability for self-accumulation is handicapped and their development inevitably restrained (Lin, Q., 1990). Furthermore, political uncertainty and risk have shortened the horizon in operation and management for private rural enterprises. Since asset specificity may limit the degree to which an asset can be redeployed to alternative use without sacrificing productive value (Williamson, 1996), the more an asset is specified, the riskier is the investment on such an asset for the entrepreneur. The private rural enterprises operating on a short horizon would consistently avoid investing in projects that require long-term investment and investment on specified assets. Therefore, private TVEs had the tendency to concentrate in sectors with less capital investment (particularly fixed or specialized capital investment) and flexible technology standards, such as trading, food services, handicrafts, and low quality consumer goods manufacturing, so that they are ready to quit business at any time (Kirsch, Worz, and Engel, 1994; Lin, Q., 1990). This distinctive feature has severely restrained the development of private enterprises in rural China. However, as discussed in section 4.1, collective property ownership and involvement of local community governments as the *de facto* owner has effectively secured the property rights for collective TVEs when facing political uncertainty and risk. Collective TVEs have thus grown at an accelerated rate and are relatively larger scaled than private TVEs.

Investment Risk: Investing to create a new firm or launching a new project is highly risky in a transitional economy. Unreasonable price fluctuation in rudimentary markets, sudden change in business environment induced by un-anticipated government policies, strict contract-enforcement with no leeway, any of these factors might be the cause of investment failure. Their difficulties begin right from the start. One of the main bottlenecks faced by rural entrepreneurs is getting the financial capital they need to start a new firm. The required capital on a reasonable scale to start a new firm in most cases is far beyond the available financial resources held by a rural private entrepreneur. Due to the extremely low level of rural net income, investing

---

[59] As many researchers observed, private TVEs had retained their extreme smallness in scale with less than three employees even up to 1996, compared to the 36.3 employee average in collective TVEs in the same year. See China TVE Yearbook, 1993-1997.

to establish a rural enterprise, even a small size enterprise, might exhaust the savings of a rural household in pervious decades.[60] Failure in investment might not only put the investing household in a miserable situation. Sometimes failure in enterprise involves a number of households, made up relatives, neighbors, and friends, who had lent out personal savings for the investment.

Local community governments' positive role in risk-sharing and absorption can not be neglected in TVEs' history, particularly in the early stage of this sector. So long as a community government served as the loan guarantor for a collective TVE, it assumed the responsibility for repayment. If the investment failed and the borrowing firm had no ability to pay back the loan, the community government might manage to repay the bad loan through its fiscal budget, through after-tax profit remittance of other firms, or by arranging for other collective TVEs to repay it. This is confirmed by many independent field studies, as well as from my own field investigation. Byrd (1990) observed:

> The community government's ability to absorb risk by varying its public expenditures may be limited, but it can spread risk across its enterprises to increase the flexibility and ability to absorb losses of any one firm. This risk-sharing is usually ad hoc and informal and is most effective when the community industrial structure is relatively diversified. Fluctuations and losses that are not life-threatening to the enterprise are absorbed by varying the flows of profit between the enterprise and the community government and, through delayed loan repayment between the enterprise and the bank.

Oi (1996) reported that: 'The debts of a village or township are the responsibility of the collective. Interviews reveal that in a number of localities, when a collective enterprise fails and defaults in its loans, the debt is paid off by the other enterprises regardless of the specifics of the contracting system.' Also as Whiting (1993) described: 'The (township) industrial corporation can also place a levy on the retained profits of the

---

[60] In 1980, the mean size of fixed capital of a TVE was 22,958 yuan, while the per capita rural net income was 191 yuan. This means that the fixed capital investment on a average-sized firm was equivalent to the total net income of thirty rural households of four members. In 1995, the mean size of fixed capital and the per capita rural net income was 58,289 yuan and 1,578 yuan respectively (China Statistical Yearbook, various volumes 1987 to 1996, China's TVEs Yearbook, 1978-87, and 1996).

successful enterprises under its jurisdiction in order to repay delinquent loans.' I observed in my field investigation that when a losing township enterprise in Doumen Township was auctioned, the township government assigned the firm's defaulted bank loan interests and partial principal to several other township enterprises. At the same time, it helped the buyers of the firm to negotiate an agreement with the bank, which allowed the buyers to repay the remaining loan principal in a 12 year span with a down payment of a certain amount.[61]

However, as pointed out by Byrd (1990), the above description applied mainly to areas in which collective TVEs development has been relatively successful. Elsewhere much of the risk may be coordinately borne by community government and local credit organization. For example, the government may help the borrowing firm, or arrange for other profitable firms, to pay the loan interests in time, in the meantime, negotiate with the loan bank or RCC to allow the firm to delay its repayment of the principal. This method is commonly used by the community governments, especially for those in more backward areas. Backward community governments may be too limited in resources to absorb much risk by themselves, and the financial performance of collective TVEs in the community may be so poor that they can not credibly cover each other's losses or take over the burden of loan repayment. Local credit organizations often have an incentive to prevent a collective TVE from failing, for once it shuts down, there is no hope of recouping loans from the community government. In this sense, as argued by Che (1995) the community government's loan guarantee is actually not legally binding.

Local community governments' risk-sharing and absorbing activities never extended to include private enterprises under their jurisdiction. The willingness of local credit organizations to absorb risks of private enterprises is also severely limited. As for coordination between the private enterprise and the credit organization by the community government, it is a rare phenomenon (Byrd, 1990). Private entrepreneurs must bear any risk associated with their investment decisions with very few exceptions, if there is any.

Operational Risk: Another kind of risk is not associated with the investment to create a new firm but, rather, stemming from un-anticipated distortion in the business environment, which could be caused by government's policy

---

[61] Informant L12, M9. Also see Case Study 8 in Chapter 3.

change, or simply due to the underdevelopment of the market system in a transitional economy. The government may take steps to liberalize the markets. This will lead to sharp fluctuation in prices -- mandatory prices, guidance prices, as well as free market prices. Such un-anticipated price fluctuation could be fatal to a firm. If the price change inflates a firm's production costs substantially, the firm may be forced to earn negative profit in order to fulfill its previously negotiated contracts. It may be punished financially, however, if it chooses to stop production and default. If the firm is a private enterprise, the entrepreneur must bear the full losses and absorb the risk by himself. With collective TVEs, such policy-induced price fluctuation might be a reasonable excuse to re-negotiate with the community government in their profit remittance or other financial obligations imposed by the government. The macroeconomic rectification campaign implemented by Chinese central government in the early 1990s resulted in tremendous increase in prices of many productive inputs and raw materials. Many township enterprises in Guohe Township re-negotiated their responsibility contracts with the township government, evaded their contracted profit remittance, or at least had it reduced to a great extent in 1993.[62] In Doumen Township, a leaseholder successfully terminated his leasing contract of the firm with the township government in early 1994, after a six months struggle under great pressure from inflated production costs.[63] As explained by the township leaders: 'The loss is not caused by poor management or wrong decisions, but by government policy changes. It is unfair to force firm managers to take full responsibility for such losses. We have no choice but bear the loss ourselves. Otherwise no one would take on the managerial positions.'[64]

During the early stage of the reform era, such fluctuations were frequent and unpredictable. Most rural individuals had very weak incentives and limited ability to bear investment and business risks in such an uncertain economic environment. The risk-sharing and absorption activities of local community government have evidently positive effects on rural enterprises development. With collective TVEs, however, firm managers did not have to bear investment risks and operation risks individually. Therefore, they could devote more of their efforts to firms' managerial affairs and production expansion. This might be one among other factors that ensured the outperforming of collective TVEs over private TVEs. However, with the

---

[62] Informant L15, L16.
[63] Informant M10.
[64] Informant L11, L14.

gradual development of the market system, the uncertainty induced by political or policy factors have been effectively reduced. Regular risk-absorbing activities continuously involving local community governments could severely damage firm managers' entrepreneurship while providing them with excuses to rely on community government to bear business losses. Undoubtedly, such activities might become inappropriate and harmful in firm efficiency improvement.

5. TVE Managers as the Agents of Local Community Government

As discussed in above sections, community public ownership of collective TVEs with community governments as the *de facto* owners had its comparative advantage over state public ownership in the performance of enterprises. It had reduced the attenuation of principal's benefit. The attenuation could be caused by the agent's abuse of control rights and deviation behavior, which in turn, is due to the separation of ownership rights and control rights in public enterprises. Under such an institutional arrangement, the community governments as the agents were under the regulation of the central government, as well as the partial monitoring of local residents. They were not as free of supervision as their counterparts in the central government. This supervision ensured that the community governments would single-mindedly pursue profit-maximization and firm efficiency improvement. In another comparison, community public ownership also had comparative advantage over private enterprises in many aspects of TVEs' development. Because of the dual role the community governments have been playing in rural social organization, they may more effectively ensure firm's property rights, gain access to resources, and absorb risks. As pointed out earlier, however, their advantages exist only when the market is imperfect. Since markets and hierarchies are traditionally viewed as alternatives for completing transactions (Coase, 1937; Williamson, 1975), local community public ownership should be viewed as the rational response of local economic entities to the imperfection of both market and government institutions in a transitional economy (Che and Qian, 1998), rather than the solution of the central government in its reform design (Chang and Wang, 1994). This means that such advantage may fade away with the development of the market system, and the community public ownership may be an optimal solution only for a relatively short period of transition.

5.1 The Re-delegation of the Control Rights from Community Government to Firm Managers

Despite the fact that local community governments have both incentives and comparative advantages in TVEs' development, in reality, operating local enterprises is not the only objective they have to pursue. As described in the above sections regarding the dual role local government leaders must play and their performance criteria specified by the cadre evaluation system, local leaders have to assume responsibilities that extended far beyond the operation of TVEs. They have many pressures that divert attention away from rural enterprises' development (Byrd and Lin, 1990; Oi, 1989; Rozelle, 1994; Walder, 1995) too. Though the development of local TVEs is the most important and direct objective of local leaders because of revenue consideration, local government leaders must deal with other affairs in rural organization and development, such as administrative affairs, provision of public goods, political stabilization and public order, growth of other local economic sectors, etc. Faced with demands from many constituencies and a diversity of objectives, local leaders may be forced to reduce their commitment of time that can be dedicated to managing the firm's day-to-day operation. Neither would they be devoting much time to learn about new directions for expansion or innovation of local enterprises. This would be particularly true as the number of enterprises grows in a given locality.

In the early years of the reform era, in the TVE sector in certain areas, conditions were such that having local leaders involved in running enterprises was almost a necessity due to the advantage they brought about (Byrd and Lin, 1990). Local leaders in most localities did not have too many enterprises or other activities, so it is easy to understand why local leaders took such an active role in personally managing firms and making most of the decisions. However, after the size and number of rural enterprises grew so rapidly in the 1980s, it became increasingly difficult for local leaders to be entirely and consistently involved in firms' day-to-day operation management. In many cases, local leaders had to seek help in running their business. They had the option of hiring professional managers to supervise and run the daily operation of the factories. In other words, local community governments, as the *de facto* owners of rural enterprises, had to delegate at least part of their control rights over the enterprises to *their* agents -- the firm managers, who were directly in charge of firms' operation. We now observe the second tier of principal-agent relationship in TVEs' governance.

By the appointment of a firm manager, the community government assigned control rights over an individual firm to the manager. To what extent the control rights had been transferred to the firm manager depended on the contractual form that governed the relationship between the community government and the manager. How such contractual form was determined for a given firm in a certain period, and how such forms had been evolving over time and varying across regions is the major focus of the following chapters. I would like to point out here that the second-tier of principal-agent proxy has created a new class of individuals -- the professional firm managers -- in rural China. This group of individuals has taken over a great degree of decision-making power in TVEs' operation from local government leaders. They have been playing the most active role in TVEs movement, and making remarkable contributions to TVEs development. Their role and their relations with local community governments will inevitably become the focus in the field of future TVEs research.

5.2 The Constitution of TVE Managers

As reported by Lin and by Byrd,[65] by the late 1980s, the main sources of private entrepreneurs in rural industry (owners and managers of private TVEs) were lower-level community government cadres, former personnel of community collective TVEs, community residents who had worked in state enterprises, and farmers who had had some business experience or special skills. However, no one to my knowledge has reported the general constitution of TVEs managers.

TVE managers comprise mainly of rural talented indigenous people with different expertise. The statistics of my 64 sample TVEs managers (Table 2.5) shows that 85.7 percent of them were local residents.[66] They were in their middle age at the mean of 43.9 years' old. The average length for them at the current management positions was 5.6 years, and the mean of their school education was 10.2 years. It is confirmed by this observation that TVEs managers are better educated than ordinary rural people, and with sufficient experience to handle various affairs in business or in life. Of

---

[65] See Byrd and Lin, ed. 1990, p.180 and p.198.

[66] 'Local residents' are defined as residents of the same township for township enterprise managers, or residents of the same village for village enterprise managers.

those sample TVEs managers, 74.6 percent were members of the Chinese Communist Party. This means that this group of people was viewed as politically reliable by the government.

Table 2.5 The Statistics of Sample TVE Managers, 1994

	Mean	Maximum	Minimum
Age	43.9	67	25
Year of School Education	10.2	15	4
Year at Current Position	5.6	22	<1

Source: Author's Survey, 1994.

Among the 64 managers, 81 percent indicated they had been appointed to their current positions by the community governments; 8 percent identified themselves as private firm owners; 9 percent became firm managers through leasing contract bidding; and only one person (less than 2 percent) identified himself as an employee-elected manager.[67] We may conclude from these observations that as late as 1994, the majority of the TVE managers, particularly those from collective TVEs, were the agents selected by the community governments. However, we also observed an alternative method -- open bidding, through which a firm manager was chosen. This is a method in which financial achievement was the main consideration. As reported by Tsai (1995), as a method it tended to be the most popular one in some areas after 1994.

Of the sample managers, 58 out of 64 responded in my field investigation regarding their previous status. Of the 58 managers, 19 percent reported they had held positions as Party cadres before getting their current managerial positions; 36.2 percent had previous been managers of other collective TVEs; 32.8 percent were former employees (mainly technicians or procurement and marketing personnel[68]) at the same firm or at other

---

[67] This is an evidence that collective TVEs are hardly labor-managed producer cooperatives.

[68] The importance of the ability to gain access to resources and markets for the success of the firm is proved by this statistic.

firms; 6.9 percent had been the former employees of state-owned enterprises; and 5.2 percent were private owners. The status constitution of TVE managers observed in the field investigation revealed that TVE managers are usually talented rural people who are endowed with business, managerial, or technical experiences. Together with the better education and working experience they have, such talents have made them advantaged candidates in the competitive potential managers' pool. A newly emerging class of professional TVE managers has formed, drawn from rural talents and it is due to these people that there is an extraordinary rapid growth and expansion of the TVE sector.

Another interesting, but not surprising finding in the observation on TVE managers' constitution is that all of the 64 sample managers are male. Extending this sample to include another group of 20 managers I interviewed during the group research trip and the preliminary fieldwork did not change such an all-male composition. Two facts may be applicable to explain such a finding. One is the traditional discrimination against females rooted deeply in Chinese culture and history. Men in rural China assume the responsibility of supporting the whole family and dealing with 'outside affairs'. Women's main responsibility was household works or 'inside affairs'. Therefore, men tend to have more school education and more opportunities to acquire working experience and skills than women do. This traditional bias toward men has put male rural residents in a greatly superior position in the competition for managerial positions. The second fact is that, in the early years of TVE development, employment opportunities in rural enterprises were allocated to each household by the community government rather than recruitment from the public (Byrd and Lin, 1990; Ma et al., 1994). In most cases, males had retained dominance in the rural households and whatever opportunities came their way would automatically go to the men. After several years working as production-line workers, these early-birds became the first group of rural residents who were familiar with non-agricultural productions. Those most talented or skilled workers in this group might be promoted to white-collar employees, then, managerial positions. In the meantime, rural female laborers did not participate in rural non-agricultural labor pool on a large scale until the late 1980s. Many females might have been excluded from the managerial positions due to the lack of necessary experience and skills because they had been excluded from the early-birds group.

5.3 The Governance of Collective TVEs

I would like to complete this chapter by introducing Figure 2.3, The Governance of Collective TVEs.

Figure 2.3 illustrates the mechanism of governance for collective TVEs. As shown by the lower portion of the diagram, a TVE is an economic entity producing for markets by available resources, namely land, labor, financial capital, human capital, technologies, and other resources. This is parallel to any 'firm' described in microeconomics textbooks. The upper portion of the diagram shows that the community government must play a dual role -- as government apparatus and as representative of local residents at the same time. Therefore, it is under the direct control and regulations of the central government, as well as (at least partially) under the supervision of local residents. As the *de facto* owner of the collective TVE, it has complete control rights over the firm. The community government has the ability to directly allocate labor, land, and other locally endowed resources to the firm. It may also have the ability to mobilize sufficient financial capital, human capital, and technologies to the firm through its influence on local branches of the central government, or through its bridging activities between the firm and the state-owned sectors. The community government's role in the governance mechanism has been illuminated in above sections.

However, a new actor -- the firm manager -- has been inserted between the firm and the community government as shown in the middle portion of the diagram. The firm manager is in charge of the daily operation of the firm, and is directly responsible for the performance of the firm. He is the agent of the community government, which has delegated its control rights over the firm to him. The extent to which the community government will delegate its control rights to the firm manager depends on the contractual form, which governs the distribution of decision-making power and of residual profit claim between these two parties.

The mechanisms that determine the current contractual form for the firm and the possible evolution of such form over time are not illustrated in this diagram. The fact is that they are seldom analyzed by researchers in TVEs studies. In the following chapters, I will attempt to provide a general framework for explaining the evolutionary pattern of the structure of the contractual forms, and to predict how this contractual form will vary temporally and spatially. That is to say, the missing details of the middle portion of this diagram will be delineated in the following chapters.

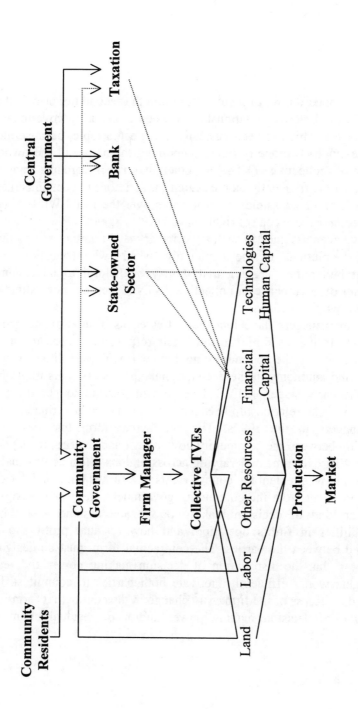

Figure 2.3 The Governance of Collective TVEs

3 The Contractual Structure of Collective TVEs

From this chapter on, we turn our attention to the second tier principal-agent relations, *i.e.*, the proxy relationship between community government and firm managers. This has been basically a neglected topic, because most of the studies in TVE property rights pinpointed the nature of the ownership structure of collective TVEs. In other words, researchers may have concentrated too frequently on the search for solutions to questions like *who* owns the firm, or *who* holds control rights over the firm? While very few have asked *how* these control rights have been assigned? Or *why* the control rights have been assigned in such a particular way? I am not saying that the search for solutions to the commonly asked 'who' questions is not important but, rather, arguing that it may be helpful to understand the mechanism of governance in collective TVEs if we pay more attention to 'how' and 'why' questions.

The firm managers have long been treated as a subordinate group of participants in the TVE movement. Their responsibility was to carry out decisions made by the community government, with very little or without initiative and autonomy in the decision making process. This might be the fact in the early stage of TVE development, but no longer the precise description of the relationship between the community government and the firm managers in the 1990s. The contractual form that governs the relationship between the community government and the firm managers has been evolving over time and varying across regions. Such contractual form determines to what extent the control rights in a firm should be delegated to the firm manager from the community government, *i.e.*, each party would hold what kind of decision making power and assume what kind of responsibilities in firm's operation; and how residual profit should be distributed between the parties. The contractual form must be designed in such a way that the distribution of decision making power and residual claim rights would efficiently motivate both parties to commit sufficient effort to the success of the firm. Any change in the contractual form is a re-distribution of decision making power and/or of residual claim rights between these two parties. In most cases, such change is for the purpose of adapting to a varying environment within which the firm is operating.

I would like to start this part of research with a detailed description of the managerial contractual forms that had been implemented in the TVE sector from its very beginning up until 1994, the year I conducted my field investigation in rural China. Seven distinctive contractual forms that were observed are discussed in Section 1. The general characteristics of each form are described, after which case studies follow to illustrate their application in the practice. A short section, Section 2, is devoted to the discussion of the eighth form -- share cooperative form (Gufen Hezuo Zhi), which was encouraged and supported by the central government in TVEs' property rights reform in early 1990s, but seems not to be as successful as expected. In section 3, I classify these observed contractual forms into three categories: fixed-wage, profit-sharing, and fixed-payment. Then I argue, that three kinds of contractual forms entitled the firm managers with significantly different degrees of decision-making autonomies in firm operation. They also established intrinsically dissimilar incentive sets for firm managers, which would consequently lead to dissimilar objectives in managers' performance pursuit. Three enlightening findings in the field investigation are elaborated upon in the last section. The three findings are: co-existence of different contractual forms in a given area, the evolution of the structure of the contractual forms over time, and the cross-regional variation of the structure of the contractual forms. The unique data set collected in the field investigation backs up these findings, which have laid the groundwork for further research focus. The core objective of the remaining chapter is to search for an inherently consistent explanation regarding these findings, *i.e.*, to clearly explain *what* determined the selection of the optimal contractual form for a given firm; and *what* induced evolution and variation in such a selection.

1. The Contractual Forms Implemented in Collective TVEs

Various contractual forms have been implemented in collective TVEs. The structure of these forms is like a ladder with the different contractual forms as its steps. These forms differ from each other as to the extent of business autonomy the firm manager enjoys, the degree of business risks the firm manager must bear, as well as the method by which residual profit is distributed between the community government and the firm manager. The contractual forms fall roughly into the following eight types: work-point system, wage/salary system, collective contractual responsibility system (Jiti Chengbao Zeren Zhi), personal contractual responsibility system (Geren Chengbao Zeren Zhi), personal mortgage contractual responsibility system (Geren Diya Chengbao Zeren Zhi), leasing (Zulin), auction, and share cooperative system. I will illustrate each of them in turn in this section, except for the eighth one, the share cooperative system, which will be discussed in Section 2.

1.1   The Work-point System

The work-point system was implemented in the pre-reform era when rural enterprises were collectively owned by communes, brigades, or production teams. The manager of a firm was usually the cadre appointed by a higher authority or by the same level authority. The authority controlled the firm directly by choosing and approving projects, providing original investment funds and other resources, assigning laborers, supervising daily operations, and finding, or at least helping to find markets for the firm's products. The so-called 'manager' played the role at most like a floor production foreperson.

The most important characteristic of this system was that the authority at each level had the rights to completely control profit distribution. The firm paid 'wages' and 'salaries' directly to the production team of which the workers or the manager[1] were members. The workers or the manager received work points instead of cash payment for their work for the firm and then participated in the collective income distribution which was made by the production team at the year's end. All the profit made by the firm belonged to the authorities, and it was the authorities who made the decisions regarding profit allocation: reinvestment in the existing firm, establishment of new firms, or investment in local infrastructure or welfare projects. Under this system, there were no formal contractual relations between the community government and the firm 'manager' with clarified rights and responsibilities to each party. The manager of the firm was not an

---

[1] Unless the manager of a commune-owned firm held the status of a formal member of the state bureaucracy system (Guojia Ganbu Bianzhi) and was on the regular government payroll, most managers of the commune, brigade, and production team enterprises who were not professional government cadres (Tuochan Ganbu) received payment from production team's year end collective distribution according to the work points they had earned.

independent economic agent with decision-making autonomy, and neither did he face business risk at all. To the manager, there was hardly any economic reward or penalty that was contingent upon the firm's performance. The manager's personal income was closely related to the overall performance of the production team, rather than to the performance of the firm. Hence, the firm manager had a very weak and indirect incentive to improve the efficiency of the firm.

1.2 The Wage/Salary System

This system was introduced in the early stage of the post-Mao reform era and shared many common characteristics with the work-point system. With the abolition of the commune system, the work-point income distribution method was abolished too. The commune, brigade, and production team owned enterprises became township or village owned enterprises and independent accounting units. The township and village community governments exercise their control over the firms in ways similar to their counterparts in the commune era, and have the rights to completely control the distribution of the profit generated by the firms. The firm managers who are appointed by the community government under this system play a role also similar to what they did under the work-point system.

The substantial difference between this system and the work-point system is that, the workers and the manager receive their wages and salary directly from the firm instead of work-point based income from the production team. However, the level of the wage or of the salary is usually independent of the firm's financial performance. It is determined by the community government that is concerned more with income equalization within the community. The main incentive for the manager to improve firm's performance is the possibility of political promotion rather than any direct economic benefits derived from such improvement.

It is worthy of note that, under this system the wage paid to workers might be in different forms -- either a fixed monthly wage or a piece rate wage,[2] but the salary paid to the manager was always in the form of a fixed monthly payment. In the later stage of the implementation of this system, the community government might pay some year-end bonuses out of the profit remittance received from the community enterprises to the firm

---

[2] The piece rate wage was first introduced to TVEs under this system, but prevailed under other managerial forms, especially after the late 1980s.

manager as well as to the workers. However, the amount of the bonus is usually determined arbitrarily, with neither unique criterion for determining the amount, nor any direct relation to the firm's financial performance.

Case Study 1 Jinxi Chemical Plant[3] (Wu County, Jiangsu Province)

This is a new village collective factory established in 1992 producing chemical products. The initial investment is one million yuan, of which 30 percent is a bank loan, 40 percent is personal borrowing, and another 30 percent is a collective fund raising from village residents (Jizi). The factory hired about 20 workers (all village residents) and went into operation in 1992. It earned profit the same year and had been operating well since then.

This factory was directly controlled by the villagers' committee. All projects and operation decisions of the factory must be approved by the committee; the control rights over the firm's revenue and expenditures rested in the hand of the committee; and the committee kept the accounting records of the factory. The current manager of this factory was appointed by the villagers' committee. His responsibility was to organize the daily production under the guidance of the committee. He earned a monthly fixed salary, which was determined by the committee at the level of an average manager income in four other enterprises owned by the village.

In 1993, this factory's sales revenue reached 6 million yuan. Since it could enjoy the new factory and the new product tax exemption preferential policy treatment for three years, it generated 2 million yuan of net profit for the village that year, and all of the profit was delivered to the villagers' committee. By using this profit remittance, the committee was able to pay back the loans, invest 500 thousand yuan to establish another village factory, and to buy a new Volkswagen sedan, and set a running water facility to every household in the village in 1994.

There are two major reasons, as I was told when I visited that village in August 1994, why the villagers' committee chose the direct control form in running this factory. The first is, this was a new factory, and the channels of raw chemical materials supply and product sales had not been well installed. The factory needed such assistance like the personal connections and contacts of the villagers' committee in order to complete the establishment of such channels for a successful operation. The second is that this was the only high-technology factory that attained a high profit rate in the village. The villagers' committee could collect money from it to

---

[3] Informant L1.

support agricultural production and village welfare projects more easily than from other village firms. The village head admitted he was unwilling to give up his direct control over it.

Case Study 2 Jiangnan Battery Factory[4] (Qingyunpu Township, Jiangxi Province)

This is a joint venture between a state-owned factory and a village. It was established in 1989 with equipment and starting funds contributed by the state-owned factory, and land and factory building contributed by the village. As stipulated by the joint-venture contract, the state-owned factory and the village each owned one half of the firm's property, and might claim one half of the after-tax profit produced by this factory. The state-owned factory was responsible for providing some of the raw materials demanded by the firm (the quantity was not guaranteed as in 1994), and marketing half of the firm's output. The entire after-tax profit of the factory must be handed to the state-owned factory and the villagers' committee at the half-half ratio. Financial loss, if there was any, would also be shared at the half-half ratio as specified by the contract. Decisions regarding the profit reinvestment were made through negotiation between the state-owned factory and the villagers' committee.

The current manager of the firm was an engineer of the state-owned factory, who was appointed by that factory to the current position, but kept his status as a state-owned factory employee. As reported by this manager, he acted as the representative of the state-owned factory rather than an independent firm manager. He must follow the directions from the state-owned factory and had very little autonomy to make decisions in firm management.[5] He expressed his dissatisfaction with such limited autonomy, though he claimed neither would he be held responsible for the firm's financial performance. Most of the managerial staff of this factory were village residents, while a few in the key posts (technical department and accounting department) were from the state-owned factory. All employees in the factory were paid fixed monthly wages or salaries. The managerial staff who belonged to the state-owned factory also received some fixed amount of subsidies every month for working in rural area. There might be some year-end bonuses to the employees. However, this decision making

---

[4] Informant M39, L9, L8.

[5] In my sample, the full score of a manager's autonomy is 32, the sample mean is 26.4, while this manager's score is 12, much lower than the sample mean. I will discuss the survey regarding managers' autonomy in detail in Section 3.

power lay in the hands of the state-owned factory and the villagers' committee instead of the firm manager.

1.3 The Collective Contractual Responsibility System

This system became the dominant pattern in the collective TVE sector after the early years of 1980s. It still prevails in some areas in the 1990s. The main characteristic of this system is that all employees -- the manager(s), managerial staff, and production workers -- of the firm act as an economic collective in signing the contract with the community government. The firm manager, who is selected by the community government in most cases, acts as the representative of this collective. The community government grants the firm the rights of control in respect to such areas as production management, employment of labor, product design, technical innovation, and purchase and sales. The firm has the responsibility of fulfilling certain operational objectives stipulated by the contract, such as total output, pre or after tax profit, labor productivity, investment, and so on. The community government reserves its rights to control in such matters as project planning, investment decisions, appointment and promotion of managerial staff, levels of wages, salaries, and bonuses, and most importantly, the distribution of firm's after-tax profit. The contract is renewed every year in most cases,[6] and the stipulated operational objectives are adjusted upon renewal. One point that commonly interested TVEs researchers needs to be clarified here: the adjustment of the stipulated operational objectives is based upon the firm's actual performance in the previous year. The targeted objectives for this year are usually a certain percentage higher than last year's actual achievement.

During the early stage of the implementation of this system, the enforcement of the contract caused trouble for the community government. At that stage, the government took all after-tax profit from the firm, then returned a certain percentage of it to the firm as a bonus paid to the workers and to the firm manager, given that all objectives had been satisfactorily achieved. This bonus accounted for a relatively small portion of the total income of the workers and of the manager. The workers, particularly the manager, thus had a weak incentive to fulfill the contract, and the contract was hardly enforceable.

---

[6] All firms in my sample operating under this system renewed their contracts with the community governments at the beginning of each year.

This problem has been solved by the introduction of the so-called 'two-stage distribution' method in early 1990s.[7] By applying this method, the firm manager and the workers are only paid the basic salaries or wages required to cover their subsistence expenditure each month.[8] Another part of payment called 'floating wages/salaries' is paid at the year-end, depending on the achievement of contracted objectives. The floating income may be as high as, or even higher than basic wages/salaries. This method exerted pressure on the manager as well as on the workers to fulfill the contract.

The community government exercises its control over a firm's after-tax profit disposition through its decisions regarding what proportion of this after-tax profit should be distributed to the firm's floating payments, the firm's reinvestment, and the community government's revenue respectively.[9] The community government may also determine the proportion of the manager's floating payment relative to the workers' floating payment.

Under this system, the manager of the firm has partial decision making autonomy, mainly on certain aspects of the firm's daily operation, even though the rights to control key aspects are still in the hand of the community government. The risks facing the manager is low, at most only the loss of his floating payment. The manager has the incentive to fulfill the contracted objectives, but a very weak incentive to pursue profit maximization[10] for fear of another rise in next year's targeted profit objective.

---

[7] Both Huazhuang and Guohe township adopted this method in 1993.

[8] 120 yuan per month for everyone includes workers and managers in Huazhuang and Guohe.

[9] Under the two-stage distribution method, the firm calculated its before-tax net revenue with the floating wage/salary included. The community government determined the distribution proportion after the taxes and fee payments had been made. In 1994, the proportions devoted to floating income, firm reinvestment, and profit remittance to the community government was 4-3-3 in Huazhuang, and about 4-5-1 in Guohe according to the report from my investigated TVEs. However, how the taxable revenue and the tax payment were calculated is not clear.

[10] When a contracted firm made over target profit, the firm must first hand 70 percent to 80 percent of this excess profit to the community government. Then, as most of this kind of contracts formulated, it could apply the remainder to its employees' bonuses.

Case Study 3   Five-ring Chemical Company[11] (Guohe Township, Hubei Province)

This is a medium sized township collective enterprise established in 1984. In the last five years before 1994, all employees of this firm signed a responsibility contract with the township government as a collective. The contract stipulated the total output value and after-tax profit as the major operational objectives to be achieved by the firm. The contract was renewed every year at the year's beginning. According to last year's actual achievement, the new targeted objectives for the contract renewal were determined through negotiation between the township government and the firm manager, who acted as the representative of all firm employees.

Table 3.1 Targeted, Realized, and Remitted After-tax Profit of the Firm, 1989-1994 (in 10 thousand yuan)

	1989	1990	1991	1992	1993	1994
Targeted after-tax profit	3.7	3.3	10	10.7	11.7	15
Realized after-tax profit	-10	-16	10.7	11	12	--
Profit remitted to township government	1[a]	1[a]	3	3.2	3.5	1.5[b]

[a] reported as 'management fee' paid to the township government.
[b] Targeted profit remittance.

Source: Author's survey, 1994.

Before 1993, as stipulated by the contract, 30 percent of the after-tax profit had to be handed over to the township government. In 1994, this proportion was reduced to 10 percent. Table 3.1 illustrates the change of each year's targeted and realized after-tax profit of the firm. We may observe the obvious co-relation between the yearly profit target and the

---

[11] Informant M23, L16.

realized profit in the previous year. However, the cause of the jump between 1990 and 1991 is not clear.

The employees of the factory including the manager, who used to be a manger of another township enterprise and was appointed by the township government to the current position, were paid only the basic wage/salary every month. In 1994, this basic wage/salary was 120 yuan per month for everyone to cover daily subsistence expenses.

Upon the fulfillment of the contracted objectives, the employees would receive the floating wages/salaries at the year-end. This part of payment was extracted from the after-tax profit left to the firm. After the township government had collected its shares, it determined the proportion of the remainder that should be allotted to the firm's reinvestment and to employees' floating incomes. In 1994, this proportion was about 5 to 4. How to allocate this overall floating payment among the firm employees was determined by the firm's manager. The township government might intervene if the relative share of the floating income between the manager and other employees was considered as unreasonable, though no explicit ceiling for manager's floating income had been set. No such intervention was reported in the past five years, however. The average floating salary for the manager was 4,000 yuan per year, while only 1,500 yuan for the staff and the workers. As reported by the current manager, the township government had the last-say in some key managerial aspects, such as investment, fund raising, managerial staff recruitment and promotion, wage/salary/bonus level determination, disposal of residual profit, etc. He himself had very limited autonomy with the exception of the firm's daily operation.

1.4 The Personal Contractual Responsibility System

The manager of the firm signs a contract with the community government as an individual agent, instead of as the representative of the collective under this system. That is the major difference between this system and the collective contractual responsibility system. There are two patterns for this system: the non-mortgage and the mortgage pattern. By applying this system, the firm manager (who may either be appointed by the community government from an other government position, or selected by the community government from the firm personnel pool) is granted partial control rights to operate the firm by the community government. His autonomy may be extended beyond those aspects under the collective contractual responsibility system and include such aspects as labor dismissal, managerial staff recruitment and promotion, wage and bonus level determination. However, the community government still has last-say in some critical aspects of the management such as the firm's medium to long term development plan, investment and reinvestment decisions, and most of all, the distribution of residual profit. Together with the business autonomy enjoyed by the manager is the full responsibility he must bear to fulfill the signed contract. The manager makes decisions regarding resource allocation within the firm; organizes, directs, and monitors the firm's daily production activities; works with sources of supply and directs product marketing to ensure fulfillment of contracted performing objectives. In most cases, the manager of the firm determines the wage rate for workers. His own salary, though, is determined by the community government.

The workers and staff members of the firm under this system act as individual employees, whose responsibility is to accomplish the work load or business task assigned to her/him by the firm manager. They may be rewarded for excellent performance (bonus or rise of wage rate) and punished for being unable to accomplish the assigned workload or task (loss of bonus, part of wage, or even the job). They respond to the contract fulfillment indirectly through the accomplishment of their individual workloads. Their income is related to the contract fulfillment in the same indirect way. Piece rate wage becomes popular under this system. The process of contract negotiation and renewal is similar to that under the collective contractual responsibility system. The community government determines the proportions for the distribution of the firm's after-tax profit. The manager has control rights over the residual share that is left to the firm after payment of the government's share and the firm's reinvestment share. We have reason to believe that a large portion of this residual share had been set aside as to the manager's personal income, the remainder went to employees' year end bonus or welfare expenses.

Case Study 4 Hongda Feed-processing Factory[12] (Qingyunpu Township, Jiangxi Province)

This village collective factory was established in 1984, then it was merged into the township 'Hongda Feed Corporation' as a branch plant in 1992. It is a relatively large village enterprise with 51 employees and 1.4 million yuan in capital. The current manager of the firm was nominated by

---

[12] Informant M32, L7.

the villagers' committee, and appointed by the corporation. The manager signed a responsibility contract with the villagers' committee every year. The contract stipulated the targeted total output value for the firm at each year's beginning. The firm must pay a 'management fee' to the villagers' committee, which was equivalent to a certain percentage of the total output value produced by the firm that year. From 1989 to 1992, this management fee was 3 percent of the firm's actual total output value; in 1993, this percentage was raised to 5 percent.

As reported by the firm manager, he had complete control rights over the firm's daily production operation, labor employment and dismissal, product design, pricing, and marketing. However, his decision on managerial staff recruitment, wage levels, capital investment, and so on had to be approved by the villagers' committee before being put into practice. The villagers' committee had tight control over the firm's profit distribution.

The workers in the factory were paid by piece rate wage, averaging about 420 yuan per month. The manager and the managerial staff were paid by fixed salaries, averaging about 350 yuan per month. By the end of the year, if the firm had fulfilled the targeted total output value and paid the contracted management fee timely, the firm manager and other employees might receive bonuses. The amount of the bonuses depended on the level of the 'net after-tax profit' of the firm. (The net after-tax profit means the firm's before-tax profit minus the tax paid to the central government, other fees paid to various government authorities, and the management fee to the villagers' committee.) As specified by the contract, this net after-tax profit would be allocated among the villagers' committee, the firm's reinvestment, and employees' bonuses. In 1993, this distribution ratio was 4-4-2 as determined by the villagers' committee, i.e., 40 percent was submitted to the villagers' committee, 40 percent left to firm for reinvestment, and 20 percent for employees' bonuses. The manager's total bonus was 5,000 yuan, the managerial staff's bonus averaged about 1,200 yuan. Since most of the workers were paid by piece-rate wages, their average bonus was 800 yuan.

Under this system, the contract is enforceable only in one direction-- rewarding the manager for contract fulfillment, but with inability to enforce in another direction-- punishing the manager for failure to fulfill the contract. In case the firm loses money instead of making a profit and can not deliver the contracted profit to the community government, the personal loss of the firm manager is only the deprivation of his extra payment or bonuses. He is not responsible for the firm's financial loss. It may be more appropriate to say that he can not be forced to take the responsibility for such loss.

The *personal mortgage contractual responsibility system* was formulated to enforce fulfillment of the contract in both directions. The firm manager, who signs the personal mortgage responsibility contract with the community government, is required to mortgage a certain amount of cash or other personal properties (such as residential house). In case the firm is unable to deliver the contracted profit to the community government because of inferior performance, the community government has the right to withdraw the amount equivalent to the shortage from the manager's mortgage fund. The contract will be terminated upon the exhaustion of the mortgage fund. If the firm has financial loss, the manager may be required to pay a proportion of that loss from his mortgage fund. This proportion is usually the same as that he may receive from the after-tax profit when the contracted objectives have been fulfilled.

The personal contractual responsibility system, particularly the personal mortgage contractual responsibility system, increases a firm manager's business autonomy while raising the risk a manager must bear at the same time. This provides a firm manager with the incentive to allocate firm resources efficiently and to improve the firm's performance.

Case Study 5   Qingyunpu Machinery Factory[13] (Qingyunpu Township, Jiangxi Province)

This township collective enterprise was established in 1979. Before 1992, this factory was operated under the township government's direct control. The township government assigned the targeted profit remittance to the firm at the beginning of each year. In case the firm over fulfilled the profit target, the township government had the perfect right to appropriate the excess, but would return 4 percent of it to the firm as bonuses to the manager and to the employees. However, if the firm failed to fulfill the profit target, a fine, equivalent to 12 percent of the shortage, would be imposed on the firm, Although in what manner and from which source the firm pays for the fine is not clear.

In 1992, the personal mortgage contractual responsibility system was applied in this factory. As stipulated by the contract, the factory must deliver 80 thousand yuan of after-tax profit to the township government in 1992, which was 10 percent higher than that firm's profit remittance in

---

[13] Informant M46, L6.

1991. After 1992, there would be a 10 percent increase of this remittance each year. The extra profit over the stipulated remittance would be shared by the township government and the firm at a half-half ratio. However, in case the factory suffered financial loss, the net loss would also be shared by these two parties at a half-half ratio.

To enforce the fulfillment of the profit delivery, the manager of the factory, who was assigned by the township government, was required to deposit 5,000 yuan cash plus his house ownership certificate to the government. An amount equivalent to the shortage in profit remittance would be withdrawn from his deposit should he be unable to deliver the contracted profit to the government. His house could be auctioned off upon the exhaustion of his cash deposit, and the contract would be terminated when his entire mortgage had been exhausted.

Case Study 6 Qilong Textile Factory[14] (Doumen Township, Zhejiang Province)

This large township collective factory was well-known in the town for its continuous and considerable financial losses before 1993. The accumulated debts of the firm totaled 3.09 million yuan, and its annual interest burden was 1.03 million yuan. In 1994, the township government decided to change the managerial form for this firm. However, leasing and auction was infeasible due to the sizable debts and the heavy interest burden. Then the personal mortgage responsibility contractual form was adopted.

The current manager was the same person as the former manager appointed by the township government in 1988. He signed the responsibility contract with the township government. This contract would be valid for 12 years. As specified by the contract, the manager had complete autonomy to manage the firm's operation.[15] It was his obligation to pay the debt interests every year. He would also pay land and employment management fees (about 15 thousand yuan per year) to the county government. Besides these payments, he would have to deliver 258 thousand yuan every year to the township government to pay back the debts. After paying all the above

---

[14] Informant M6, L12.

[15] As reported by the manager in the investigation, he was completely autonomous in all listed managerial aspects except for two: investment decisions and establishment of joint ventures with other firms. For these two aspects, he had partial autonomy.

items, the manager had entire autonomy to dispose of the remainder of the profit.[16]

To make this contract enforceable, the township government required a 100 thousand yuan cash deposit from the manager as mortgage. In case the contract signer was unable to fulfill the contracted payment, the township government had the right to withdraw the amount equivalent to the shortage from this deposit.

Since the implementation of this system was less than one year, the effect of this contractual form transition was hard to evaluate in October 1994 when the field investigation was conducted.

However, the critical characteristic of the contractual responsibility systems, no matter collective or personal, non-mortgage or mortgage, is that the residual profit is proportionally shared by the community government and the firm (as a collective) or the firm manager. The excess profit created by a firm's superior performance is shared by both parties and may lead to an increase of the targeted profit objective upon contract renewal. The objective function of the firm manager is thus the achievement of the contracted objectives rather than profit maximization. In the meantime, the loss caused by inferior managerial performance may also be shared by both parties. Therefore, the manager will always have the incentive to overstate loss and understate excess profit.[17]

---

[16] This contract is actually more similar to a fixed-payment contract in essence. However, it differs from a fixed-rent leasing contract in two major aspects: one is that the firm manager was appointed by the community government, not selected through contract bidding. The second is that the payment was determined by other factors, rather than by the value of the assets that were leased out to the leaseholder as in the case of a leasing contract.

[17] As I was told when interviewing TVE managers, they would never report their excess profit to the community governments if they were not forced to do so; they would overstate their losses, if they would not be punished for such losses, to obtain tax exemption or reduction, which might be enough to offset their loss of profit shares.

1.5 Leasing System

Leasing has been the prevailing contractual form in many areas[18] since 1993, especially for small and medium sized TVEs. Under this system, the community government retains its *de facto* ownership of the land and the capital (such as factory buildings, equipment, vehicles, tools, and so on) used by the firm, and exercises control through such ownership rights over the firm, *i.e.*, it grants the managerial control rights in the firm to a selected lease-holder in exchange for a contracted rent payment in a given period.

The community government sets the rent for the firm to be leased to the individual agent based upon the land area and the assessed value of the capital. Usually, the community government would formulate a unique rent scale for land in different locations before calculating the land rent for leased firms in the community. Such scale is based on both the area and the location of the land.

The calculation of the rent for the capital used by the firm is complicated. A common method is to set this rent equivalent to the prevailing interest rate. In some cases, the community government may enforce an additional condition. For example, the firm must always maintain the value of the capital so that it is no less than it was when the leasing contract was signed; or the firm must withdraw an appropriate depreciation fund each year before the manager dispenses the residual profit. These additional terms are made in the effort to avoid loss of capital value through excess depreciation caused by any abuse of capital during the contracted leasing period. However, I have observed more than a few leasing contracts without such additional terms. In some cases, the rent calculation was not based on the assessed capital value or land area but, rather, upon terms resulting from the negotiation between the community government and the leaseholder.

The leaseholder may be selected through a formal or informal bidding process, or through personal negotiation. When a leaseholder has been selected, the community government will grant him control rights in almost all aspects of the firm's management. The manager's autonomy under this system will be extended over such areas as investment and reinvestment decisions, and distribution of residual profit. It is obligatory that the manager should pay the contracted rent on time each year. Top priority must be given to the rent payment in the firm's after-tax profit distribution

---

[18] Even in Wuxi, well known for its collective ownership and community government managerial control in TVEs' operation, this form was widespread after 1994. See Appendix of Chapter 6.

process. In case the firm performs poorly, the manager as the lease-holder may risk the loss of his whole year's income, or even the loss of personal properties.[19]

The leasing contract is usually valid for a period of three to five years. The rent is fixed during this period. However, the rent may be adjusted upon the renewal of the leasing contract in accordance to the price index and the interest rate at the time. The crucial distinction between the leasing contract and the responsibility contract is that, the contract adjustment upon renewal is related to given exogenous factors under the leasing system, but related to the firm's actual performance under the responsibility system. This will lead to different results with regard to the manager's incentives.

The leaseholder under the leasing system has perfect control rights over the firm's residual profit, given that the rent is paid on time. He would act like a professional manager maximizing profit.

Case Study 7   Liuyue Fabric Factory[20] (Doumen Township, Zhejiang Province)

This is a large township collective enterprise with 222 employees and over 5.5 million yuan of capital. It was established in 1980 and was operated under the direct control of the township government from 1980 to 1989, then under a collective responsibility system from 1990 to 1993. During this period, all profit produced by this factory has to be submitted to the township government. The government determined the distribution of the profit. The manager as well as the other employees might receive a year-end bonus depending on the quantity of the profit remitted. The manager, however, had no responsibility for carrying financial loss of the factory.

---

[19] The leasing contract is legally enforceable. I have not observed any instance where the leasing firm was unable to pay the rent in time since all of the leasing firms in my sample had been under this system less than two years. However, I did hear in Shaoxing County of Zhejiang Province that the leaseholder of a leasing firm was unable to pay the rent and suffered business loss during the leasing period. He had managed to terminate the contract before it expired by paying the financial loss (about 30,000 yuan) to the community government from his own savings, with the excuse that the policy-induced inflation of his production costs of material inputs was beyond his ability to bear. The township government was forced to resume the collective responsibility contractual form in the firm, while seeking a buyer to take over it. It looks as if the enforceability of the leasing contract may still be an open question under some circumstances.

[20] Informant M8, L12.

In 1994, the township government decided to lease out this factory. The current leaseholder, who obtained the leasing contract through bidding, used to be the procurement and marketing manager of the factory.

As specified by the leasing contract, the leasing period was 6 years, and the rent would be unchanged until the contract expiration date. The rent was determined according to the assessed fixed capital the factory employed (equal to 7 percent of the value of fixed capital), and the land the factory occupied. As reported by the manager, after this contractual form had been implemented, he had perfect control over the firm's business decisions and complete rights to dispose of the firm's after-tax, after-rent profit; on the other hand, he had complete obligation for the firm's loss as well.

Because of the un-anticipated rapid rise of the price of chemical fiber, the costs of this factory were 50 percent higher in 1994 than in 1993, meanwhile the sale of chemical fabrics (which was this factory's final product) had fallen. The manager expected a serious business loss in 1994. However, in October 1994 when the field investigation was conducted the actual result was still unknown.

1.6 Auction

Strictly speaking, auction is not a contractual form in firm's governance itself, but a method through which the community government changes the ownership structure of a previously collectively owned TVE. This method has been extensively adopted by many community governments in order to dispose of small and/or unsuccessful TVEs since 1993.[21]

The community government transfers through auction ownership of the fixed capital of a TVE to an individual, who is to be the owner of the firm, while reserving ownership of the land occupied by the firm.[22] The basic

---

[21] Even in Wuxi (including the suburbs of the city and three counties that belong to the city), more than 1,000 collective TVEs were auctioned in 1994. The funds received by the various levels of government from the auction totaled 1.7 billion yuan. The largest factory auctioned was worth 60 million yuan. According to updated information of 1997, a considerable portion of collective TVEs in Wuxi has been auctioned to private owners. For example, a township in Wuxi County used to have thirty township-owned enterprises. In 1997, only seven maintained their township-owned status after auction and merger (Informant L18).

[22] In some cases, the community government may also reserve the ownership of factory building(s). What has been auctioned off is the fixed capital other than building(s). This is a commonly adopted method in Wuxi after 1994 (Zhou and

auction price is based upon an evaluation of the capital. To be equitable, the auction should be open to the public, and the new owner should be selected through a competitive bidding process.[23]

The buyer of the firm may either pay the total cash value of the firm to the community government at one time, or pay only part of that amount and take over the firm's debt as the remaining payment. The community government transfers its control rights over the firm to the buyer upon receiving the payments. The buyer, as the owner of the firm, has complete business control rights and rights to all of the residual profit of the firm. At the same time, he has to bear all the business risks as well. His only obligation is to pay the rent for the land the firm occupied and a regular management fee to the community government on time. The firm is privatized. The manager, usually the new owner of the firm, acts as an independent profit maximizing economic agent.

Case Study 8 Fushihao Printing and Dyeing Mill[24] (Doumen Township, Zhejiang Province)

This collective factory established in 1983 was a primary deficit firm in the township having turned into a nightmare for the township leaders before 1993. The average financial loss was 1 million yuan per year. In august 1993, a capital assessment of this factory revealed a negative net capital, *i.e.*, its existing total capital was 5.14 million yuan, while its debts was totaled 8.19 million yuan. The township government decided to sell this factory through auction open to public.

The basic auction price was set at 4 million yuan, approximating the existing fixed capital value of the factory. Three buyers, including the former manager, competed through bidding. The current owner, a family including the parents and their four sons, obtained the factory at the price of

---

Zhou, 1996). The community governments hold the ownership of factory buildings, auction or lease productive equipment to private managers. The latter are responsible to provide the operating capital while have the rights to run the firms as private owners (Fangchan Gongyou, Shebei Zulin, Zicou Zijin, Geti Jingying).

[23] I use the word 'should' because I did hear about a few 'auctions' that were actually at prices agreed upon personal negotiation, instead of through competitive bidding. However, most of the auctions in my sample did have at least a nominal bidding process.

[24] Informant M9, L12.

4.208 million yuan.[25] The price was paid in two parts. The first part was 0.628 million yuan of cash[26] directly paid to the township government after the auction; the second part was a contract that the buyer would take over 3.58 million yuan of the factory's debt to the bank and pay it back in twelve years.[27] The buyer paid another 0.23 million yuan of cash to buy the factory's inventory and the stocked raw materials.

After the auction, this factory became a complete private firm owned by the said family. The township government transferred all of its control rights over the factory to the current owner. The firm had the obligation to pay interest on the debt (about 0.5 million yuan per year) to the bank; rent for the land occupied by the factory (about 36 thousand yuan per year); and management fee (equal to 0.3 percent of total sales revenue) to the township government. The current manager had perfect autonomy in the firm's operation, investment decisions, profit disposal, and assumed sole responsibility in risk-taking.

The factory dismissed about half of its existing workers after the ownership transition. Then they built a new building to contain a new printing machine imported from Italy. Ten months after the auction it started making profit instead of losing money.

Case Study 9 Friendship Casting Factory[28] (Huazhuang Township, Jiangsu Province)

This small village factory with about 35 workers cast machinery parts for large factories. In 1994, the factory due to its unprofitable operation was 'auctioned' by the villagers' committee. The basic price was set at 0.38 million yuan, which was equal to the net capital (= total capital + credit - debt) the factory had. However, nobody bid in the open auction. The villagers' committee then negotiated with the former manager of the factory, asking him to buy it. The buyer was given preferential treatment. He was allowed to pay the price by installments stretched out into three years, and the interest of the remaining two payments would be waived on

---

[25] The members of this family had been working as technicians or marketing staff in this or other printing factories for more than ten years. The former manager left the factory after the auction.

[26] The cash was from the family's savings and personal borrowing from friends and relatives.

[27] The remaining debts of this factory were assigned by the township government to other profit-making township enterprises.

[28] Informant M71, L3.

condition that they would be made on time. All the credit and the debt were transferred to the buyer at the time when this factory was sold, and the factory became a private firm. After this 'auction', the owner of the factory no longer had the obligation to deliver profit to the villagers' committee. However, he still had to pay rent for the land (5,000 yuan per mu/year) and for the electricity facility it used (500 yuan per kw/year).

The main obstacle in the auction of collective TVEs is the lack of available financial resources for private entrepreneurs to buy a desirable firm, particularly relatively large sized firms. The absence of capital market and underdevelopment of credit institutions have prevented many potential buyers (private entrepreneurs, current managers and personnel of collective TVEs, local government cadres, etc.) from becoming private owners of rural enterprises. However, local government leaders understand this problem very well. Quite a number of community government leaders during my field investigation indicated to me that leasing was just a transitional contractual form. Their real aim in implementing the leasing system was in the hope that the leaseholder could accumulate sufficient financial capital funds from their disposable residual profit to buy the firm in the near future.[29]

2. The Share-cooperative System

This section is devoted to a brief discussion of another form of ownership and management in the TVE sector -- the share-cooperative system. This system was a very hot topic in TVEs studies between 1992 to 1994, particularly among the researchers in China. This system was introduced as an institutional innovation in the reform experiments to attempt to 'clarify the property rights' of the collective TVEs, and 'separate government's administrative intervention from firm's daily operation' so as to improve firm's efficiency. It was explicitly encouraged and supported by the central government, and thus led to its great popularity with local community governments. In many areas, local governments at different levels even intended to set a timetable to accomplish the transformation of all local collective TVEs into share-cooperatives.[30]

---

[29] Informant L1, L6, L11.

[30] See 'Sum up the experiences, actively support and guide, in order to promote a healthy development of rural share-cooperatives: an investigation on the

The general method in transforming a former collective TVE into a share cooperative firm is to divide the firm's existing capital into shares to be held by the community government (as the representative of the community citizens), the firm, the manager(s), and the employees of the firm.[31] The firm sells cash shares at the same time to its employees (in some cases to local residents as well) to increase the firm's total capital.[32]

Under this system, the distribution of residual profit becomes easier since each party can claim its clearly defined shares. However, the control rights over the firm do not seem to be clearly defined. A share-cooperative firm is nominally under the control of the Board of Directors. The firm manager is 'recruited' or appointed by the board and runs the firm under the close guidance of the board with important decisions made at the board meetings. Since the community government holds the majority of the shares,[33] the manager of the firm is usually appointed in the desire of the community government. He must follow the community government's decisions in most cases since the community government controls the majority of votes in the board.

Case Study 10 Jiangnan Iron and Steel Company[34] (Huazhuang Township, Jiangsu Province)

This is a primary township collective enterprise established in 1983 with the initial investment from the township government. In 1993, it had 382 million yuan of capital and 752 employees, accomplished 489.6 million yuan of sales and delivered 2 million yuan to the township government.

In March 1993, this factory was selected by local (county and township) governments as the experimental firm to implement the share-cooperative system. On the basis of a capital evaluation, the firm's existing net capital 55 million yuan was transferred into shares held by the township government. In the meantime, the firm sold 5.3 million yuan of cash shares to its employees and local residents at the price of 100 yuan per share. After

---

implementation of share-cooperative system in TVE sector', The Finance Research Institute, People's Bank of China, Jiangxi Province Branch, 1994, Nanchang, China.

[31] As observed in my investigation, the individual holders of this part of shares had only dividend distribution right, but no ownership rights to the assets. These shares were not transferable should the holder leave the firm.

[32] The holders of this part of the shares had both an ownership right and a dividend distribution right to the assets. These shares were transferable.

[33] Accounted for 70 percent to 90 percent in the investigation sample.

[34] Informant M49, L3.

this transition, the collective shares (those held by the township government) accounted for 91 percent of the total shares, and the private shares accounted for 9 percent. The private shares cannot be withdrawn, but can be transferred within the firm after one year of possession, and then can be inherited or given away.

As specified by the firm's 'Rules of New Share-cooperative Company', the manager should be selected by the Board of Directors. However, until October 1994, the current manager was still the same person appointed by the township government. The manager's responsibility was specified by the 'Rules' as to direct the firm's daily productive activities, design and schedule the firm's development project, plan the firm's budget and distribution scheme, and recruit, allocate, or dismiss employees.[35]

The after-tax profit distribution was as follows: 10 percent of the after-tax profit would be extracted first as the firm's collective accumulation fund; then 40 percent as the firm's development fund; the remainder was the dividend distributed to the share holders (including the township government). After these two extracts, if the firm should make an extremely high profit with the dividend exceeding some 'normal' limit, the firm should withdraw a certain amount of the after-tax profit as a 'dividend reserve fund'. Only then would the remainder be distributed to the shareholders. The collective accumulation fund can not be distributed to shareholders. However, the development fund belonged to the shareholders, and it might be turned into new shares in future for the existing shareholders in accordance with the initial shares they held. The 'dividend reserve fund' might be applied to dividend distribution in subsequent years in case the firm could not pay a 'normal' dividend to its share holders due to failure to make a high enough profit rate. In 1993, the dividend rate was 30 percent, well above the prevailing interest rate.

Case Study 11 Triflower Group Corporation[36] (Xinchang County, Zhejiang Province)

This large township enterprise was developed from a small agricultural tool repair workshop established in 1967. In 1993, its output was 87.2 million yuan, before-tax profit was 14.7 million yuan. It had 67 million

---

[35] However, the manager of this firm indicated only partial autonomy in employee recruitment and promotion in response to my investigation.

[36] 'Undertaking the property rights reform, forming a modern corporation', a report at Hangzhou International Conference on the Property Rights Reform in China's TVEs. August 1994, Hangzhou, China.

yuan of capital and 1,200 employees. This firm was converted into a share-cooperative company in August 1993.

Based upon a capital assessment conducted by Shaoxing City State Capital Assessing Center, the firm had 28.89 million yuan of net capital before this transition. 7.9 million yuan, which was equivalent to the total tax exemption the firm enjoyed in the previous years, was extracted from this net capital to set aside for a 'risk fund'. The remainder of the net capital was turned into shares and divided into two parts: 20 percent of that was owned by the township government, and 80 percent was 'firm owned collective shares', or 'shadow shares' as called by local residents. The 'shadow shares' were owned by the firm, but the right of dividend income distribution of these shares was allocated to firm employees depending on their positions and working years in the firm.[37] This part of the shares was non-transferable.

In the meantime, everyone who accepted the 'shadow shares' had to buy the firm's cash shares at the proportion of one to one half (*i.e.*, every 1 'shadow share' accepted must be combined with the purchase of 0.5 share of the cash shares). The sold cash shares totaled 8.27 million yuan. The cash shares were allowed to be transferred, inherited, or given. However, withdrawal was prohibited.

The firm was under the managerial control of the Board of Directors, which was consisted of nine members including the representatives of the township government and the firm employees. The board appointed the manager, who was the former manager appointed by the township government. Since the manager was allocated with more 'shadow shares' than the ordinary employees, he had to invest more in the cash shares. As a consequence, he would either enjoy more dividend income, or suffer more losses depending on the firm's financial performance.

Ten percent of the firm's after-tax profit had to be set aside as the collective accumulation, and 5 percent as collective welfare funds. The remainder (85 percent) of the after-tax profit was distributed as dividend to the shareholders.

It was found after nearly two years of practice that the share-cooperative system was not as successful as expected with regard to the purpose of property rights reform in TVEs. Local government leaders in many areas

---

[37] Among these shares, 25 percent was allocated to the members of the Board of Directors, 20 percent to the managerial staff, and 35 percent to the workers and other employees.

came to realize this and reduced their enthusiasm in support of the practice, and turned their attention to leasing and auction in the second half of 1994.

It is not difficult to understand why the share-cooperative system did poorly as a means to 'clarify' the property rights of the collective TVEs. As observed in the investigation, the majority of the shares that were transferred from the existing capital of the firm was held by the community government as the so-called 'public shares', or by the firm as a unit as 'collective shares'. The cash shares that were actually owned by the private investors accounted for a relatively small proportion in the total capital. This ownership structure made only a minor difference from the community public ownership of the firm. Due to such majority holding, the community government could not withdraw itself from the firms' operation but exercised control indirectly through its power in the Board of Directors. Therefore, the two major objectives -- to clarify the property rights of the collective TVEs, and to separate the government's administrative intervention from firm's operation failed in practice.

Regarding the managerial autonomy of the firm manager, several of my interviewed managers complained of losing rather than gaining decision-making autonomy during such practice. As the manager of a share-cooperative firm said:[38] 'I had only one mother-in-law (Popo) -- the township government -- to follow before the reform, but I have to serve many mothers-in-law now. The shareholders who are completely ignorant about business strongly demand higher dividend distribution at the expense of reinvestment in long-term development of the firm. They even threaten to withdraw in order to put pressure on me to oppose my proposed project. I was really upset. I would much rather go back to the previous (personal responsibility contractual) system.'

Many local leaders and firm managers admitted that the real objective for them to promote such change so enthusiastically was to acquire more financial capital. The money was needed to overcome the capital bottleneck caused by the macro-rectification of the central government in the early 1990s.[39] Therefore, the property rights reform experiment became a means of fund raising because it gave the community government a good excuse to squeeze financial resources from firm employees and local residents. China is not a fully mature market economy, few people understand what 'investment' really means, especially in rural areas. The only way to entice

---

[38] Informant 17.
[39] Informant L10, L11, L17.

the urgently needed financial resources from the peasant households is to promise a higher rate of return than the prevailing savings interest rate. Some community governments announced a 'rule' in the share-cooperative practice: for all cash shares invested by individual investors, the government would 'guarantee the principal, guarantee the interest, and pay dividend' (Baoben, Baoxi, Fenhong). This means that privately owned cash shares would not risk any financial loss of the firm. They would be paid by a guaranteed rate at least the same as the prevailing interest rate, plus a dividend income if the firm made profit.[40] With such a promise, the implementation of the share-cooperative system became infeasible for most of the rural enterprises. Only unusually profitable firms had the ability to pay high enough dividends to attract potential shareholders. In many cases, the firm could sell its cash shares only with certain degree of coercion as we observed in Case Study 11.

3. Three Categories of the Managerial Contractual Forms

In Section 1 we discussed the managerial contractual forms. If we rank the forms according to how fully firm manager enjoyed decision making autonomy and how much risk he was liable, we may observe a monotonic increasing locus from the work point system to auction. We may classify these contractual forms into three major categories distinguishing them from each other by the residual profit distribution between the community government and the firm manager: the *fixed-wage* form, which includes the work point system and the wage/salary system; the *profit-sharing* form, which includes the collective contractual responsibility system, and the personal contractual responsibility system (non-mortgage and mortgage); the *fixed-payment* form, which includes leasing and auctions.[41]

During extensive interviews throughout eastern and central China, it became clear that the idea that views TVE managers as subordinate community government employees assigned no property rights of the firm has been getting increasingly outdated. Some managers appear to have become much more autonomous, explicitly and implicitly assigned more and more property rights of the firm. They have begun to share an interest

---

[40] Informant L13, L14.

[41] We may view all private TVEs as belonging to this category, since they have to pay the rent to the community governments to use the land, sometimes buildings, that are publicly owned properties.

in the economic performance of the firm too. As a way of increasing their incentive to work harder and exercise more responsibilities, community government leaders have made managers more than mere wage-earning forepersons. By the late 1980s, profit-sharing arrangements were being offered to them. In a sense, managers have become partners in TVE development and operations. In some instances (especially in the recent years since Deng's trip to south China in spring 1992), fixed-payment leasing arrangements have been adopted to enlist firm managers' whole-hearted dedication. Community government leaders give up substantial amount of control over property rights of TVEs in return for a single, lump-sum payment.

The fixed-wage form entitled the community government to take over the profit produced by the firm in its entirety. The remuneration of the firm manager is not contingent on the financial performance of the firm. It is rather, contingent on other considerations of the community government, such as income equalization within the firm or among firm managers in the community. Therefore, the firm manager is not motivated by his personal economic benefit in the firm's operation. He has very weak incentive to improve the efficiency of the firm.

Under the profit-sharing contractual form, the profit is shared between the community government and the firm manager. Although the community government has decisive power to make the decisions regarding the distribution of the residual profit, it acknowledges that the firm manager has the right to share the benefit derived from the firm efficiency improvement. The community government understands that such profit sharing arrangement is necessary because it would give the firm manager the desirable incentives to exert more effort to the improvement of firm's efficiency. Such efficiency improvement without doubt would mainly benefit the community government.

The community government grants the entire residual claim rights to the firm manager under the fixed-payment contractual form, but retains its ownership rights over the properties that are publicly owned by the community. After collecting the rents -- the cost the producer must pay in order to use the valuable properties in a market system -- it is with the community government's approval that the firm managers can have entire residual profit of the firm at their disposal. As an exclusive residual claimant, the firm manager has very strong incentive to made full commitment to the firm's efficiency improvement.

People may be puzzled when they note that the profit objective and the profit distribution share were explicitly stipulated upon the responsibility contract renewal in the beginning of the year. The targeted profit remittance to the community government was known to the firm manager when he entered his contractual relations with the community government. If over-targeted profit is left at the firm's sole disposal as observed in some cases, the contracted profit remittance becomes a fixed amount, while the firm or the firm manager remains the exclusive residual claimant. Can we still distinguish this kind of responsibility contracts from the leasing-kind fixed payment contract? The answer is 'yes'.

Two critical features make this kind of responsibility contract distinguishable from the leasing-kind fixed payment contract. The first, as illustrated in Section 1, the contracted profit remittance is determined by the actual financial performance of the firm in the previous year when a responsibility contract is signed. The contracted rent payment, however, is determined by the formulated rent scale of the land and the assessed capital value of the firm when a leasing contract is signed. The second, the yearly contract adjustment upon renewal enables the community government to share the benefit of firm efficiency improvement under the responsibility systems, since the profit increase of the firm is always followed by the profit target lifting as the consequence. However, the rent under a leasing contract is fixed for a certain period without fluctuation related to the firm's actual performance. The leaseholder is thus the only beneficiary of the firm efficiency improvement in this period. These two features result in dissimilar incentives for the firm manager. The firm manager has the incentive to fulfill the contracted profit objective when working under the responsibility contract, but will not pursue profit maximization. The reason is because he can benefit as the sole residual claimant only for a very limited period, at the cost of inflating performance objectives in the following period. The firm manager with a fixed payment contract, in contrast, is motivated to pursue profit maximization since he is the sole residual claimant for a relatively long period.

Generally speaking, a contractual form is designed in such a way that compensation to the agent should be sufficient enough to motivate him to exert a desirable degree of effort toward his responsibilities. The more responsibilities assigned to a firm manager, the more he must be compensated for. A positive correlation between the compensation a firm manager may receive and the responsibilities he must assume is evident in the TVEs' contractual forms. A firm manager will have more decision-making autonomy when he is assigned more responsibilities. At the same time, he will receive a more favorable compensation package. As observed in my investigation, firm managers working under the fixed-wage contractual form had limited decision making autonomy and basically in minor aspects of firm's operation. With profit-sharing contractual form, managers share decision making power with the community government as they share the profit, but the key decisions are made by the community government. The third group of managers, those with fixed-payment contracts took full responsibility for making decisions in business operation, but share decision making power with the community government in some critical aspects.

My survey provides convincing evidence that decision-making autonomy of the firm manager differed across these three contractual categories. I asked the interviewed TVE managers to rank the degree of independence of their decision making power in sixteen managerial tasks. The rank is on a scale of 0 to 2. When the respondent answered '0', the local government leaders had complete control; when '2' was answered, the manager had nearly entire autonomy; while a '1' indicated that the decision was jointly made by both parties.[42]

Table 3.2 summarizes the survey results by grouping the 64 TVE managers interviewed into three categories: fixed-wage, profit-sharing, and fixed-payment, then calculating the mean score of each group for the corresponding managerial task. We may see from the table that as the managerial contractual form of the TVE moves across the spectrum from a government leader-operated fixed-wage management regime to a profit-sharing arrangement to a fixed lease arrangement, managers are granted increasing autonomy.

The firm managers enjoyed a remarkably higher degree of decision-making autonomy in almost all of the sixteen managerial tasks when working under fixed-payment contractual forms. The profit-sharing firm managers were more autonomous in making decisions than their counterparts under the fixed-wage arrangement, but at a less significant level and not in all of the listed managerial aspects. However, the divergence of decision-making autonomy in more critical managerial tasks was ample between these two categories.

---

[42] In most cases, the firm manager made the decision, but the decision could not be put into practice until it was approved by the community government.

**Table 3.2 The Degree of Firm Manager's Decision-making Autonomy
in Sample Township and Village Enterprises, 1994**

	Fixed Wage	Profit Sharing	Fixed Payment
Production Planning	1.9	1.9	1.9
Production Management	2.0	1.9	2.0
Product Design	1.7	1.6	2.0
Technical Innovation	1.7	1.7	2.0
Product Pricing	1.4	1.8	1.9
Marketing	1.7	1.8	2.0
Contracting with Other firms	1.8	1.9	2.0
Worker Employment	1.7	1.8	1.9
Worker Dismissal	1.5	1.7	1.9
Wage Level Determination	1.2	1.3	1.9
Bonus Level Determination	1.3	1.5	1.9
Managerial Staff Recruitment	1.3	1.2	1.8
Fund Raising	1.4	1.7	2.0
Investment	1.1	1.4	1.8
Profit Distribution	0.9	1.1	1.8
Establishing Joint-Venture	1.1	1.2	1.7

Source: Author's Survey, 1994.

A closer look will reveal that the discrepancy in the degree of decision-making autonomy varies notably across managerial tasks. It was hardly possible to find any cross-category variation in such aspects as production planning and production management. Only a minor difference was observed across the three categories or between the fixed-wage and the profit-sharing forms in tasks such as worker employment, contracting with other firms, and technical innovations. However, significant cross-category divergence existed in respect to some more important managerial decisions such as bonus level determination, fund raising, investment, and profit distribution. As shown by Figure 3.1, after grouping these sixteen tasks into four major management fields[43]-- production management, marketing, labor decisions, and investment and profit distribution, we find a homogeneous decline in autonomy in firm managers working under all three contractual forms from 'production management' to 'marketing', to 'labor decisions', then to 'investment and profit distribution'. It appeared that the community government leaders showed less inclination to share decision-making responsibility with the firm managers on more strategic aspects of the firms' operation. The cross-category autonomy variation, however, is increasing from 'production management' up to 'investment and profit distribution' decisions, indicating that the substantial distinction among these three contractual forms is embodied in the firm manager's ability to make crucial decisions on the firm's operation independently.

To summarize, as the managerial contractual form of the collective TVEs moves across the spectrum from a government leader-operated managerial regime to a profit-sharing arrangement to a fixed-payment lease contract, the firm managers are granted increasing autonomy in operation decisions. They are also compensated by increasing rights in the firms' residual profit claim to motivate them into taking more responsibilities and business risks to improve firm efficiency.

---

[43] Production planning, production management, product design, and technical innovation are sorted as 'production management'; product pricing, marketing, and contracting with other firms as 'marketing'; worker employment, worker dismissal, wage level determination, bonus level determination, managerial staff recruitment as 'labor decisions'; and the remaining four, i.e., fund raising, investment, profit distribution, and establishing joint venture with other firms as 'investment and profit distribution'.

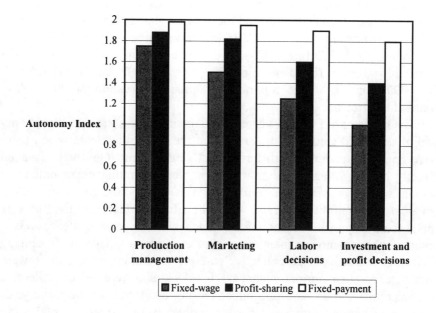

**Figure 3.1 Degree of Decision-making Autonomy for Various
Operations under Alternative Contractual Forms
in Sample TVEs, 1994**

Source: Author's Survey, 1994.

4. The Coexistence, Evolution, and Cross-regional Variation
in the Contractual Structure of Collective TVEs

The nature of formal and informal contractual relations between local
government leaders and TVE managers has important implications for the
efficient operation of firms and the expansion of the sector. These relations
vary greatly from place to place. They also change for a given firm over
time and vary from firm to firm within the same place. These are the three
fundamental findings revealed in my extensive fieldwork. These three
findings -- the coexistence of alternative contractual form in a given area,
the dynamic evolution in the structure of the contractual forms, and the

cross-regional variation of this structure -- have laid the ground work for the theoretical modeling and the empirical tests of this research work.

Many researchers have reported their observations on the coexistence of different ownership forms of TVEs in a given area (Jin and Qian, 1998; Putterman, 1994; Whiting, 1995), or on the cross-regional disparity of the ownership structure (Byrd and Lin, 1990; Liu, Y., 1992; Parris, 1993; Yang, D., 1990), but few have reported a similar observation on the TVEs' contractual structure.

I was first amazed when I visited a village in Jiangsu Province during my preliminary field studies and learned that the five village enterprises there were operating under four different contractual forms. One was managed directly by the villagers' committee, two were operating under collective responsibility contracts, the fourth one was run by the manager with a personal responsibility contract, while the fifth was leased to the manager for a fixed payment.[44] I soon found such simultaneous existence was a common phenomenon in many areas. For example, a village in Huazhuang Township had ten village collective enterprises. Among which, three were auctioned to their former managers in 1994, six were under collective responsibility system, and one under leasing contract.[45] In the same year, three township collective enterprises among twenty-eight in total were leased out in Guohe Township, while the remaining twenty-five were operating with collective responsibility contracts.[46]

Based on the study sample of 64 firms in eastern and central China, it is found the structure of TVEs contractual form has changed sharply through time (Figure 3.2). In the early reform era, local community governments not only were responsible for the strategic decisions of the firm, they also took an active role in the everyday production and marketing affairs. Over 80 percent of sample firms were in this sense leader operated, or in fixed-wage contract style. Managers generally were considered hired technicians. Only about 10 percent of early TVEs considered the manager to be in an important enough position to warrant a profit-sharing agreement. Fewer managers had lease rights to the enterprise's assets.[47]

---

[44] Informant L1.

[45] Informant L4.

[46] Informant L14, L15.

[47] Four enterprises in the study sample were private firms in substance, but under the title of 'village collective enterprise' and paid a fixed rent to the villagers' committee for the land and the building they were using. I identified them as fixed-payment firms. (See footnote 38 of Chapter 2.)

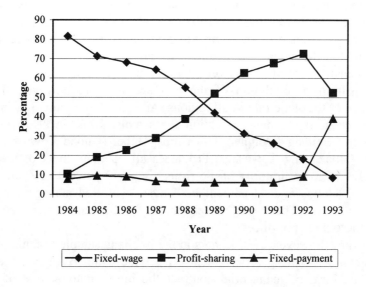

Figure 3.2 Evolution of Contractual Structure in Sample TVEs, 1984-1993

Source: Author's Survey, 1994.

During the 1980s, however, the mix of firms changed. Leader-operated firms monotonically fell to a point that by 1993 less than 10 percent of the sample firms were under the primary management control of local government leaders. During most of the 1980s, local officials chose to give more responsibility to professional managers, changing the contractual structure of the firm to one characterized by a profit-sharing arrangement between the firm manager and the community government. By 1990, firms managed by individuals with profit-sharing arrangement accounted for more than 60 percent of all TVEs in the sample.

During this swift transition towards profit-sharing arrangement, few leaders were willing (or perceived as a need) to auction off or lease out the assets of their firms. Although their role had changed to one concentrating more on external management issues, local government leaders remained heavily involved in TVEs' operation. Beginning in 1991, and accelerating in 1992, local leaders in the sample townships began to take a further step in modifying the form of the contractual relations that governed the management of their TVEs. By 1993 (the last year of the sample) over 30 percent of the firms were being operated by managers who paid a lump-sum payment to the local community governments in return for more comprehensive control rights over the firms' business operation.

The pattern of evolution of the contractual form, however, has not proceeded at the same rate in all regions. As shown by Figure 3.3, in 1984, the first year of the data collection for sample firms, local government leaders in Zhejiang (Doumen Township), Hubei (Guohe Township), and Jiangsu (Huazhuang Township) Provinces all operated most of the firms themselves. Only a minority of the firms -- e.g., 17 percent in Zhejiang, 14 percent in Hubei, and 44 percent in Jiangsu -- offered managers a profit-sharing contract. There was no lease-like, fixed-payment arrangement in any of these three provinces.

Over time, however, local leaders in the Zhejiang sample became the first to adopt profit-sharing arrangement on a wide-scale. By 1987, they had made this form of managerial contract the most common one of TVEs governance (60 percent of firms -- Figure 3.3, panel 2). By 1993, another transformation had occurred. During this more recent interval, government leaders replaced profit-sharing contracts with fixed-payment leasing arrangements. Fully 80 percent of firms were run by nearly complete autonomous managers by the end of the survey period.

The structure of managerial contracts in the Hubei and Jiangsu study sites, however, evolved slower. By 1987, only 29 percent of Hubei firms (up by only 15 percent from 1984), and 50 percent of Jiangsu firms (up by only 6 percent) had begun sharing management responsibilities with a professional manager who shared in the profit of the firm. While profit-sharing arrangement became nearly universal by 1993, local government leaders in these two provinces had not begun to use fixed-payment contracts.[48]

---

[48] Fixed-payment schemes, however, were just becoming more common in Jiangsu during the field investigation in the late 1994. Local community governments in the Jiangsu sample township leased out or auctioned off more than 20 percent of the firms in their jurisdiction (86 out among 387 township and village collective enterprises in total). No similar change has been observed in Hubei sample township. See the Appendix to Chapter 6.

1984

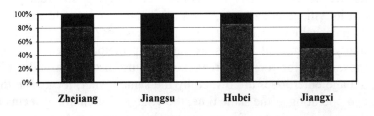

1987

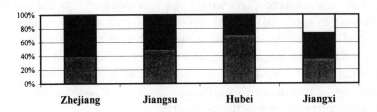

1990

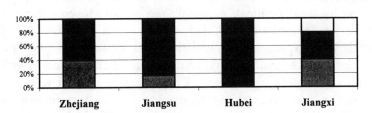

1993

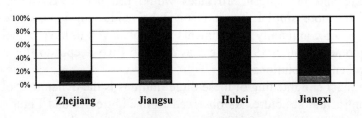

☒ Fixed-wage ■ Profit-sharing ☐ Fixed-payment

Figure 3.3 Evolutionary Transition of Contractual Structure in Sample Provinces, 1984-1993

Source: Author's Survey, 1994.

Questions surfaced immediately after these findings.

When we observe a villagers' committee applying different contractual forms to its village enterprises, not surprisingly we want to know: what is the rationale behind such discriminative decisions? If we assume that the community government leaders are rational principals, then, there must be some advantage for them to treat their agents discriminatingly. Since all these village enterprises are owned by the same owner, located in the same area, and operating at the same time, the villagers' committee seems to have no coherent grounds to discriminate unless there exists some degree of heterogeneity among the firms that makes such distinction a rational behavior. For instance, it would be reasonable for the community government to apply differential contractual forms to the village enterprises if the cost-benefit calculation associated with each form deviates from firm to firm. Then, the question becomes: under what conditions does such calculation vary? Or, how such calculation variation may affect the community government's decisions in the selection of alternative contractual forms for a specific enterprise?

The cause of the cross-regional variation in the structure of TVEs' contractual form is another question. Needless to say, the disparities embodied by local political, economic, geographic, even cultural features could be on the solution list. However, such a list may fall short of consistency in explaining the variation. For example, it may not be so surprising that the evolutionary contours in Zhejiang and Hubei differ, given the differences in the rates of development of their respective rural economies. A more perplexing enigma is raised by the similarities of the paths of contractual structure change experienced in Hubei and in Jiangsu. A priori, it might be expected that decisions by community governments in Zhejiang and in Jiangsu Provinces would produce TVE structures that would be more similar, yet it is in Hubei and Jiangsu Provinces where decisions of community governments were observed to have coincident set of outcomes through 1993. We may have to dive deeper to dig out more comprehensive solutions.

The most enlightening of these three findings is the dynamic evolution of the contractual structure. As observed from Figure 3.2 and Figure 3.3, the contractual structure of TVEs has been moving toward a unique direction, *i.e.*, moving away from the more government leader dominant fixed-wage regime toward a more efficiency oriented fixed-payment structure, though not proceeding at the same rate in all regions. If we view such evolution as an institutional innovation with a unique direction, the logical result of such innovation is pointing to an endogenous privatization in collective TVEs with abundant evidences. Then, where is this 'invisible hand' that has pushed the TVE sector toward a direction in which the government, at least the central government, has no intention of pursuing? If we agree that an existing contractual form for a given firm is the optimal choice made by the principal and the agent, then why was such choice replaced by other choices in a relatively short time span for the very same firm? In other words, what happened in the environment, within which the firm is operating, that forced the principal and the agent to take action to search for a more appropriate contractual form in the firm's operation? And, through what kind of mechanism does such outside variation lead to the evolutionary adaptation in the firm's contractual structure?

According to Coase (1992, p.718-719), the research *'inspiration is most likely to come through the stimulus provided by the patters, puzzles, and anomalies revealed by the systematic gathering of data'*. The search for answers to these questions may shed light on an understanding of the whole mechanism of the governance in the TVE sector, and of the organizational transformation in a reforming transitional economy. Since the form of the managerial organization will undoubtedly affect the efficiency of the firm's operation as well as the long run performance of China's rural industrial experiment, the challenge is not only to explain the coexistence of various managerial contractual forms, but also to explore the factors that may have had influences on the transition of these forms over time. Therefore, the goal of the following chapters is to provide a general framework for explaining the evolutionary pattern of the structure of contractual forms in the TVE sector, and to predict how this structure will vary temporally and spatially.

4 Modeling the Contractual Structure of Collective TVEs

In order to dive into the heart of answers to the questions arisen in the end of Chapter 3, a consistent theoretical framework must be developed. This chapter will serve as the 'theoretical chapter' of this book. In the first section, I briefly review the theories of institutional economics and induced institutional innovation. The transaction costs theory of firm governance structure and the environmental disequilibria induced institutional innovation of the new institutional economics have laid the theoretical foundation for the entire research, and guided the search for the factors that may have had influences in TVEs' contractual form determination and innovation. These factors are demonstrated in Section 2. A principal-agent model is formulated in the third section to capture the effects of those factors, and to illustrate the mechanism through which the external variations are translated into the determination and evolution of TVEs' contractual structure. In Section 4, the theoretical model is simulated to generate comparative static results. These results predict the possible correlation between exogenous factors and the contractual form of the firm in a testable format.

1. Institutions and Induced Institutional Innovation: A Brief Review of Institutional Economics

The contractual form applied to a firm defines the governance structure of the firm. It governs the relationship between the principal and the agent in the operation of the firm. Any change in the contractual form is a re-distribution, to a more or less extent, of the property rights over the firm. Such re-distribution assigns control rights from one party to another in conjunction with the re-allocation of residual claim rights over the firm, which is to compensate for the altered distribution of responsibilities between the principal and the agent. The exploration of the factors that may have had influences on the contractual form alteration is the main focus of institutional economics, but beyond the research scope of conventional economics.

1.1 Institutions and Institutional Economics

As defined by Douglass North (1991):

> *Institutions are the humanly devised constraints that structure political, economic and social interaction. They consist of both informal constraints (sanctions, taboos, customs, traditions, and codes of conduct), and formal rules (constitutions, laws, property rights).*

In other words, institution is a set of ordered relationships among people that defines their rights, exposures to the rights of others, privileges, and responsibilities (Schmid, 1972).[1]

Institutions are important, because individuals in a society acting in pursuit of self-interest are under the constraint of existing institutions. Their incentive and feasible behavioral choices are shaped by institutions, for *'Yesterday's institutional framework provides the opportunity set for today's organizations and individual entrepreneurs (political or economic)'* (North, 1991, P.109). And also *'it makes little sense for economists to discuss the process of exchange without specifying the institutional setting with which the trading takes place, since this affects the incentives to produce and the costs of transacting'* (Coase, 1992, p.718). Variations in institutions will change the opportunity set for individuals, and hence motivate them to alter their decisions in political and economic activities. The integrated effects of such individual decision alteration will lead to changes in direction and speed in the development of an economy. As described by North,

> *Throughout history, institutions have been devised by human beings to create orders and reduce uncertainty in exchange. Together with the standard constraints of economics they define the choice set and therefore determine transaction and production costs and hence the profitability and feasibility of engaging in economic activity. They evolve incrementally, connecting the past with the present and the future; history in consequence is largely a story of institutional evolution in which the historical performance of economies can only be understood as a part of a sequential story. Institutions provide the incentive structure of an economy, as that*

---

[1] Also see North, 1984a; and Bromley, 1989.

> *structure evolves, it shapes the direction of economic change toward growth, stagnation, or decline* (North, 1991, p.97).

Conventional economics recognizes the existence of institutions such as political, legal, monetary and other systems in an economy. However, these systems in a classical economics doctrine were either *'regarded as neutral in their effects on economic events and ignored; or taken as given and then specified in so perfunctory a way as to suggest that institutional influence was not so much important'* (Furubotn and Richter, 1991, p.1). In order to overcome such neglect, institutional economists pinpoint the relationship between institutions and the economic performance of an economy. This is because they believe that: *'The central issue of economic history and economic development is to account for the evolution of political and economic institutions that create an economic environment that increasing productivity'* (North, 1991, p.98).

According to Furubotn and Richter, *'Modern institutional economics focuses on the institution of property, and on the system of norms governing the acquisition or transfer of property rights'* (1991, p.3). Distinct from neoclassical economics, which emphasizes the effectiveness of markets and regards 'getting the price right' as the main strategy in economic reform and development pursuit, institutional economics pays greater attention to the property rights structure, arguing that the reform strategy should give priority to 'getting the property rights right' (Williamson, 1996, p.323-324). However, as argued by Williamson (1996), 'Getting the property rights right' is still too narrow a conception in institutional economics. The more general need is perhaps 'getting the institutions right', in the recognition that property rights structure is only one part of the institutions. *'....the idea of getting the institutions right can be viewed as an exercise in (general) theory or an exercise in governance/mechanisms. The former tends to be more ambitious and normative, and the later is more partial and positive'* (Williamson, 1996, p.325).[2]

The 'new institutional economics' (or 'the transaction cost economics approach to economic organization' as described by Williamson) focuses its research on the governance structure of the firm, which is operating within

---

[2] G. Rausser and L. Simon (1992) have illustrated the 'ideal formulation' of such general theory. See their paper: 'The Political Economy of Transition in Eastern Europe', in C.Clague and G. Rausser eds. *The Emergence of Market Economies in Eastern Europe*, Cambridge, MA: Basil Blackwell, p.245-270.

an economy where transaction costs are greater than zero. According to Williamson (1996, p.322),

> *The main divide is between the institutional approach, which is more a macro perspective and is concerned with the political and legal rules of the game, and the institutions of governance, which is more a micro-perspective and deal with firm and market modes of contract and organization.*

Although agreed that the former of these two is arguably more pertinent to economic development and reform, Williamson is working predominantly from the governance perspectives, as described by himself: '*I adopt a bottom-up, rather than a top-down approach to economic organization*' (1996, p.322). This is because there exist too many unsolved 'mysteries' in real economic life at the level of firms or transaction units with respect to the conventional economics. Observations in empirical studies have revealed lots of phenomena that are seemingly inconsistent with the market economic system, and regarded as non-optimal solutions in economic activities by conventional economics, yet persistently exist. As pointed out by Coase, his pioneer and Nobel Prize winning research was built on the basis of the observation that various industries were organized in different ways, and the fact that a firm's operation was organized through administrative planning and managerial coordination within the firm. This observation puzzled him for their seeming contradiction against the classical economic doctrine, one in which the 'invisible hand' -- the system of prices -- would automatically coordinate the economy to reach its highest efficiency.[3] Furubotn and Richter described the development of the new institutional economics as a gradual process over time in response to the failure of conventional economics to explain such observations. They illustrated (1991, p.1):

> *The 'new institutional economics' is sensitive to organizational issues and seeks to extend the range of applicability of neoclassical theory by considering how property rights structure and transaction costs affect incentives and economic behavior. ....the tendency to introduce greater institutional detail into economic model has come about gradually over time because of the recognition that standard neoclassical analysis is overly abstract and incapable of dealing effectively with many current*

---

[3] See Coase (1992): *The Institutional Structure of Production*, The American Economic Review, 82(4), p.713-720.

> *problems of interest to theorists and policymakers. ....conventional*
> *microeconomics fails in those (every-day) situations where transaction*
> *costs are greater than zero, and where property rights to resources take*
> *forms different from the idealized pattern hypothesized for classical*
> *capitalism.*

1.2 Institutions of Governance

Institutions of governance are distinguished from institutional environment in the new institutional economics. Davis and North (1971) defined institutional environment as the set of fundamental political, social and legal ground rules that established the basis for production, exchange, and distribution; while institutions of governance (or the 'institutional arrangements' as their concept) as contractual agreements among principals or between principals and agents that govern the ways in which these units can cooperate and/or compete to maximize their wealth by realizing the gains from trade. As by Williamson (1996), '*One of the salient differences between the institutional environment and the institutions of governance is that the former mainly defines -- can be thought of as constraints on -- the environment of the later. ....Taking the institutional environment as given, economic agents purportedly align transactions with governance structures to effect economizing outcomes*' (p.5). He emphasized: '*....Institutions are the mechanisms of governance*'.

Williamson described a three-layer schema of institutional economics as in Figure 4.1.[4] The main effects in the schema are shown by solid arrows, while dashed arrows represent the secondary effects. Williamson illustrated the middle layer -- the 'governance' -- as an organization that has a life of its own. In the meantime, it is defined by the upper layer -- the 'institutional environment', as well as by the lower layer -- the 'individual'. The 'institutional environment' defines the governance because it defines the rules of the game. Any change in the institutional environment may lead to change in the governance given that such a change is strong enough to bring about variation in the comparative costs of governance structures. The 'individual' sector defines the governance in the sense that the behavioral attributes of individuals underlie the transaction costs of the governance structures. Therefore, any studies in the governance with the transaction

---

[4] See Williamson (1996), *The Mechanism of Governance*, Oxford University Press, p.223-225.

costs as the main research means must include the assumption with respect to the individual behavior. When the 'governance' is determined, it has feedback effects on the institutional environment, for it may demand certain improvement or modification in the rules to make the game more efficient and fair. The feedback effects from the 'governance' to the 'individual' is described as 'endogenous preference' formation. The individual acting in an economy is influenced by both the governance and the institutional environment, because they shape the opportunity set for the individual.

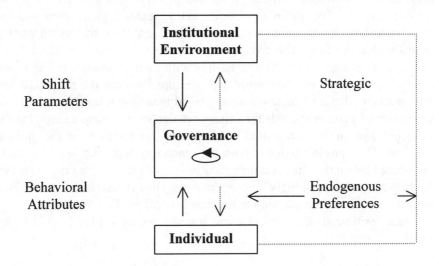

Figure 4.1 The Three-layer Schema of Institutional Economics

Source: Williamson: *The Mechanism of Governance*, 1996, Oxford University
        Press.

    The research focus in the new institutional economics is on the governance structure of the firm, while the institutional environment is treated as the shift parameters influencing the governance. '....*the institutional environment and the institutions of governance .... are joined by interpreting the institutional environment as a locus of shift parameters, changes in which parameters induce shifts in the comparative costs of governance*' (Williamson, 1996, p.119). This research field had long been neglected in conventional economics. As pointed out by Williamson (1996), '.... *economics was too preoccupied with issues of allocative efficiency, in which marginal analysis was featured, to the neglect of organizational efficiency, in which discrete structure alternatives were brought under scrutiny*' (p.100). Williamson attributed such neglect to the definition of 'firm' in neoclassical economics: '*Neoclassical firm is defined as a production function (a technological construction), transaction cost economics describes the firm as a governance structure (an organizational construction). Firms and markets are alternative modes of governance. The allocation of activities between firms and markets is not given, but to be derived*' (p.7). By defining 'firm' as a technological construction, neoclassical microeconomics left no room for research on the organizational issues within the firm. The governance structure of a firm is a 'black box', and treated as a given solution consistent with market functions. Therefore, the multiplicity of existing contractual relations between the principals and the agents is difficult to understand and almost impossible to explain in conventional economics. All the other organizational forms, except for the idealized one, must be regarded as temporary deviations from the optimal solution. They are inconsistent with the market system, and would thus be eliminated by market forces automatically in a capitalist economy. The fact is, however, the seemingly non-optimal organizational forms exist in a persistent style in contradiction to the neoclassical predictions.

Coase criticized the neoclassical microeconomics (1992, p.714) by arguing that:

> The firm in mainstream economic theory has often been described as a 'black box', and so it is. This is very extraordinary given that most resources in a modern economic system are employed within firms, with how these resources are used dependent on administrative decisions and not directly on the operation of a market. Consequently, the efficiency of the economic system depends to a very considerable extent on how these organizations conduct their affairs.

From his standpoint, non-market organizational forms are not non-optimal solutions to be eliminated by market forces but, rather, optimal solutions supplementing fundamental market organizations under certain circumstances in an economy where transaction costs are greater than zero. As he noted (1992, p.716):

....in a competitive system there would be an optimum of planning since a firm, that little planned society, could only continue to exist if it performed its coordination function at a lower cost than would be incurred if it was achieved by means of market transactions and also at a lower cost than this same function could be performed by another firm. To have an efficient economic system, it is necessary not only to have markets but also areas of planning within organizations of the appropriate size. What this mix should be, we find as a result of competition.

Therefore, in a new institutional economics perspective, any existing organizational form in the governance structure is an optimal choice. This optimal choice is reached by the economic units involved in the transaction to make the combined production and transaction costs the lowest. Since transaction costs are not identical across economic activities, it is not surprising that multiple organizational forms coexist as optimal solutions in firm's governance structure across industries. Changes in the institutional environment and/or in individuals behavioral attributes may become the stimulus to inspire transformation in firm's governance structure, because such change may affect the transaction costs calculation, *ceteris paribus*. On the other hand, the creation of institutions driven by a search for an organizational structure that will optimize the social behavior of people may result in spontaneous development in the institutional environment according to the new institutional economics.

1.3 Contracting with Positive Transaction Costs

The organizational form, or the governance structure, of the firm is closely related to the property rights structure. This is because under certain governance structure it must be clearly defined as to who owns the firm, who holds the control rights in the management, which group of individuals is assigned what kind of responsibilities and how efforts are compensated. All of these must be specified by contract.

As Furubotn and Richter described (1991, p.10):

The firm (an institution) is a legal entity that concludes written or non-written contract with a number of owners of 'productive factors' who are cooperating within the framework of the firm. The contracts indicate (broadly) which tasks are to be done by which member of the firm and under what conditions and how the coordination of the division of labor within the firm is to occur. Among other things, then, the contracts specify the particular organizational structure of the firm. Fundamental ownership

> *rights (i.e., income, control, and transfer rights) are, in effect, partitioned and assigned to different individuals. The ultimate rights to give orders in the firm is reserved, normally, for those people who own firm-specific resources and who are thought to have superior ability to assume risk and ascertain the 'state of nature' ruling any time.*

Therefore, contracts and the contracting process play central roles in the research of institutions of governance. Institutional economists are particularly interested in analyzing contractual provisions and in finding rational explanations for the multicity of contractual organizations observed in the business world.

The classical contract is comprehensive and a complete one in which *'performance and its quid pro quo provisions are fixed ex ante for all eventualities, and for the entire duration of the contract. Any matters left open by the parties are covered by the law of contract'* (Furubotn and Richter, 1991). This is because in conventional economics, individuals undertaking economic activities are defined as 'maximizing men', and assumed to have perfect information regarding their contracting partners, and perfect rationality in their own decision-making behavior. The contracting process is assumed costless, and the contracts are effectively enforced by the given legal system without costs. Therefore, the classical contract implicitly assumed zero transaction costs. The objective function of the orthodox 'maximizing men' is to minimize production costs under given technologies.

However, just as using the price system is not cost-free as argued by Coase, contracting incurs various costs too. Such costs may include the time and resources committed to the following tasks[5]: searching for and making contact with potential partners; collecting and conveying information; decision-making and contract negotiating; contract writing; contract policing and monitoring; etc. In short, the transaction costs involved in the contracting process are searching costs, writing costs, executing costs, and enforcing costs. Granted that the sum of these transaction costs is positive, individuals undertaking economic activities in new institutional economics are defined as 'contracting men', whose objective function is to minimize the combined costs of production and transaction.

Furthermore, these 'contracting men' are assumed to have bounded rationality. As argued by Herbert Simon (1957, 1961), economic actors are

---

[5] See Dahlman(1979): *The Problem of Externality*, Journal of Law and Economics, v22, p.141-162.

intendedly rational, but only limitedly so. '*It is only because individual human beings are limited in knowledge, foresight, skill, and time that organization are useful investments for the achievement of human purpose.*' Under the bounded rationality assumption, the information the contracting individuals have is imperfect, their ability to foresee eventualities over the contract duration domain is limited. Another assumption regarding individual behavioral attributes in new institutional economics is the existence of *ex post* opportunistic actions.

Due to the assumption of bounded rationality and of *ex post* opportunistic behavior, contract in new institutional economics is incomplete. '*It is costly for agents to write detailed long-term contract that precisely specify current and future actions as a function of every possible eventuality and that, as a result, the contracts written are incomplete and will be subject to renegotiation later on*' (Hart and Moore, 1990, p.1122). Moreover, the impossibility to agree *ex ante* on all future eventualities that may affect the contracting relationship brings about a gap in the contract. The law of contract can not guarantee to close such a gap in the agreement due to high transaction costs when the legal system is used.

1.4 Governance Structure and Transaction Costs

Under the conditions described above, the 'contracting men' -- the economic actors in new institutional economics -- may search for the optimal solution(s) out of the market system by adopting alternative organizational form or reforming existing organizational form in firm's governance. With given production costs and transaction costs and organizational knowledge, rational economic actors seeking their own welfare will tend to choose a governance structure (*i.e.*, an institution) that minimizes transaction costs. '*Nonmarket forms of organization tend to be sought in order to minimize the constraining effects of bounded rationality and, at the same time, to safeguard transactions from the hazards of opportunism*' (Furubotn and Richter, 1991, p.5). For example, institutional economists see integration as a way of reducing opportunistic behavior and holdup problems when a contract is incomplete and the enforcing costs are high (Coase, 1937; Hart and Moore, 1990; Williamson, 1996).

In institutional economics, market and hierarchy are regarded as alternative organizational forms to complete transaction. Special governance structures of hierarchy style may supplant standard market-cum-classical governance as an efficient solution when transaction costs are high. As illustrated by Williamson (1979, p.246):

> *Governance structures, however, are properly regarded as part of the optimization problem. For some transactions, a shift from one structure to another may permit a simultaneous reduction in both the expense of writing a complete contract (which economizes on bounded rationality) and the expense of executing it efficiently in an adaptive, sequential way (by attenuating opportunism).*

Because of diversified attributes of transactions, the efficient solution(s) in the search for optimal organizational forms could deviate from the unique and idealized market solution hypothesized in conventional economics. The multiplicity of existing contractual relationships is no longer inconsistent with the market system but, rather, a more deliberate description of real business life.

The puzzling problem of the persistent existence of non-market organizational forms is solved in a way, one in which such variation is coherently explained by the underlying difference in the attributes of transactions. Efficiency purpose is served by matching governance structure with the attributes of transaction in a discriminating way. Which governance structure is chosen at any time by a rational, though bounded, business unit is dependent on the properties of the transaction being undertaken. The contracting parties will presumably make arrangements to shape their contractual relations so as to minimize the *ex post* total costs of supervision and adaptation to the continuously changing environment.

Williamson characterizes transactions by certain major properties they possess: specificity of investment, uncertainty and frequency of transactions. As he noted in his 1979 paper,

> *....(the) governance structure -- the institutional matrix within which transactions are negotiated and executed -- vary with the nature of the transaction. ....the three critical dimensions for characterizing transactions are (1) uncertainty, (2) the frequency with which transactions recur, and (3) the degree to which durable transaction specific investment are incurred.* (p.239)

The type and the degree of asset specificity are critical in identifying the difference of transactions. Assets involved in transactions such as physical capital, human capital, brand name, production site, etc., may be transaction-specific in greater or lesser degree. '*Asset specificity has reference to the degree to which an asset can be redeployed to alternative uses and by alternative users without sacrifice of production value*' (Williamson, 1996, p.105). The higher the degree of transaction-specificity an asset is, the less possible it can be redeployed to alternative uses without value sacrifice, and hence, the higher the transaction costs will be incurred to the asset supplier and demander to re-negotiate and adjust the contract between them in *ex post*. When a transaction entails a high degree of transaction-specified investment, the contracting parties may be 'locked into' such transaction, just as discussed by Williamson (1996):

> *When a buyer induces a supplier to invest in specialized physical capital of transaction-specific kind, inasmuch as the value of this capital in other uses is, by definition, much smaller than the value of the specialized use for which it has been introduced, the supplier is effectively 'locked into' the transaction to a significant degree. This is symmetrical, moreover, in that the buyer cannot turn to alternative sources of supply and obtain the item on favorable terms, since the cost of supply from unspecialized capital is presumably great. The buyer is thus committed to the transaction as well* (p.240).

When the transaction is characterized by such specificity, a mutually agreed transaction-specific contractual form (or 'relational contract') may be better than the classical market organizational form for cost reduction. Such a form may effectively overcome the *ex ante* bounded rationality problem and prevent *ex post* opportunistic behavior to make contracted obligations credible. However, the transaction-specific governance structure is more beneficial to recurrent transactions than to one-shot or occasional transactions.

When a transaction involves a high degree of uncertainty, writing a complete contract becomes an even more infeasible effort. A transaction-specific organizational form that may effectively attenuate opportunism and enforce the contracted obligations, perhaps by some administrative means, is highly desirable. When an industry matures, however, the extent of uncertainty in the business will decrease. Then, benefits that accrue to the hierarchy type of governance structure will presumably decline too. Accordingly, greater reliance on market contracting will become commonly feasible for transactions of recurrent trading in mature industries.

In principle, as concluded by Williamson (1996, p.259):

1. Nonspecific transactions, either occasional or recurrent, are efficiently organized by market;

2. Occasional transactions that are nonstandardized stand most to benefit from adjudication;

3. A transaction-specific governance structure is more fully developed when transaction are (1) recurrent, (2) entail idiosyncratic investment, and (3) are executed under greater uncertainty.

1.5 Induced Institutional Innovation

The currently optimal governance structure chosen by the contracting parties is not functioning in isolation, but rather, within certain institutional as well as economic environment. Variations in the environment, such as reform in political system or legal system; alteration in laws or property rights constitutions; important progress of technologies; significant change in resources endowment; etc., may bring about fundamental changes in the governance structure. These variations will affect the cost (production and transaction) -- benefit calculation of the contracting parties, which will in turn stimulate them to search for a more cost-efficient organizational form in their contractual relations. In this sense, the creation of institutions is driven by arising economic needs, given that such institutional innovation is cost effective.

As pointed out by Bardhan (1989b), in the long-run historical-evolutionary process, economic factors play an important role in the shaping of institutions. Among others, Marxists have a well-known endogenous theory of institution.[6] They view the economic structure of a society as consisting of property relations and corresponding to the level of the development of the productive forces (which include all means of production and technology). The central driving force behind institutions is the forces of production. Changes in the forces of production, particularly technological changes, produce over time some tension between the existing structure of property rights and productive potential of the economy, and it is through class struggle that this tension is resolved in history, with the emergence of new institutions. The nature of this tension, and the

---

[6] Bardhan (1989) described three kinds of endogenous theory of institution: Marxist, Coase-Demsetz-Alchian-Williamson-North (CDAWN School), and Imperfect Information School. As he pointed out, these three schools have some broad similarities, as well as sharing some weakness and problems.

interaction between institutions and the utilization and development of the forces of production have been studied with much greater rigorous and micro-analytic details by institutional economists.

According to the endogenous theory of institutions of the new institutional economics, transaction costs, and institutions that *evolve* to minimize these costs, are the key to the performance of economies. '*North and many other neoclassical institutional economists believe that the basic source of institutional change is fundamental and persistent changes in relative prices, which lead one or both parties in a transaction to perceive that they could be better off under alternative contractual and institutional arrangements*' (Bardhan, 1989a, p.6). The institutional innovation resulting from relative price changes consists of organizational changes, instruments and specific techniques and enforcement characteristics that lower the costs of transactions participation (North, 1991).

Williamson (1996) viewed institutional innovation as the adaptation of institutions in response to disturbances in the environment. He distinguished cooperative adaptation from autonomy adaptation. As he noted, adaptation is the central problem in economics. Hayek insistently argued that '....*economic problem arise always and only in consequence of change*', and '*the economic problem of society is mainly one of rapid adaptation in the particular circumstances of time and place*' (1945, p.523-524). In neoclassical economics, the price system, as compared with central planning, is an extraordinarily efficient mechanism for communicating information and inducing changes. Changes in the demand or supply of a commodity are reflected in price changes, in response to which, 'individual participants' (or the 'maximizing men') are able to take the right action. Williamson (1996) defined such adaptation as 'autonomy adaptation', in which consumers and producers respond independently to parametric price changes so as to maximize their utility and profit respectively. As argued by Williamson, however, autonomy adaptation is not always possible. Some disturbances require coordinated responses, or defined by Williamson, a 'cooperation adaptation'. This is particularly true when the adapting parties bear long term bilateral dependency relations to each other. They must respond to such disturbances in a coordinated way to fill the gap in their incomplete contract. Failure of coordination may arise because each party may read and react to the signals differently if they respond in an autonomous way, though their original purpose is to achieve a timely and compatible combined response. As concluded by Williamson (1996), the market organizational form is superior with respect to autonomous adaptability, while hierarchy governance enjoys an advantage in bilateral and multilateral adaptability. Therefore, the attributes of transactions matter in institutional innovation since they define the transaction costs incurred in the adaptation.

Ruttan and Hayami have a more comprehensive explanation with respect to induced institutional innovation, which stems from their empirical studies on the property rights transformation of mid-nineteenth century Thailand. According to Ruttan and Hayami, the underlying source that may lead to institutional innovation is a disequilibria in the environment.

> ....*The changes in institutional arrangements governing the use of production factors were induced when disequilibria between the marginal returns and the marginal costs of factor inputs occurred as a result of changes in factor endowments and technical change. Institutional change, therefore, was directed toward the establishment of a new equilibrium in factor markets* (Ruttan and Hayami, 1984, p.209).

> *The growing disequilibria in resource allocation due to institutional constraints generated by economic growth create opportunities for political entrepreneurs of leaders to organize collective action to bring about institutional changes* (p.204).

Since disequilibria imply potential gains by moving from disequilibria to equilibrium, inspired economic actors will respond by taking innovative actions. As argued by North and Thomas (1970) and Schultz (1975), anticipation of latent gain to be realized by overcoming the disequilibria resulting from changes in factor endowment, product demand, and technical change represents powerful inducement to institutional innovation. The incentives in the institutional innovation may first advocate modification in governance structure or so on, then, when such modifications cumulate to a certain level, a more fundamental innovation in institutions may take place.

> *In some cases, the demand for institutional innovation can be satisfied by the development of new forms of property rights, more efficient market institution, or even by evolutionary changes arising out of direct contracting by individuals at the level of the community or the firm.*

> ....*the basic institutions such as property rights and markets are more typically altered through the cumulation of 'secondary' or incremental institutional changes such as modifications in contractual relations or shift*

in the boundaries between market and non-market activities (Ruttan and Hayami, 1984, p.205).

However, the recognition of latent gain associated with the elimination of disequilibria is not always translated into actual innovations. Whether or not the innovation incentive will elicit actual innovative action is reliant greatly on the cost-benefit calculation of such proposed innovation(s). In conjunction with potential gains, institutional innovation inevitably incurs transaction costs -- the resources that will be dedicated to the realization of such innovation. Hence, actual innovation will be carried out only if expected gains are larger than the estimated transaction costs for the parties who intend to undertake such an innovation. Ruttan and Hayami (1984, p.213) declared: '*We hypothesize that institutional innovation will be supplied if the expected return from the innovation that accrues to the political entrepreneurs exceeds the marginal cost of mobilizing the resources necessary to introduce the innovation.*'

Furthermore, the latent gain is probably asymmetric to the parties involved in the transaction. Each party's cost-benefit calculation may differ markedly from each other. Then the situation can be described as one in which:

> *The supply of institutional innovation depends critically on the power structure or balance among vested interest groups in a society. If the power balance is such that the political entrepreneurs' effort to introduce an institutional innovation with a high rate of social returns are adequately rewarded by greater prestige and stronger political support, a socially desirable institutional innovation may occur. However, if the institutional innovation is expected to result in a loss to a dominant political bloc, the innovation may not be forthcoming even if it is expected to produce a large net gain to society as a whole.*

> *To the extent that the private return to the political entrepreneurs is different from the social return, the institutional innovation will not be supplied at a socially optimum level.* (Ruttan and Hayami, 1984, p.213-214)[7]

---

[7] These arguments provide an insightful view in explaining the divergent attitudes between the central government and local community governments towards the property rights and organizational form reform in China's rural enterprises. I have briefly discussed this problem in Chapter 2 with respect to the different functioning

Besides political powers, cultural endowments like religions, ideologies, morals, ethics, etc., may exert strong influences on the supply of institutional innovations,[8] because '*they make some forms of institutional change less costly to establish and impose severe costs to others. .... ideology can be a critical resource for political entrepreneurs and an important factor affecting the supply of institutional innovations*' (Ruttan and Hayami, 1984, p.215, p.217).

However, the theory of induced institutional innovation is still in its primitive stage as pointed out by Ruttan and Hayami. The research in this field has basically depended on historical and case studies as the primary methodology, and the mechanisms through which innovation incentive has been translated into innovation practice remain still a 'black box'. Obviously, the correlation between institutional innovation and change in the external environment perceived in research strongly support the hypothesis of induced institutional innovation. However, as to *how* individuals -- political leaders, private entrepreneurs, farmers, firm managers, etc., -- respond to the changes in their external environment, (such changes as in political constitutions, legal systems, or resources and cultural endowments), and *how* their responses help to shape the new form of institutions, our knowledge is still very much limited. Ruttan and Hayami (1993) admitted that,

> *a limitation of the induced innovation model developed so far has been the 'black box' nature of the internal working mechanism. Induced technical and institutional changes were modeled as a response to changes in economic opportunities with relatively little analysis of the mechanism and process with which changes in incentives are translated into action by private and public agents to result in technical and institutional change. This is especially the case in our work on institutional innovations* (p.31).

The relationship between the institutional or economic environment and the institutions of governance is in essential recursive. As illustrated by Williamsons' three-layer schema,[9] both the external environment and

---

objectives of the central government and of the local community governments. I will return to this problem in the last chapter.

[8] Weitzman and Xu (1994) emphasized the cooperative tradition in Chinese culture as the critical factor in the success of community public ownership of TVEs.

[9] Recall Section 1.2.

individual behavioral attributes have direct effects on the governance structure. In the meantime, however, the governance structure exerts its feedback effects on both the institutional environment and individual incentives. Moreover, the evolving environment induced innovations in governance structure may lead to reform in the institutional environment. The recursive feature of this relationship has made the model complicated and econometric testing of the hypothesis difficult. Ruttan and Hayami (1993) gave high priority to a more rigorous research approach in this field as they illustrated:

> ....*the model of induced institutional change maps the general equilibrium relationship among resources endowments, cultural endowments, technology and institutions. The empirical testing of the model remained incomplete. The recursive relationship among the several elements of the model do not lend themselves to econometric testing as ready as the earlier induced technical change hypothesis.* (p.10)

> *It is quite clear that the tests we have been able to make of the induced institutional innovation hypothesis thus far represent case-study 'plausibility tests' rather than the more rigorous econometric tests that we have been able to make of the induced technical change hypothesis. A more rigorous approach to understanding the process of institutional innovation should rank high on the economic development research agenda.* (p.26)

To summarize, the fundamental difference between conventional economics and institutional economics resides in their view toward institutions. According to conventional economics, institutions are given and neutral in their effects on economic performance; whereas according to institutional economics, institutions are among the determinative factors that shape the direction and speed of change in an economy. The new institutional economics focuses its research on the institutions of governance, which is distinguished from the institutional environment. The latter is viewed to define the former, because it is the institutional environment that determines the comparative costs of alternative governance structures. Due to the existence of positive transaction costs in the contracting process and bounded rationality, contracts in new institutional economics are incomplete. Various governance structures will be chosen as efficient solutions to overcome *ex post* opportunistic behavior, and safeguard the credibility of contracted obligations. Most important of all, they are chosen to minimize the combined costs of production and transactions. The selection of the optimal governance structure is determined by the attributes of the transaction. In response to changes in the external environment, new forms of institutions will be created to realize latent gains that could be generated by moving away from disequilibria. The induced institutional innovation hypothesis is supported by empirical observations. However, further econometric tests should be done in the future to make it more rigorous.

In order to provide comprehensive and consistent answers to the questions that arose at the end of Chapter 3, I will structure my theoretical research on the basis of the institutional economics briefly reviewed above. I shall go over two major dimensions, which have been summarized by Furubotn and Richter (1991, p.16) as follows:

> *An adequate theory of this (property rights) transformation process must achieve two objectives. In the first place, the theory has to establish what the factors are that affect the cost-benefit ratio associated with the 'production' of new rights. Further, the theory must indicate the general mechanism through which changes in the cost-benefit condition are translated into the development of property rights.*

They have also pointed out some special factors to look at, which have laid out the ground for the exploration to start with:

> *.... the factors responsible for changes in cost-benefit calculation include such things as: technical progress, the opening up of new market, the introduction of new products and changes in resources endowments. In other words, a dynamic economy tends to generate new price configurations and thus provides opportunities and incentives for the restructuring of property rights* (p.16).

2. What Factors May Determine the Contractual Form of TVEs?

To explore the factors that may have had influences on the determination and evolution of TVEs' contractual structure, we start from an obvious fact that there are two kinds of management distinguishable from each other: internal management and external management.

'Internal management' is defined as managerial activities including such tasks as organizing daily production, allocating productive tasks to employees, scheduling production process, supervision of the work force, monitoring and coordinating, quality control, etc. 'External management', on the other hand, is defined as managerial tasks in fields including finding the supply sources of and procuring inputs (such as raw materials, energy, capital funds, equipment, etc.), finding markets for outputs and marketing them, acquiring technologies and other relevant information from formal and informal sources, recruiting human capital, organizing and directing research and development (R & D) activities, etc.

On the basis of this distinction between internal and external management, one may find that the distribution of managerial responsibilities varies systematically across three types of contractual regimes described in Chapter 3. When a firm is operating under a fixed-wage contractual form, local community government leaders have both internal and external management responsibilities on their shoulders. The firm manager will take over both kinds of managerial tasks from the local leaders when the firm moves to a fixed-payment contractual arrangement. Between these two contractual forms, *i.e.*, when a firm is under a profit-sharing contractual form, the managerial tasks are shared between local community leaders and firm managers in such a way that the former is responsible for external management while the latter mainly for internal management.

As I discussed in Chapter 2, the underdeveloped markets (especially factor markets during the 1980s) did not allocate resources or distribute products efficiently during the early part of the reform era. Local community government leaders were more effective at launching new enterprises than private entrepreneurs by using their political, social and personal connections to more consistently find sources of capital, allocate land, mobilize labor, acquire technology and human capital, etc. They were able to help their collective TVEs to gain formal or informal access to planned or lower priced material inputs and other scarce resources. They particularly had an advantage over private individuals in interfacing with those outside of the local community's jurisdiction. In other words, they were in a unique position to furnish external management functions that others were not able to provide as effectively. In the early 1980s, moreover, local community government leaders also frequently involved themselves in the day-to-day operation of the firm in addition to performing external managerial tasks. Even where there was a production foreperson (who was sometimes called a manager), the local leaders were inevitably found on the factory floor supervising and managing the work of the factory and providing the entrepreneurial impetus for making these primitive enterprises function.

One reason that the community government leaders were able to assume both kinds of managerial responsibilities is that they did not have so many collective TVEs to personally manage in this period. The costs were low in acquiring information regarding the firm's business, monitoring the firm manager's performance, or enforcing the manager's obligation. This is because the community government leaders controlled the firm's input and output flow directly and made most of the managerial decisions themselves, leaving very limited room for the firm manager to perform with initiative.

Furthermore, because of the extraordinary strong demand in the consumer markets and relatively weak competition in the supply side during this period, access to planned or scarce resources was a good deal more important for the success of the firm than other factors such as product design and quality, or timely delivery. Therefore, external management to a great extent at this stage outweighed internal management. The community government leaders would not perceive the need to motivate the firm manager to take over more managerial responsibilities until later on.

It is obvious that, if China had been a fully mature market economy, exchanges of the firm with the outside would have been automatically organized by the price system. Then the external management would not have been weighted so crucially to the success of a firm. Private entrepreneurs or individuals bestowed with full property rights over the firm might have a comparative advantage in operating an enterprise relative to a bureaucrat. Such advantage might be particularly pronounced in enterprises that require careful and intense monitoring of workers (*i.e.*, when firms use technology where the effort of workers is an important part in the production process and the link between effort and output is difficult to assess. For example, firms using labor intensive technologies). Nevertheless, China is not a fully mature market economy but one in transition. Thus, the community governments had conceivable reasons to choose the fixed-wage form in the governance of collective TVEs in the early stage of their development.

However, having community governments as entrepreneurs could be costly. As discussed in Chapter 2, the multiple performance objectives of the community government leaders may force them to deviate from the profit-maximizing goal and to sacrifice the efficiency of the firm. There may be a tradeoff between keeping the local leaders (with superior external management skills in planning-type economies) closely involved in the operation of TVEs, and in providing the individual entrepreneurs with rights to the residual firm profit as a way of creating incentives for a more efficiency-oriented management. When markets are poor, the inherent inefficiency of having a busy leader in charge of a firm may be outweighed by the services that the leader can provide. When markets develop, the relative contribution of the leader's political and social connections for arranging external management function may diminish, making the net cost of the inefficiency of leader-provided management rise. If the inefficiency from having local community government leaders run the day-to-day operation of the business is high, there may be one important cost saving measure that could be used by local leaders to keep their enterprises competitive: reorganizing the form of the managerial contract between the community government and the individual who may run the firm independently.

The tradeoff between taking advantage of the external management skill of the community government leaders and internal management skills of individual managers may be the catalyst in the evolution of the structure of contractual organization in China's TVE sector. Indeed, as the reforms proceeded, the traditional community government leader-headed firm -- so familiar in the mid-1980s -- rapidly disappears. Since the mid-1980s, the local community governments have constantly reorganized the operation of collective TVEs to effect innovative change.

A crucial difference distinguishing the mid-1980s from the early stage of the reform era is the liberalization of markets, and increasing competition in the economy. As argued by Naughton (1994), one of the important causes of rapid TVE growth is the distortion that existed in the socialist system. Most TVE start-ups were in manufacturing, where state planning price controls kept profitability high in the early 1980s, so that the state could harvest revenues from state-owned-enterprises (SOEs). In the meantime, TVEs entered primarily empty niches for which SOEs had failed to produce. They also enjoyed low tax rate preferential treatment. However, such distortions, at least a part of them, were eliminated by the mid-1980s. For example, in 1980, only 6 percent of TVEs' profit was paid to the state as taxes. This rate climbed to 20 percent after 1985 (China Statistical Yearbook, 1992, p. 390). What characterizes this period is that, market creation in commodity was accelerated, but the development of input markets lagged significantly. By the mid-1980s, markets and market prices existed for nearly all commodities. Markets for land, labor, and other production factors, however, emerged gradually until the 1990s, and financial institutions were still in the midst of a gradual process in their adaptation to market forces as late as the 1990s (Naughton, 1994).

Due to the accelerated liberalization of the commodity markets and the rocketing expansion of the TVE sector,[10] market competition among rural enterprises became a remarkable phenomenon in the mid-1980s. Both the 'after-tax profit per 100 yuan of original value of fixed assets' and the 'pre-tax profit per 100 yuan of funds' declined sharply at a constant pace from 1984 through 1991, except for a slight increase in 1988 (see Table 4.1).

Table 4.1 Profitability of TVEs, 1984-1993 (yuan)

	After-tax Profit Per 100 Original Value of Fixed Assets	Pre-tax Profit Per 100 Funds
1984	22.4	24.6
1985	22.8	23.7
1986	17.0	19.7
1987	15.3	17.0
1988	16.4	17.9
1989	12.5	15.2
1990	10.6	13.0
1991	10.8	12.7
1992	13.8	14.3
1993	21.2	19.0

Source: ZGTJNJ (China Statistical Yearbook), various volumes, 1988 to 1996.

Local community government leaders, who were then unable to commit sufficient time in personally managing each firm's operation when the number and the size of their enterprises expanded, had to rely on the firm managers to perform managerial tasks mainly in the internal management

---

[10] Recall Table 1.1, the number of TVEs increased by more than 8 times 1980 to 1985, the average firm size was more than doubled in the same period.

dimension. However, the delegation of control rights in external management from the community government leaders to the firm managers still fell far short of feasibility. The reason for this was because the liberalization and creation of inputs markets were considerably lagged behind. Problems in a variety of ways rose with the reallocation of the control rights over the firm. As the principal, the community government leaders had to dedicate some resources to monitoring the firm manager's behavior after withdrawing themselves from the personal day-to-day management in the firm. It was extremely difficult to evaluate the firm manager's real performance since it was distorted greatly by the unpredictable policy changes and prices fluctuation in rudimentary markets, though the costs in information collection were low when the community government leaders were still heavily involved in the firm's external management. The inability of the community government leaders to exert direct supervision and to measure the efforts of the firm manager brought them to a situation, which called for an alternative organizational arrangement. This new arrangement would have to reduce the moral hazard problem in contract enforcement and to motivate the firm manager to perform his obligation to a desirable standard. Letting the firm manager share the benefit of efficiency improvement in the firm was thus a feasible option to the community government.

As the agent, firm managers, who were responsible for the internal management of the firm by this time, were also seeking a desirable organizational form. They recognized that they must depend on the community government leaders in the supply of external management for a successful operation. If the community government leaders were not appropriately motivated, they might 'shirk' in performing their external managerial tasks, or perform their obligations in a discriminating way giving preference to certain firms and disregarding others. Since no one of the firm managers wanted to be among the 'others', they would choose the profit-sharing contractual form to reduce moral hazard problem and compete for more support from the leaders. The responsibility contracts are the formal form of such profit-sharing organizational arrangement; while the frequently reported observations of bribes or side-payments from the firm managers to the community government leaders are the informal form of profit-sharing.

By the early 1990s, commodity markets in China had nearly been fully liberalized (See Table 4.2). Over ninety percent of retail goods was priced through free market in 1993, leaving less than five percent priced by the government. At the same time, the markets for production factors had adequate development as well. By 1993, only less than twenty percent of the production factors was either priced directly by the government or under government's pricing guidance, while the majority -- over eighty percent -- of those factors was priced at markets.

Table 4.2 Proportion of Goods under Different Pricing Systems, 1989-1993 (in percentage)

	1989	1990	1991	1992	1993
Retail Goods					
government pricing	31.3	29.8	20.9	5.9	4.8
guided pricing	23.2	17.2	10.3	1.1	1.4
market pricing	45.5	53.0	68.8	93.0	93.8
Agricultural Goods					
government pricing	35.3	25.0	22.2	12.5	10.4
guided pricing	24.3	23.4	20.0	5.7	2.1
market pricing	40.4	51.6	57.8	81.8	87.5
Production Factors					
government pricing	60	44.6	36.0	18.7	13.8
guided pricing	40*	19.0	18.3	7.5	5.1
market pricing	--	36.4	45.7	73.8	81.1

* 'Guided pricing' and 'market pricing' combined share.

Source: ZGWJNJ (China Price Yearbook), 1990, 1994.

With the gradual maturity of the commodity markets (apart from a few products that were produced as special intermediate goods for other industries or state-owned sectors) the lion's share of TVEs' output was completely distributed through markets. Since the early 1990s, even state-owned enterprises had to procure their material inputs from markets rather than through planning channels. The provision of planned material inputs by the SOEs to TVEs was terminated in most cases as reported in Chapter 2. The bridging function of community governments between state-owned sectors and TVEs in the acquisition of scarce resources input had virtually vanished. During this stage, markets gradually became the most important media to complete transactions. Most rural enterprises had to compete for input supplies and output markets in a relatively fairer competitive environment and rely on their own marketing and procurement staff and not on the community government in accomplishing their market trading. Because of such development in the whole market system, the community government leaders were no longer able to personally undertake or direct the vast, frequent, and trivial market transaction activities for each of their enterprises. The best the community government could do was to give certain privileged access to limited number of resources that were still within their reachable scope to the 'key' revenue generating firms in its jurisdiction, at the same time, leaving most of the 'ordinary' TVEs to compete in markets independently. One hundred percent of my sample TVEs reported procuring their material inputs through free markets in 1993. Only three out of sixty-four firms obtained some material inputs from their state-owned joint-venture partners at a non-guaranteed base and with the amount declining markedly from previous years.

By this time, managerial responsibilities -- both internal and external -- were unilaterally performed by the firm managers. The community government had lost its power and authoritativeness to a great extent in firm's operation after withdrawing itself from the external management. As described by an executive of Township Industrial Office (which is a branch of the township government in charge of local TVEs)[11]: 'Our office used to be the busiest and powerful branch in the township government. Since we controlled the allocation of raw materials and other materials badly needed, the managers of local TVEs came to our office very frequently to beg for help. However, nobody is coming to our office now, because we have nothing to allocate but statistical report sheets that are hated by the firm managers so much.' As I observed on the day I visited that office, four of the staff were playing Ma-Jiang (a Chinese game) with another three watching for the entire afternoon during office hours. No one came in for business. The firm managers as the agents, on the other hand, became increasingly independent of their principal in the firm's operation.

---

[11] Informant L7.

Severe problems arose in the profit-sharing contract enforcement at this stage. Since the firm manager directly controlled the input-output flow of the firm, and transactions were completed through markets, it became more and more difficult for the community government leaders to obtain precise information regarding the firm's actual financial performance. How reliable the firm reported figures were depended, to a considerably large degree, on the firm manager's honesty instead of on a workable measurement. In the meantime, firm's financial performance was still frequently distorted by policy changes. It was a common complaint of firm managers.[12] Thus, there could hardly be a fair and environment-neutral evaluation for the firm manager's efforts. The firm manager might understate the firm's profit or overstate the firm's financial loss, but it would be too costly to verify every transaction data reported by the firm even though the community government was suspicious. When the actual profitability of the firm is unknown, or known only at an extremely high cost, 'profit-sharing' is a hollow arrangement and the enforcement of the profit-sharing contract becomes virtually infeasible. The community government leaders must find an alternative organizational arrangement in response to such changes. If the reduction in contract enforcement cost is more than enough to compensate for any possible loss in the shared-profit under a well-enforced profit-sharing regime, then, the fixed-payment governance structure will be adopted. For instance, if the community government could receive $100 of profit remittance under a profit-sharing contract, but had to spend $50 to verify financial information and enforce the remittance, the community government would undoubtedly adopt a fixed-payment arrangement, which might entitle them to $80 of rent payment but with zero enforcement cost. As indicated by a township leader[13] that, the township government might have to double its staff if it had to verify the reported firm financial performance by checking each firm's original transaction records to enforce the profit-sharing contracts.[14] Hence, 'we would rather adopt some simple

---

[12] As reported by the interviewed government leaders and firm managers, the taxation scheme and scale were changed twice during one year in 1993. Such change forced the community governments to re-negotiate with the firm managers before the expiration of the contracts, because the changed taxation scheme had remarkable effects on firms' profit calculation. Informant L12, L16, M10, M49.

[13] Informant L6.

[14] As he pointed out, this was perhaps still not an effective way. Because it was so difficult to distinguish the fake receipts from the real ones, and get sufficient evidence to prove they were fake.

scheme which will make things easier for both sides. Under a leasing arrangement, the government just collect the fixed rents from the firm with no reference to its actual performance. Whether the firm manager overstates or understates his profit, we are not going to verify so long as he pays me the agreed rent timely. This (leasing) method has saved us lots of trouble'. The firm managers may also benefit from this move in that they do not have to rack their brains to hide the true statistical records, bargain with the government leaders, and risk penalty if caught. They can commit their full effort to firms' management and assuredly claim the residual profit as the fixed-payment contract specified.

However, despite the similarity in the changing external environment, the process of adaptation of the firm contractual structure to market forces differed notably from firm to firm. The attributes of firms' technical structure might have played an important role in causing such divergence. The following case study could be a good example to explain such concern.

Case Study 12 Huangxi Food Factory and Jiangu Aluminum Building Material Company (Qingyunpu Township, Jiangxi Province)[15]

In the first case, the community government could really do nothing with this village enterprise but had to let it become a private firm. The main business of this village factory was to purchase sunflower seeds, pumpkinseeds, watermelon seeds, peanuts and soybean from local peasant households. The seeds, nuts, and beans were roasted or fried with spice, then sold to nation-wide food markets. The most valuable asset the factory had was a truck along with woks, stoves, ovens, steamers and containers. The production of the firm was fully market-oriented with fewer transaction-specified assets, external management seemed much less important than monitoring its thirty hired workers and controlling the quality of products for a sustainable business operation. It would be extremely costly to enforce any kind of profit-sharing arrangement. This is because ascertaining the firm's true input costs and sales revenues was almost an impossible task even with high detecting costs. The villagers' committee simply sold those production assets to the firm manager in 1989, but kept the ownership of the factory building to collect a certain amount of rent and management fees every half year.

At the same time and in the same village, however, another village enterprise had a completely different story. It was then a newly established

---

[15] Informant L9, M34, M48.

factory manufacturing alloy aluminum window frames. The main machinery equipment was imported from Singapore, and the plant building was new. However, the factory itself was struggling for survival. The crucial problem resided is the lack of experienced technicians and marketing channels. Since no one in this factory knew how to operate the machinery, the production line was below its designed capacity and the output quality was inconsistent. The factory was also suffering an over stock of output, because it had not been able to find appropriate buyers to purchase an adequate amount to absorb this factory's output. The previous manager resigned after two years' failure to overcome its financial deficit. Afterwards no one even wanted to sign a responsibility contract with the villagers' committee. As explained by the village head, with more than 10 million yuan of investment put down on the machinery equipment, it was too risky for any single individual to take over the complete managerial responsibilities to run the firm, especially when the marketing channel was still rudimentary. 'If the investment fails, the expensive machinery equipment will become a stack of garbage, even we (the village leaders) can't take on the responsibility for such a loss, let alone an individual firm manager!' In 1994, the villagers' committee with the help of the township government managed to recruit a young college graduate from Nanchang City Machinery Import-export Company (a state-owned company). The committee guaranteed him one thousand yuan fixed monthly salary, plus year-end bonus if the firm became profitable under his management. He was assured that he would not be held responsible for the firm's existing loss and debts, but he was required to solve the technical problems to bring the production line up to normal and smooth function. At the same time, the villagers' committee sought marketing channels by contacting with several construction companies within or out of the province. The township government also seemed to be anxious to help, because on several occasions, both the secretary of the township party committee and the executive of the township industrial office asked if I had any personal relations that might help this enterprise to establish marketing channel.

In this case, external management (including the recruitment of human capital from outside sources) obviously outweighed internal management for the success of the firm. Both the community government leaders and the firm manager preferred a bilateral dependent organizational structure to share responsibilities and risks. The community government's major concern was to establish a feasible profit-sharing contract, rather than the profit-sharing enforcement.

Business risks were also closely related to the attributes of the firm's technical structure and the nature of its transactions. The more 'sunk' fixed capital is involved in a firm's technical structure, particularly when such fixed assets consist mainly of machinery equipment with a high degree of specificity, the more risk some party must bear to complete the business operation. On the other hand, if a factory is producing for the market in general, *i.e.*, its products are in demand by markets in many localities and consumed by various groups of individuals, or if the factory can easily adapt to the changing market demand by altering its existing production means without much difficulty, the degree of business risk will be lower, though the profit rate will also be lower. In contrast, suppose a firm is producing some kind of product that was specially designed for a downstream user by employing specified assets, when the bilateral business relationship is constant and stable, the firm may earn a higher profit rate. However, in case some distortions affect such partnership relations, the firm will face considerable trouble in adaptation, for its market is extremely narrow and finding alternative downstream buyers is not always an easy task. Therefore, business risk is positively related to the specialization degree of the firm's technical and business features.

As discussed in Chapter 2, because of the inability of private entrepreneurs to bear significant investment or business risks,[16] the community governments were forced to assume the risk-absorption responsibility in the development of rural enterprises. When the risk degree increases in a firm's operation, the community government becomes less able to withdraw itself from its management obligations in the firm. Therefore, the firm's technical structure and business attributes, *ceteris paribus*, will have influence on the contractual structure determination of the firm through the risk embraced in its business.

Another factor that may affect the determination of the contractual structure of collective TVEs is the location of the firm. Quite a number of researchers have reported the observed relations between TVEs' ownership structure and their geographic locations (Byrd and Lin, 1990; Huang, 1990; Liu, Y., 1992; Parris, 1993). However, my research emphasizes the relationship between firm's contractual form and firm's location, which has been an empty niche in TVEs studies.

---

[16] The ability and the willingness of the private entrepreneurs in risk bearing have been increasing, particularly after the early 1990s. I will return to this concern in the last chapter, Chapter 6.

This is a straightforward and obvious consideration nevertheless. In a locality where the community government has many TVEs to manage and direct, the time and effort the community government leaders are able to commit to the management of each of the firms is limited. The amount of each single firm's profit remittance relative to the total revenue of the community government is insignificant. In contrast, the community government in a relatively backward area will have just a sprinkling of enterprises to control. The community government leaders will be anxiously involved in each firm's management, since they value to a great extent the financial revenues they may acquire from the firm. The contract enforcement costs for the community government are positively related to the development of local rural enterprises, *i.e.*, the number and the size of the enterprises a community has, *ceteris paribus*. The relative importance of each firm's profit remittance to the community government is inversely related to the development of local rural enterprises. Needless to say, the discrepancy in such cost-benefit calculation will inevitably elicit a corresponding divergence in the organizational form of TVEs across regions. The evidence of such consideration is not difficult to find. As observed in the investigation, Wuxi, one of the developed areas with a sizable TVE sector was prepared to take further steps in firms' property rights reform (moving toward fixed-payment contractual form) towards the end of 1994, though this area was famous for collective ownership in its TVE sector. Contrarily, the government leaders of Guohe township indicated their preference for profit-sharing arrangement against the fixed-payment contractual form, arguing against the latter that 'the collective wealth would be channeled to the private pockets of the firm managers through leasing contracts and significantly impair the township government's revenue'.[17] In recent years, Wuxi faced the problem of local labor supply shortage and labor costs inflation. Local government leaders sought to establish joint-ventures with collective TVEs in other coastal developed areas rather than with inland areas where labor costs were much lower. When asked the reason why the community governments in Wuxi was doing so, the local government leaders pointed out that the primitive infrastructure and low education and skill of the labor was not in their major concern. What had made them hesitant to establish cooperative relations with relatively backward inland areas was the fear that the community governments in those areas might abuse their power. Due to their

---

[17] Informant L16.

extraordinary limited source of financial revenues, they might frequently intervene in the firm's business decisions and to extract financial benefit from the firm in an exploitative way, which would undermine firm's long-run growth.[18]

In conclusion, the development of the entire market system, the attributes characterizing a firm's technical structure and transactions, and the economic setting of a locality in which a firm is operating, may all have some influence on the determination of the contractual form of the firm. A theoretical model will be formulated in the next section to illustrate the effects of all these factors.

3. The Model

Local community government leaders and firm managers have contributed to the success of TVEs. The managerial contractual form between local government leaders and the firm managers governs not only each party's decision making power and degree of involvement in firm business operation, but also each party's claim on the residual profit produced by the firm. In the end, the contract defines the incentives impelling those involved in the contract and determines how the services of the individuals are employed in the firm, two elements that will have an important bearing on the ultimate profitability of the enterprise. Such a contract must be established on the basis of mutual dependence and mutual benefit. But in the end, since the ultimate property rights reside with the local government leaders as curator of the community collective assets, the leader will make the choice on contractual form in a manner that most further his/her interests. Local community government leader's interests are assumed to be consistent with profit maximization.[19] In this section, a theoretical model is presented that allows local government leaders to endogenously determine the most profitable managerial contract form for their firm, given the locality's economic setting.

---

[18] Informant L2.

[19] Rozelle (1991, 1994) has shown that concern with profits is one of the most common compulsion local leaders use to further their goals. Leaders are also concerned with employment and growth, but in China's increasing competitive rural industrial sector, search for maximum profits would be consistent with these other goals.

One way of characterizing this relationship between local government leaders and firm managers is that each party brings something to the contract that the other party does not have, or can not provide as efficiently. If the factor brought by one or both parties are not available for purchase on the market, then to the extent that each factor is needed for profitable operation, it becomes necessary to get each party to use the factor in the enterprise as effectively as possible. Hence, it might be hypothesized that if the connections of local community government leaders (or *Guanxi*) are much more important for the profitable operation related to the close supervision of a hard working manager, then one might expect to find a fixed-wage contractual form and to find local leaders heavily involved in the day-to-day operation of the firm.

If, on the other hand, factors and goods and services can be purchased on the markets with no more difficulty than found in any business environment, and if local government leaders are busy with other activities (including the case where they have so many firms that they are unable to devote any degree of substantial time to any single firm), then the 'connections' of local leaders may be relatively less valuable to the profitable operation of the firm. In a relative sense, the need to have an inspired, hard working supervisor of the business practices of the firm becomes more important. Under these circumstances, profit-maximizing leaders may grant a fixed-payment contract to the manager, collect the rent, and let the manager independently manage the firm.

A third case might also exist. It may be that both parties can provide equally valued inputs for the profitable operation of the firm. If the community government leaders can manage the external affairs of the firm efficiently (especially when compared to the firm manager), the firm manager may find it advantageous to rely on the local leaders' connections (for such things as acquiring needed inputs). At the same time, the local community government leaders may be overwhelmed by the work load, handicapped by experience, or in a lack in the supervisory skills of a full time manager, they find it expedient to rely on the firm managers to monitor the firm's daily operation. If this break down of responsibilities is chosen, and it is deemed appropriate to offer the manager part of the profits as an incentive to exert himself in his management duties, a profit-sharing contract could be used.

However, the degree to which each party's provision of their respective skills proves to be more valuable to the profitable operation of the firm basically depends on the economic environment. This economic environment includes both the entire economic system and the local economic setting in which the firm is developing. It may also depend on the firm's technical structure that determines the firm's demand for what each party can bring to the contract. For example, leaders ε in a locality with better factor markets and easier access to product market may decide to run the firm differently than the leaders in an isolated area with incomplete markets. Likewise, leaders may decide to manage a firm producing a product that has a labor intensive manufacturing process (in which the link between worker effort and output is difficult to observe) differently than if that firm had a capital intensive production process.

Eswaran and Kotwal (1985) developed a model explaining choice of contractual form in land tenure contracts between landlord and tenants on the basis of unmarketed inputs. Following this idea, their approach has been adapted in this research to capture many of the features of the problem faced by local community government leaders in determining how to operate their TVEs. The construction of the model begins as follows.

Suppose in a community, all the initial assets of TVEs are collectively owned by local citizens and the property rights for managing the firm are controlled by the local leaders. The official, as the principal, can choose to run the firm in three ways: as a leader-run firm, paying a foreperson a fixed wage (or under a fixed-wage contract); jointly with a manager under a profit-sharing arrangement (or under a profit-sharing contract); or lease it to a manager with complete autonomy for a lump sum payment (or under a fixed-payment contract). The optimal contractual form is determined by the one which returns the highest level of profit to the local official who is the *de facto* owner of the collective assets.

The difference in the profitability of each form is derived from the provision of unmarketed, but necessary inputs for the firm's production activities. Besides physical inputs, such as labor, L, and capital, K, two kinds of managerial inputs are required: internal management and external management. Internal management, s, is defined as the time spent on internal managerial tasks. The efficient labor input, E, is:

$$E = g(s, L; \varepsilon) \qquad\qquad (1)$$

Where g is a linearly homogenous aggregator which is increasing and concave in s and L, and ε is a parameter ($0 \le \varepsilon \le 1$) characterizing the aggregator to capture the relative importance of internal management in a unit of efficient labor.

External management, m, is defined as the time spent on those external management tasks.

The firm's production function may be expressed as:

$$q = F(m, E, K) = f(m, s, L, K; \varepsilon)$$ (2)

Where f is linearly homogenous and increasing in its first four arguments.

It is assumed that the firm manager always has superior ability in internal management for he is closely involved in the daily production process of the firm. Likewise, the local leader has superior ability in external management due to his connections. This idea of differential ability is quantified by means of two parameters, γ_1 and γ_2 ($0 \leq \gamma_1, \gamma_2 \leq 1$), where 1 refers to the local leader, and 2 refers to the manager. It is assumed that one hour of the leader's time devoted to internal management is equivalent to only a γ_1 fraction of one hour devoted to internal management by the manager; and one hour of the manager's time devoted to external management is equivalent to only a γ_2 fraction of one hour devoted to external management by the local leader.

The model is also based on the assumption that the local leader and the manager each has one unit of time which they must allocate between the firm's production activities and their alternative activities. The opportunity income of the leader is v, and that of the manager is u. The wage rate for hired workers is w, the interest rate is r, and the price of the output is P. The parameters, v, u, w, r, and P are all assumed to be exogenously determined, and the labor market is competitive.

Under the *fixed-wage* contract (denoted by superscript fw), the local government leader maximizes expected net income:

$$\Pi^{fw1} = \max_{m_1, s_1, K, L} [Pf(m_1, \gamma_1 s_1, K, L) - rK - wL] + (1 - m_1 - s_1)v$$ (3)

where $0 \leq m_1 \leq 1$; $0 \leq s_1 \leq 1$; and $0 \leq m_1 + s_1 \leq 1$.

Under the *fixed-payment* contract (denoted by superscript fp), the expected net income of the manager prior to delivering the payment is:

$$\Pi^{fp2} = \max_{m_2, s_2, K, L} [Pf(\gamma_2 m_2, s_2, K, L) - rK - wL] + (1 - m_2 - s_2)u$$ (4)

where $0 \leq m_2 \leq 1$; $0 \leq s_2 \leq 1$; and $0 \leq m_2 + s_2 \leq 1$.

Given the existence of a perfectly elastic supply of managers and competitive contract bidding, the payment will be bid up until the manager is at (or marginally above) his opportunity income, u. The fixed payment to the local leader for use of the factory is:

$$R = \max\{ 0, \Pi^{fp2} - u \} \tag{5}$$

and the local leader's income is:

$$\Pi^{fp1} = v + R \tag{6}$$

Under the *profit-sharing* contract (denoted by superscript ps), the local leader and the firm manager each provides one of the unmarketed inputs and the profit is shared according to some endogenously determined, but mutually agreed upon rule. For the purpose of tractability, we make the assumption of complete specialization.

Define the restricted expected profit function, $\Pi(s, m)$, which is obtained by optimally choosing K and L for parametrically given m and s :

$$\Pi(s, m) = \max_{K,L} Pf(m, s, K, L) - rK - wL \tag{7}$$

Under the most general of profit sharing rules, the manager gets:

$$S_2 = \alpha + \beta\Pi^{20} \tag{8a}$$

where α and β are constants to be endogenously determined. At the same time, the local leader gets:

$$S_1 = -\alpha + (1 - \beta)\Pi \tag{8b}$$

Under these circumstances, the manager and the leader choose s_2 and m_1 to maximize their expected income by solving:

$$\max_{s_2} \beta\Pi(m_1, s_2) + (1 - s_2)u \tag{9a}$$

---

[20] Under the responsibility contractual implemented in TVE sector, α is equivalent to the basic salary a manager may receive, while $\beta\Pi$ is the floating salary.

where $0 \leq s_2 \leq 1$, and:

$$\max_{m_1} (1 - \beta)\Pi(m_1, s_2) + (1 - m_1)v \qquad (9b)$$

where $0 \leq m_1 \leq 1$, and (9a) and (9b) will give the best response functions:

$$s_2 = \sigma(m_1, \beta) \qquad (10a)$$

$$m_1 = \tau(s_2, \beta) \qquad (10b)$$

At a Nash equilibrium pair $[m_1^*(\beta), s_2^*(\beta)]$, which is shown by Eswaran and Kotwal to exist and be unique, (10a) and (10b) are simultaneously satisfied.

Before making the final agreement on a set of endogenously determined contractual terms, the leader chooses β to maximize expected income as long as the manager's expected income is no less than his/her opportunity income. The endogenously determined value, β^*, of β is that which solves:

$$\max \; -\alpha(\beta) + (1 - \beta)\Pi[\, m_1^*(\beta), s_2^*(\beta)\,] + [\, 1 - m_1^*(\beta)\,]v \qquad (11)$$

The leader's expected income under profit-sharing contract is thus:

$$\Pi^{ps1} = \Pi[m_1^*(\beta^*), s_2^*(\beta^*)] + [1 - m_1^*(\beta^*)]v + [1 - s_2^*(\beta^*)]u - u \qquad (12)$$

After solving each of these programs *ex ante*, the criteria used by the local community government leader to select the managerial contractual form under which each TVE is operated in the locality is simple: compare expected income under all three contractual forms, (3), (6), and (12), and choose that form which maximizes the local leader's expected income.

4. Model Simulations and Implications

In this section, the theoretical model formulated above will be solved for a Cobb-Douglas specification. Then, its comparative static results will be presented to illustrate the predictions of the model.

If the production function is specified as:

$$q = Am^{\delta_1}K^{\delta_2}E^{\delta_3}$$

where A, δ_i, (i = 1,2,3) are positive constants, and $\sum_{i=1}^{3}\delta_i = 1$; and:

$$E = s^{\varepsilon}L^{1-\varepsilon}$$

where $0 \leq \varepsilon \leq 1$. When reasonable values are chosen for the exogenously determined parameters A, δ_1, δ_2, δ_3, ε, r, w, v, u, and P, then the model is closed and numeric values for Π^{fw1}, Π^{ps1}, and Π^{fp1} can be calculated and compared. After a reasonable baseline is established, parameters can be varied and simulations can be performed to check the sensitivity of the model to certain key assumptions, and to analyze the impact of structural and policy changes on TVEs operations.

To simplify, the base values of the exogenously determined parameters in the simulation are chosen as follow: r = w = P = 1; v = 1.25; u = 1; A = 4; and ε = 0.5. The input shares in the production function, *i.e.*, the values of δ_i, however, need further consideration. According to several researchers who estimated industrial production function for China's TVEs (Chen, et al, 1988; Jefferson, Rawski, and Zhen, 1992b; Jin and Du, 1993), the share of capital ranged from 0.45 to 0.55, while the share of labor varied from 0.39 to 0.52. However, no one has ever, to my knowledge, tried to include 'management' -- either external management or internal management -- as a separate input in his or her estimation of TVEs' production function. Though 'management', especially 'external management', has been recognized by many researchers in the TVEs studies as an important, possibly one of the most important inputs, to the success of TVEs' operation. However, it is extremely difficult to include this factor in the production function estimation due to the availability of applicable data and measurement problems. In my field investigation, I was able to collect data regarding sample TVEs' employment constitution by distinguishing managerial staff from production-line workers, and distinguishing managerial staff in marketing and procurement ('external') from those in other positions ('internal'). Using this data set, I estimated the production function coefficients (δ_1, δ_2, δ_3) for external management, m; capital, K; and labor, L. Estimates of the coefficients from restricted (to constant returns to scale, *i.e.* $\Sigma\delta_i = 1$) and unrestricted production function with and without fixed effects are shown in Table 4.3.

Table 4.3 Estimates of Production Parameters for Use in Simulations

	Unrestricted Production Function Estimates		Restricted Production Function Estimates[a]	
	Without Fixed Effects	With Fixed Effects	Without Fixed Effects	With Fixed Effects
Constant	0.98 (3.27)	1.91 (3.88)	1.90 (6.48)	2.28 (7.17)
Inputs				
Capital	0.69 (9.14)	0.58 (6.79)	0.62 (9.60)	0.54 (6.28)
Labor	0.17 (1.34)	0.30 (2.36)	0.16 (1.60)	0.29 (2.17)
External Management	0.41 (3.03)	0.33 (2.21)	0.23 (2.18)	0.16 (1.70)
Province Effects				
Zhejiang	--	-0.51 (-2.49)	--	-0.21 (-1.07)
Jiangsu	--	-0.89 (-3.92)	--	-0.58 (-2.95)
Hubei	--	-0.46 (-1.90)	--	0.54 (2.16)

[a] Restricted model estimated with sum of coefficients of inputs equal to one (or impose constant returns to scale). T-ratio is in parentheses.

Source: Author's survey, 1994.

As demonstrated by this table, the contribution of capital to production ranges between 0.54 and 0.69, those of labor ranges from 0.16 to 0.30, and those of external management from 0.16 to 0.41. With the references from other researchers' estimates, I set the baseline parameters of production, δ_i, as following: $\delta_1 = 0.2$, $\delta_2 = 0.5$, and $\delta_3 = 0.3$. After the baseline simulation, a number of comparative static exercises will be run with different values of δ_i to capture the variations in the firm's technical structure.

4.1 The Space Partition of Dominant Contractual Form

This is the baseline simulation. All the values of the exogenous parameters applied in this simulation are those indicated above. If γ_1^c and γ_2^c are defined as the critical values of γ_1 and γ_2 at which the local community government leader will choose to switch from the profit-sharing to fixed-wage contract, and switch from profit-sharing to fixed-payment contract, then γ_1^c and γ_2^c can be used to partition the contractual space into three areas where fixed-wage, profit-sharing, and fixed-payment contracts are optimal and will be observed. The determination of these critical values can be executed by simulating the model (solving the three problems of the local leader and comparing to find which generates the highest expected income) across a grid of γ_1 and γ_2 values (varying from 0 to 1). The result of such an exercise is demonstrated in Figure 4.2.

For high enough value of γ_1 (> 0.4) and relatively low value of γ_2, the fixed-wage contractual form prevails. Since the leader is less inefficient than the manager in the firm's internal managerial tasks, while the manager is unable to perform the external managerial tasks as efficiently to a desirable level. The fixed-payment arrangement will prevail when γ_2 climes to above 0.64, implying that the manager is capable enough to perform the external managerial tasks, while γ_1 is below its critical value 0.4. However, even though γ_1 is pretty high, the leader may still choose the fixed-payment contract if γ_2 is higher than certain level. The ultimate case is where γ_1 equals one, but γ_2 is greater than 0.86. This is because with a very capable manager who can perform the external managerial tasks independently and efficiently, the leader can earn the most by leasing the firm to the manager under a fixed-payment arrangement. The leader can withdraw himself from the firm management completely to undertake alternative activities to earn his opportunity income. By this way, he will earn more total income than under any of the other contractual forms, though he himself is almost perfect in performing the internal managerial duties.

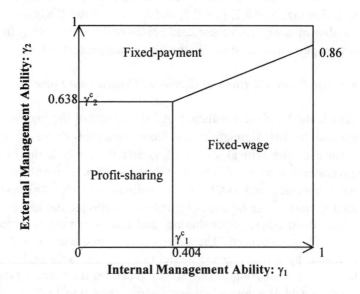

Figure 4.2 Baseline Realization of Optimal Contractual Form under Varying Degree of Comparative Advantage for Leader- and Manger- Supplied Inputs

For low values of both γ_1 and γ_2 (both are smaller than their critical values γ_1^c and γ_2^c, respectively), profit-sharing contractual form prevails. Since each party can only perform one kind of managerial tasks efficiently, they must rely on each other to operate the firm in an efficient way. The leader will choose this contractual form for it is the one that may generate the highest expected income for him.

The basic results from Figure 4.2 can be used to gain some idea about why the form of contract between local leaders and managers has changed over time. The ability of the manager and the leader to perform external and internal management duties are not constant over time. With the gradual movement to a market-oriented rural economic system from one dominated by planning, the manager's ability to perform external managerial tasks (γ_2)

may increase over time, especially relative to the leader. For example, where once only a phone call to political crony should gain access to some key input, with increasing markets, input suppliers will be more easily accessible through normal economic channels. Likewise, as TVEs grew and the size of the local economy expanded, the ability of the leader to perform internal management functions in a firm would decrease (or γ_1 would get smaller). With a declining γ_1 and an increasing γ_2 when markets gradually replace the planning, the profit-sharing contractual form will first supplant the fixed-wage contractual form, and then go on to give way to the fixed-payment form. In China's rural economy-in-transition, one might expect that the form of the managerial contract for a TVE would be moving away from the fixed-wage form to profit-sharing form and ultimately to fixed-payment form (as shown by the dashed arrow in Figure 4.3). The reason for such movement is the changes in the relative ability of actors providing unmarketed inputs (or internal and external management).

It is noteworthy that, the profit-sharing form is presumably a transitional governance structure in TVEs' development. In other words, it is an optimal organizational solution only under certain institutional environmental conditions, *i.e.*, when both market and government are imperfect. The comparative advantage of this contractual form during this very special stage of economic reform and transition is its ability to pool otherwise unobtainable resources to allow the application of a superior input bundle to the growth of rural enterprises. As argued by Eswaran and Kotwal (1985), such ability '*results in the possibility of the agricultural yield under sharecropping being higher than that under any other contract despite the disincentive effect operating in sharecropping*' (p.360). Similarly, the disadvantage of the disincentive effect of the profit-sharing contract has been outweighed by its advantage of a superior input combination. Therefore, its financial performance compared favorably with state-owned enterprises and the rural private sector as illustrated in Chapter 2. However, the imperfections in both market and government are a temporary rather than a persistent institutional phenomenon in a transitional economy. As the institutional environment evolves, the disadvantage of the disincentive effect in a profit-sharing form may reveal itself as a more severe obstacle to the growth of the firm, as compared with the unavailability of external management input. Hence, sooner or later it is doomed to be eliminated by the growth in market forces, exactly the way the fixed-wage form was eliminated.

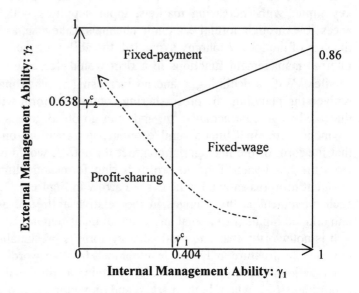

Figure 4.3 Simulation of the Evolution of the Contractual Form During Period of Market Development

From Figure 4.3, the first prediction of the model can be drawn:

> *Prediction 1*: The dominant contractual form in a given area at a particular time depends on the level of market development in that region and in the whole economy. The more developed the market is, the more prevalent profit-sharing and fixed-payment contracts will be.

Figure 4.2 and Figure 4.3 explain the determination and the evolution of the contractual form for a representative firm. However, they do not explain the co-existence of two or more contractual forms in the same geographical area at the same time. The new institutional economics, as illustrated in Section 1.4 of this chapter, explains the multicity of governance structure by the underlying differences in the attributes of transactions. Introducing heterogeneity in firm's technical structure into the model will help to outline the more realistic aspects in the determination of the contractual form for various firms.

4.2 The Divergence in Firm's Technical Structure

Figure 4.4 illustrates the result of the second comparative static exercise, namely, the simulation in the purpose to explore the effects of change in the importance of capital relative to labor in the firm's technical structure (δ_2/δ_3).

In this exercise, the values of all the exogenous parameters are set in the same way as in the baseline simulation, except for those of δ_i The share of the external management is fixed at $\delta_1 = 0.25$. The sum of the labor share and the capital share is thus 0.75 ($\delta_1 + \delta_2 = 0.75$). I perform the exercise from the stating point $\delta_2/\delta_3 = 0.15$ ($\delta_2=0.1$, $\delta_3=0.65$), then increase δ_2/δ_3 until it reaches 14 ($\delta_{c2}=0.7$, $\delta_{c3}=0.05$). For each of δ_2/δ_3, a pair of the critical value of γ_1 and γ_2, γ_1^c and γ_2^c, have been discovered. The critical values γ_1^c and γ_2^c as functions of the capital intensity of the firm's technical structure are shown in Figure 4.4a.

An increase in the importance of capital relative to labor input (or an increase in δ_2/δ_3) lowers γ_1^c and increases γ_2^c. In other words, the area covered by the fixed-wage contractual form increases, while that covered by the fixed-payment form shrinks, like the dashed space partition compared with the solid partition in Figure 4.4b. Hence, when a firm's technical structure is more capital intensive, there will be a greater propensity for it to move back into (or not to move out of) a fixed-wage contract. When there are fewer workers to supervise, the local community government leaders have little incentive to remove themselves out of the floor-line manager's role. It also may be in these circumstances that connections of local leaders to their superiors in echelons above are relatively more valuable since the capital intensive technology may very well have come from a state-owned enterprise or another collective TVE run by a fellow cadre. Moreover, as more fixed capital is invested in a capital-intensive firm, its operation conceivably incurs more risks. Inevitably, the contractual form is favored where community government leaders are more directly and frequently involved in the firm's operation in person to help spread or absorb risks.

Panel A   Simulation of Change in Capital Intensity

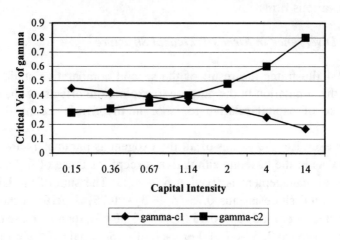

Panel B   Change in the Space Partition of Contractual Form

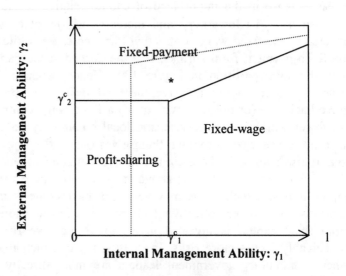

Figure 4.4   The Effect of Capital Intensity on Firm's Contractual Form

On the other hand, a decline in δ_2/δ_3 results in higher γ_1^c and lower γ_2^c, the area covered by the fixed-payment contract will be enlarged relative to the area covered by fixed-wage form. Therefore, a labor-intensive firm will favor the fixed-payment form more than other contractual forms, because such a firm highly values appropriately motivated and monitored efficient labor input in its operation.

Obviously, with uniquely given combination of the internal management ability endowed by the leader and the external management ability endowed by the manager (γ_1, γ_2), (say at * in Figure 4.4b), the optimal contractual form will differ for firms with divergence in their technical structures. For a relatively labor-intensive firm (solid space partition), the optimal choice is the fixed-payment contract; but for a capital-intensive firm (dashed space partition), the fixed-wage form is the choice.

This comparative static exercise gives us the second model prediction:

> *Prediction 2*: The optimal contractual form for a specific firm depends on the firm's technical structure. The more capital intensive a firm's technology is, the more likely the fixed wage form will be selected by the local leaders, and the less likely will the local leaders to select a fixed-payment contractual form.

4.3 Changes in the Relative Importance of External Management

Figure 4.5 sketched out the results of the third simulation, which demonstrates the effects of changing importance of internal management relative to external management in the determination of firm's contractual form.

In this simulation, all the other exogenous parameters are fixed at their base values. The capital share, δ_2, is fixed at 0.3, which leaves the sum of the efficient labor share and the external management share to be 0.7 (*i.e.*, $\delta_1 + \delta_3 = 0.7$). The simulation starts from $\delta_3/\delta_1=0.17$ ($\delta_3 = 0.1$, $\delta_1 = 0.6$). Then δ_3/δ_1 is increased until it equals 6 ($\delta_3 = 0.6$, $\delta_1 = 0.1$). With the increase of δ_3/δ_1, more weight is given to the efficient labor input relative to the external management input in a firm's operation.

We may see from Figure 4.5a that the critical values γ_1^c and γ_2^c are sensitive to the changing contribution of efficient labor input and of external management in the firm's operation. γ_1^c is positively, while γ_2^c is negatively, related to δ_3/δ_1. With greater δ_3/δ_1, the area covered by the fixed-wage contractual form will be smaller as shown by the dashed space partition in Figure 4.5b as compared with the solid partition. At the same time, the area covered by the fixed-payment contract will become larger. In other words, when the external management input is counted less to the success of the firm, or the firm depends on the effort of its employed workers to a greater extent in accomplishing its business, the fixed-payment contract will then be revealed a more effective form of organization, and *vice versa.*

This result explains the observation that small, more labor-intensive, and fully market-oriented firms are targeted first when the community government considers leasing out or auctioning off their collective TVEs. Large-scaled enterprises with more fixed capital investments, or enterprises that need special marketing and/or procurement channels, on the other hand, are the last. One of the basic reasons is due to the fact that such enterprises generally need more resources that are either scarce or difficult to acquire through markets, for instance, financial capital or highly specified human capital. Therefore, this kind of firms will appreciate the personal commitment of local community government leaders in the firm's external management more than labor efficiency, since the firm manager is perhaps unable to perform such external managerial tasks as effectively.

Then we have the third model prediction:

> *Prediction 3*: If a firm's operation relies more on labor effort than on external management input, then there is more possibility that the firm manager is granted a fixed-payment contract.

A deducible inference from the above two simulation results is that the optimal contractual form to firms with different technical structure in a certain economic environment may differ from another even if the two are in the same locality. This could be one way that this theory will be useful in explaining how different contractual forms coexist in the same locality.

Panel A   Simulation of Change in Relative Importance of External Management

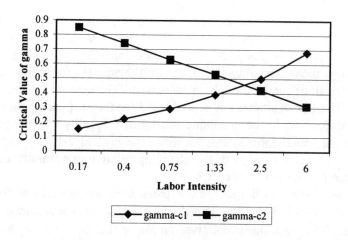

Panel B   Change in the Space Partition of Contractual Form

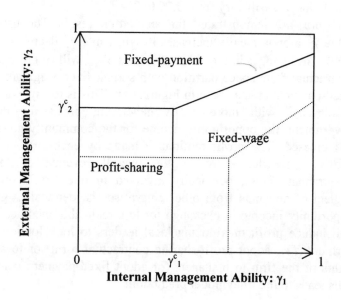

Figure 4.5   The Effect of Relative Importance of External Management on Firm's Contractual Form

4.4 Changes in Opportunity Incomes

The local leader's opportunity income changes if a local economy has grown to a point where the demand on local officials is such that it becomes increasingly difficult for them to spend time on internal management functions. Given a level of market development and given a firm's technology, the opportunity cost of the local leader (v) for spending time on the factory floor can be thought as increased if the community reaches such a point. The fourth simulation is performed for the purpose of assessing the relationship between the economic setting of a locality and the prevailing TVEs' contractual form in that locality. The critical values γ_1^c and γ_2^c are estimated to correspond with the changing relative opportunity income of the leader and of the manager, v/u.

The base values of the exogenous parameters are selected as following: $r = w = P = 1$, $A = 4$, $\varepsilon = 0.5$. The shares of inputs, δ_i, are assumed to be the same as in the baseline simulation, $i.e.$, $\delta_1 = 0.2$, $\delta_2 = 0.5$, $\delta_3 = 0.3$. The opportunity income of the manager is fixed at 1 (as we assume that there exists a competitive market price), the opportunity income of the leader is assumed to vary in the range from 0.25 to 2. It is similar to say in this simulation v/u will vary from 0.25 to 2.

Figure 4.6 demonstrated the simulation result. The estimated critical value γ_1^c monotonically increases in v/u, while γ_2^c decreases in v/u (Figure 4.6a). The changes in the value of γ_1^c and of γ_2^c will result in a change in the contractual form space partition with shrunk fixed-wage area and extended fixed-payment area as seen in Figure 4.6b. This is to say, when a given area gets richer with more TVEs generating profit for the community government, the opportunity income for the community government leader is increased. The profit remittance made by each firm will count for a relatively smaller share in the overall revenue of the community government. Being personally involved in one firm's operation to the neglect of demands from other enterprises is identical to giving up more opportunity income in exchange for less realizable income. Therefore, this will induce profit maximizing local leaders to look for joint management partners (*i.e.*, adopt profit-sharing contractual form) or to assign property rights of the firm to managers (or adopt fixed-payment contractual form). This leads to the final model prediction:

Panel A: Simulation of Change in Relative Opportunity Income

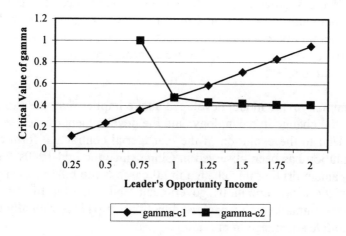

Panel B: Change in Space Partition of Contractual Form

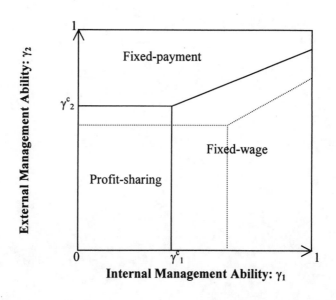

Figure 4.6 The Effect of Leader's Opportunity Income on Firm's Contractual Form

Prediction 4: The more wealthy a region is (the more TVEs it has, or the smaller a given firm's profit remittance is relative to the community government's total revenue), the more likely that local community government leaders are willing to move away from fixed-wage contract and towards profit-sharing and fixed-payment contracts.

To summarize, the model developed above implies that, the expansion of markets, the change in technology, and the development of local economies may all lead to the evolution of the managerial contractual form of TVEs. This evolution has been observed in China since the mid-1980s. Moreover, the mechanism driving this change in all cases is the relative change in the ability of the local community government leader and the firm manager to perform the unmarketed managerial functions in which originally each had a comparative advantage in providing.

5 Explaining the Contractual Form Innovation in Collective TVEs

The model developed in Chapter 4 has provided a general theoretical framework to explain the determination and evolution of the contractual form in the TVE sector. The model simulations result in four predictions that relate the contractual form of a TVE to several exogenous factors: the development of the market system, the technical structure of the firm, and the economic setting of the locality in which the firm operates. These predictions are helpful in understanding temporal and spatial variations of the contractual form structure in the TVE sector. However, how good may these predictions approximate to the real situation in the TVE sector is still open to question. In other word, we would like to know the predictive power of the model.

On the basis of the intensive field investigation conducted in rural China in 1994, the model predictions will be examined in this chapter in two ways. In the first section, a series of descriptive statistics are used to check the predicted correlation between the exogenous factors and the contractual form of the firm. The focus of this section is to test if these predicted forces can be appropriately applied to the explanation of the three findings in the contractual form demonstrated in Chapter 3. A multinomial logit model is then formulated in the second section to provide a more rigorous econometric test to explore the relative importance of these exogenous factors in their influence on the determination and the evolution of the contractual form structure.

1. Empirical Tests of the Model: The Explanatory Power of Model Predicted Factors

In this section, all the predicted relevant exogenous factors will be examined to verify their influences on the determination and the evolution of the contractual structure of TVEs in a one-by-one sequence. The observed attributes or variations of each exogenous factor will be compared with corresponding contractual forms in order to confirm whether such predicted correlation exists.

1.1 The Development of Markets

The first model prediction suggests that with the development of the market system, the prevailing managerial form will move away from a fixed-wage contract and toward a fixed-payment contract. In other words, the development of the market system is a critical factor in explaining the evolutionary pattern of the contractual structure in the TVE sector.

Recall Table 4.2, the share of goods allocated through markets has grown rapidly in China since the late 1980s. In 1989, less than half of retail goods, and only 40 percent of agricultural goods were distributed through non-planning market channels; less than 20 percent of production factors was purchased by producers in free markets. By 1993, however, more than 75 percent of retail goods, agricultural products, and even factors of production were distributed through markets.

Table 5.1 summarizes the statistical data of free market development in China. The 'price adjusted per capita free market transaction value' is obtained by dividing each year's reported total free market transaction volume[1] by local population (by national population in 'nationwide' column) in the same year, then adjusted by local overall retail price index (by national overall retail price index in 'nationwide' column). The price adjusted per capita free market transaction values are thus comparable cross provinces and over time for they are all in 1978 prices. The value of per capita free market transaction has been increasing since the mid-1980s. In the mid-1980s the average resident in China completed only about 50 yuan of transaction in a single year. By 1993, that same resident was making more than 170 yuan of transactions (in real term). Both market liberalization and free market development had sharply accelerated after 1991. The share of market priced goods (under any of those three categories) and the nationwide per capita free market transaction value had a sharp 'climb up' in 1992 as seen in Table 4.2 and Table 5.1.

---

[1] Including rural as well as urban free market transaction values, since sizable production factors are traded in urban markets, especially in 1990s.

Table 5.1 Development of the Free Market in China, 1984-1993
(Price Adjusted Per Capita Free Market Transaction Value, in yuan)

	Nationwide	Jiangsu	Zhejiang	Jiangxi	Hubei
1984	37.2	42.2	47.7	32.6	38.7
1985	46.6	49.3	66.1	40.7	55.1
1986	61.7	64.2	100.8 ·	54.3	82.9
1987	72.7	76.6	124.5	66.3	90.2
1988	84.5	96.1	149.2	75.0	98.7
1989	86.1	89.9	155.9	79.1	85.9
1990	91.4	98.3	168.5	83.9	89.4
1991	105.7	117.1	205.0	93.9	90.3
1992	134.1	151.5	299.5	99.2	96.5
1993	176.8	n.a.	n.a.	115.2	123.6

Source: ZGTJNJ (China Statistical Yearbook); Statistical Yearbook of Jiangsu, Zhejiang, Jiangxi and Hubei. Various volumes, 1984 to 1994.

With better markets, the need to rely on local community government leaders to perform external management activities, such as finding access to inexpensive, planned inputs or locating scarce commodities, might be expected to diminish. This would reduce the comparative advantage of the local leaders relative to a firm manager in performing the external management functions (or, it would increase the γ_2 of the firm manager). Other things equal, when managers can perform external managerial tasks on a more equal footing with local community government leaders, as predicted by the model, the leader would more likely offer profit-sharing contract since its relative profitability is higher. With even higher γ_2 which is correlated to market development, the leader may consider offering a fixed-payment contract to the firm manager. Figure 5.1 combines the over time development of the contractual structure (Figure 3.2) with the development of free markets. We may see from the figure that the market development visibly explains the gradual expansion of profit-sharing contracts between 1984 to 1992, and the partial replacement of profit-sharing contracts by fixed-payment contracts after 1992. The first prediction of the model is thus confirmed by the facts observed.

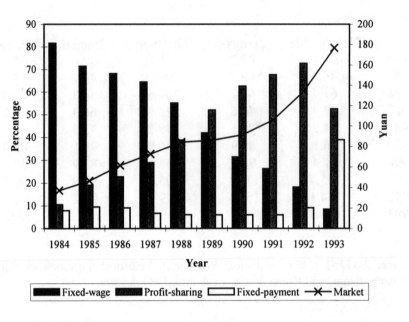

Figure 5.1 Market Development and the Evolution of Sample TVEs' Contractual Structure, 1984-1993

Source: Author's Survey and ZGTJNJ (China Statistical Yearbook).

Table 5.2 The Proportion of Market Priced Goods in Four Sample Provinces (%)

	1991	1992	1993
Zhejiang			
Retail Goods	59.9	95.4	92.8
Agricultural Goods	68.4	88.8	86.6
Production Factors	41.7	84.0	88.7
Jiangxi			
Retail Goods	68.0	95.9	95.9
Agricultural Goods	59.2	79.2	90.6
Production Factors	35.3	74.5	78.4
Hubei			
Retail Goods	68.3	93.0	89.7
Agricultural Goods	65.5	76.0	84.4
Production Factors	43.2	68.2	82.7
Jiangsu			
Retail Goods	61.7	90.2	94.9
Agricultural Goods	56.2	72.5	81.4
Production Factors	33.4	69.9	77.7

Source: China Price Yearbook, various volumes, 1990 to 1994.

The level of market liberalization and development may be one of the factors that even explain the cross-regional variation in the evolutionary pattern of the contractual structure of TVEs. People might wonder why the contractual structure evolution in the Zhejiang research site differs significantly from that in the Jiangsu site (recall Figure 3.3). Both the Jiangsu site and the Zhejiang site in the sample are relatively developed coastal areas with high per capita rural income and a sizable TVE sector. However, the local community government leaders in Zhejiang had led other regions in their adoption of the fixed-payment contractual form, but the Jiangsu site apparently lagged behind in such a move. According to most general indicators of market development, markets in Zhejiang expanded faster (from 48 yuan per capita free market transactions in 1984 to 300 yuan in 1992) than any other sample provinces. Residents in Jiangsu Province on average made only 152 yuan of transactions in 1992 (up from 42 yuan per capita in 1984). It was only about half in real term of that made by residents in Zhejiang Province. In the comparison of the level of market liberalization among the four sample provinces (Table 5.2), Jiangsu was also lagged behind. For example, nearly 90 percent of production materials was distributed through markets in Zhejiang in 1993, while this share in Jiangsu was less than 80 percent. Moreover, these secondary statistics in some sense reflect observations made during the field investigation. Interviews revealed that while in 1993, 85 percent of electricity used by TVEs in Jiangsu sample township (60 percent in Hubei sample township) was still allocated by the township government. Whereas the Zhejiang sample township had removed the government from this role completely (*i.e.*, 0 percent of the electricity energy was arranged through bureaucratic channels). It is perhaps that part of the observed regional difference in the managerial contract structure may be explained by the variation in regional market development.

If the rate of market development is the only factor that leads to cross-regional disparity in the pattern of TVEs' contractual structure evolution, then we might expect Jiangsu leaders to have progressed more towards profit-sharing and fixed-payment contract than their counterparts in Hubei, since markets are better developed in Jiangsu as seen from Table 5.1. However, the observation shows that the contractual structure evolution of the two sites was in a similar stage (Figure 3.3). To explain this observation and the coexistence of different contractual forms, we turn our focus into the next two model predictions.

1.2 The Technical Structure of the Firm

Prediction 2 and 3 state that the technical structure -- the relative importance of capital input to labor input or the external management input to internal management input -- of a firm partially explains the optimal contractual form applied to the firm. In fact, in the entire sample the form of the managerial contract appears to be closely related to the technical structure of the firm (Figure 5.2).

In 1993, 80 percent of the sample enterprises running under fixed-wage contracts (i.e., local leaders still running the factory mainly by themselves) were capital-intensive. Only 17 percent of the firms running under fixed-payment contracts had fallen into the capital-intensive category, however. In contrast, 83 percent of the leaders who chose to work with managers under the fixed-payment contractual arrangement were engaged in labor intensive sectors.

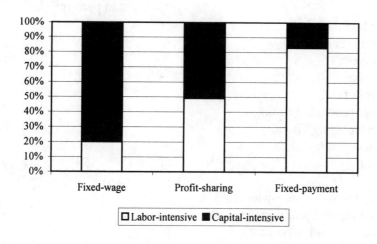

Figure 5.2 Constitution of Labor-intensive and Capital-intensive Firms under Various Managerial Contracts in Sample TVEs, 1993

Source: Author's Survey, 1994.

Table 5.3 Industrial Sector Distribution of Sample TVEs under Various Contractual Forms, 1994

Industrial Classification[a]	fixed-wage firms	profit-sharing firms	fixed-payment firms
		In percent[b]	
Labor Intensive Industries			
Food processing	--	6	5
Garment	20	6	13
Textiles	--	15	30
Furniture	--	4	--
Paper products/Printing	--	9	9
Metal casting/Foundry	--	9	22
Other	--	--	4
Subtotal	20	49	83
Capital Intensive Industries			
Smelting and pressing	40	--	--
Electrical and telecommuni-cation equipment	20	3	--
Machinery	20	21	4
Chemical products	--	15	4
Construction materials	--	12	9
Subtotal	80	51	17

a. Firms are categorized by their primary product of output. Firms are capital intensive if capital per worker of sector exceeds 5,000 yuan according to State Statistical Bureau (1993); otherwise firm is counted as labor intensive.
b. Each column sums to 100 percent.

Source: Author's Survey, 1994.

Table 5.3 provides a more detailed description regarding the industrial sector distribution of sample TVEs under different contractual forms. The enterprises in the 'fixed-wage' category were mainly involved in production of smelting, manufacturing of electrical communication equipment and machinery. They were typical capital intensive sectors with heavy specialized fixed capital investment. The firms under fixed-payment contracts, in contrast, were clustered in labor intensive manufacturing and service sectors, such as textile, garment, and metal casting. These industries employ large labor force that uses a great deal of expensive materials in the manufacturing process, hence require intensive and careful monitoring of their labor force. Firms running under profit-sharing arrangements were split equally between those in capital intensive industries and those in labor intensive ones. Apparently, the more labor intensive a firm is, the less effective a local community government leader can be in operating the firm directly. (This is equivalent to say that γ_1 of the leader in internal management is relatively lower.) Such situation would lead to a greater propensity to make the profit-sharing or the fixed-payment agreements with the firm manager.

Table 5.4 illustrates from another angle the congruence of the technical structure of the firm and its form of managerial contracts. Local community government leader-run enterprises had more capital, especially fixed capital, but hired fewer employees than their counterparts under other managerial contracts. The average fixed capital a sample fixed-payment firm had was less than half of that used by a fixed-wage firm. However, the average amount of production-line workers hired by the former was more than double of that hired by the latter. The fixed-wage firms are more than twice as capital intensive as firms run under profit-sharing or fixed-payment agreements. Fixed-wage firms averaged 68,000 yuan of total capital (fixed plus operating) per employee (managerial staff plus production-line workers) and 69,000 yuan of fixed capital per production-line worker. Firms that had been leased out to autonomous managers had only 24,000 yuan of total capital per employee and 16,000 yuan of fixed capital per worker, by contrast. The capital intensity measurement for profit-sharing firms was in the middle between fixed-wage and fixed-payment categorized enterprises, as predicted by the model.

Table 5.4 Technical Structure of Sample TVEs under Different Contractual Forms[a]

	fixed-wage firms	profit-sharing firms	fixed-payment firms
Technology of Firms			
Total Capital (million yuan)	5.4	5.0	3.8
Fixed Capital (million yuan)	4.5	2.4	2.2
Total Number of Employees (each)	79	144	159
Number of Production-line Workers (each)	64	125	144
Capital Intensity (thousand yuan per person)			
Total Capital per Employee	68	35	24
Fixed Capital per Worker	69	20	16
Management Intensity (Workers to Managers Ratio)			
Workers to Total Management Staff Ratio	5	9	14
Workers to Production Managerial Staff[b] Ratio	8	14	19
Workers to Marketing Managerial Staff[c] Ratio	13	28	56

a. All figures are three years' average (1991-1993).
b. Includes monitors, technicians and accountants.
c. includes staff in marketing and procurement department.

Source: Author's Survey, 1994.

The third portion of Table 5.4 suggests close correlation between a firm's contractual form and the relative management intensity of the firm's technical structure. Generally speaking, fixed-wage firms are more management intensive relative to firms run under profit-sharing and fixed-payment arrangements. A managerial staff in average manages 14 workers in a fixed-payment factory. This number is reduced to 9 in a profit-sharing firm, then to 5 in a fixed-wage firm. However, the need for more careful internal management to monitor the labor force in fixed-payment enterprises, and for more intensive external management effort in marketing and procurement in fixed-wage enterprises can be seen by comparing workers to management ratio of different contractual categories in this table. The comparison of 'workers to production management staff ratio' is 8:19 corresponding to firms with fixed-wage and fixed-payment contracts. Such comparison becomes 13:56 when referring to 'workers to marketing management staff ratio', implying that fixed-wage firms had much higher external management intensity technology than their counterparts under fixed-payment contractual forms. It is interesting to note that once again profit-sharing firms appear to be in the middle between fixed-wage and fixed-payment firms in this measurement. Hence, the descriptive statistics do suggest a strong correlation between the managerial contractual form and the technical structure of a firm. The predictive power of the model is thus verified.

From the above discussion, it is now clear why Jiangsu research site firms looked more like Hubei site firms rather than those in Zhejiang site in the late 1980s and early 1990s (Table 5.5 and Figure 5.3). The difference in the technical structure of sample TVEs in the investigation sites may in fact be the explanation. While more developed in a market sense (which would tend to make leaders adopt profit-sharing or fixed-payment contractual forms), firms in the Jiangsu site were larger in size (used more capital and hired more employees) and more capital intensive in their technologies. They used more than 127 thousand yuan per employee of capital and had 91.5 thousand yuan per worker of fixed capital (Table 5.5, column 3). In contrast, Zhejiang firms used less than one third of the capital per employee and Hubei firms less than one sixth (column 1 and 2).[2] Hence, when markets began developing in Hubei, local community government leaders responded by expanding the role of firm managers, providing them with more incentive by making them profit-sharing partners. But markets had not

---

[2] See footnote 3 of this chapter.

reached the level found in Zhejiang, where markets had become good enough so that local leaders found their 'connections' increasingly less important for providing good external management. This greater level of market development may have induced local leaders to adopt a fixed-payment scheme in the Zhejiang site. During the same time, the external management services of local leaders in the Hubei site were still sufficiently valuable to require their active participation in the operation of the firms.

The community government leaders in Jiangsu site, however, might not have chosen to move to a fixed-payment arrangement for another reason. Prediction 2 states that despite relatively good markets in Jiangsu, the degree of capital intensity of TVEs in the Jiangsu site might prevent the local leaders from moving ahead to a fixed-payment regime. As seen in Figure 5.3, TVEs in the Jiangsu site were overwhelmingly clustered in the capital-intensive sector (80 percent of sample TVEs in the Jiangsu site concentrated in machinery manufacturing or smelting and pressing industries). While TVEs in the Zhejiang site, in contrast, were clustered in labor intensive sectors (most of them are textile or garment factories). With higher degree of capital intensity, the operation of TVEs in the Jiangsu site involved more risks and was in greater need of external management services (*e.g.*, for upgrading technologies, obtaining timely technician services and financial capital inputs, etc.). Hence, there is less pressure for leaders to give up their role in the firm, but greater pressure for managers to rely on the community government leaders for their assistance to absorb risks and provide external management services. Due to such marked difference in their firms' technical structure, local leaders and firm managers in the Zhejiang site were motivated differently against their counterparts in the Jiangsu site. It is not surprising that they would select different contractual forms for their TVEs. This fundamental disparity in TVEs' technical structure can obviously serve as a critical factor in explaining the cross-regional variation between the Zhejiang and Jiangsu sites, no matter whether or not market development in these two areas were at a similar level.

Table 5.5 Technical Structure Disparity of Sample TVEs in Four Provinces, 1993

	Doumen Township Zhejiang	Guohe Township Hubei	Huazhuang Township Jiangsu	Qingyunpu Township Jiangxi
Total Capital (million yuan)	6.58	2.05	39.4	1.38
Fixed Capital (million yuan)	4.31	0.95	22.85	0.98
Total Number of Employee (each)	192	137	310	62
Number of Production-line Workers (each)	177	120	250	51
Capital per Employee (thousand yuan)	34.2	14.9	127.2	22.2
Fixed Capital per Worker (thousand yuan)	24.3	7.9	91.5	19.4

Source: Author's Survey, 1994.

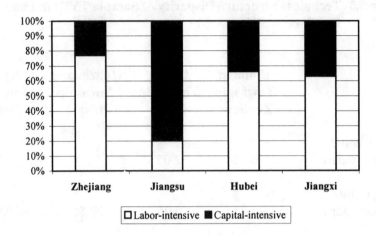

Figure 5.3 Labor- and Capital-Intensity of Sample TVEs from Four Provinces, 1993

Source: Author's survey, 1994.

1.3 The Economic Setting of the Locality

The fourth model prediction suggests that, when there exist more TVEs in a given locality, and the local community government can collect a larger amount of the total revenue from existing TVEs, a lessening in anxiety can be expected when local leaders deal with a single firm's operation. If a township government has to limit the number of cadres on its payroll, as the number of firms expands, in some sense the opportunity cost of serving any individual firm increases. Under these circumstances, local leaders would prefer to adopt the fixed-payment contractual form and move away from the fixed-wage arrangements. This prediction may have provided another reason why the Zhejiang and Jiangxi sites (and more recently, the Jiangsu site) have moved further towards assigning property rights to firm managers, while the Hubei site has lagged behind, especially when comparing it with its seemingly analogous counterpart, the Jiangxi site.

As shown by Figure 5.3 and Table 5.1, sample TVEs in the Hubei site (Guohe Township) and in the Jiangxi site (Qingyunpu Township) had quite similar technical structures, and the markets in Hubei and in Jiangxi were equally developed too. Although the average size of sample TVEs in the

Hubei site was larger relative to that in the Jiangxi site (Table 5.5),[3] they are less capital intensive. All these observations imply that the Hubei site should have progressed toward the fixed-payment contractual form as its counterpart in Jiangxi site had done rather than staying behind in such move, if other things being equal. However, other things were not equal. The economic setting may have had an influence on such cross-regional variations as predicted by the model.

Referring to Table 5.6 that Guohe of Hubei Province is the largest township among four sample townships in both area and population. However, it was the poorest one in 1993 in that it had the lowest total output value (agricultural plus industrial) and per capita income. Labor in Guohe produced only 6800 yuan of annual output in average, accounting for about 12 percent of an average labor produced in Qingyunpu (56,200 yuan per labor) the same year. The township government collected 122 thousand yuan of revenue from its enterprises, less than 30 percent as much as did its counterpart in Qingyunpu Township. Undeniably, such comparison will have notable effects on the cost-benefit calculation of the township governments in these two areas. Granting complete residual claim rights to the firm manager under a fixed-payment contract would cost the township government more relative to the benefit that is generated by moving away from profit-sharing arrangement in Guohe, for it had a very much limited source of financial revenues. With relatively abundant revenue sources, the opportunity cost of personally managing an individual firm to the neglect of other enterprises would be higher for the township government in Qingyunpu. Therefore, the Qingyunpu Township government has decided to move further to adopt fixed-payment contractual form, while at the same time, the Guohe Township government preferred to keep profit-sharing contract as the dominant organizational form in an attempt to protect its revenue against decline. Hence, the fourth model prediction also passed an empirical examination.

---

[3] One reason for this larger average size is that all sample firms in the Guohe site are township enterprises, no village enterprise is included. In the other three sites, the ratio of township enterprises to village enterprises in the same sample is about half-and-half. Therefore, the 'average size' of TVEs shown in the table is possibly artificially enlarged relative to its actual size for the Guohe site. However, this fact will not affect any conclusion to be made in this research.

Table 5.6 Descriptive Statistics of Sample Townships in Four Provinces, 1993

	Doumen Township Zhejiang	Guohe Township Hubei	Huazhuang Township Jiangsu	Qingyunpu Township Jiangxi
Area (km^2)	42	128	37	16
Population (thousand)	46.5	74.2	44.6	21.4
Labor (thousand)	23.0	37.4	23.5	10.3
Agricultural Output (million yuan)	115.0	111.1	49.2	33.9
Industrial Output (million yuan)	1005.6	144.7	2519.6	545.2
Total Output per Labor (thousand yuan)	48.7	6.8	109.3	56.2
Per Capita Income (yuan)	1872	924	2888	1436
Number of TVEs (each)	312	28[*]	450	539
Government's Revenue from TVEs (thousand yuan)	2363	122	3770	442

* Figure includes township enterprises only.
Source: Author's survey, 1994.

2. Empirical Tests of the Model: The Relative Importance of Model Predicted Factors

The predictive power of the model developed in Chapter 4 has been verified by the tests demonstrated in the last section. The tests confirm the model-predicted correlation that illustrates the effects of exogenous factors on the determination and the evolution of the contractual structure in the TVE sector. The model predicted exogenous forces have proved powerful in explaining some puzzling or anomalous observations such as the evolutionary pattern and cross-regional variation of the contractual structure. However, in order to discover the relative importance of each of these exogenous factors in the contractual form determination, a more rigorous quantitative measurement is required. We need a precisely formulated econometric model to perform the quantitative measurement. With such a model, the effects of each of relevant exogenous factors can be quantified through coefficient estimation, and the dominant factor(s) can be identified. The entire mechanism through which the exogenous forces have been translated into the innovation of contractual institutions can be fully clarified. Further reform strategy analysis and policy suggestions can then be built upon a solid foundation. In order to achieve this goal, a multinomial logit model is developed in this section, the data collected in the author's field investigation is then applied to run the regressions. The hypotheses formulated by the theoretical model are further tested by the regression results.

2.1 The Model and the Variables

To reveal the correlation between a firm's contractual form and a number of exogenous forces, a multinomial logit model is specified in the following form:

$$Y_t = C + \beta_1 X_{t-1} + \beta_2 Z_{t-1} + \beta_3 V + \mu$$

The dependent variable Y_t is a qualitative variable that represents the contractual form choice of a given firm in period t. The community government leader, as the principal of the firm, may choose from three managerial contractual forms -- fixed-wage, profit-sharing, and fixed-payment -- to run the firm in a given period. His choice is constrained by a number of exogenous factors that have impacts on his cost-benefit assessment associated with each contractual form. The form that maximizes his expected net income will be chosen as the optimal solution and applied to the firm. This is the one observed in the investigation. We define:

Y_t = 1, when the fixed-wage form is observed;
Y_t = 2, when the profit-sharing form is observed; and
Y_t = 3, when the fixed-payment form is observed.

Local leader's decision in the contractual form selection is expressed as a function of a series of explanatory variables. There are three sets of explanatory variables in the model: X_{t-1}, Z_{t-1}, and V.

X_{t-1} is a vector, consists of four firm specified variables characterizing each firm's technical structure and its position in the economy in period t-1. They are 'capital intensity', 'labor intensity', 'profit remittance', and 'input market'.

'Capital intensity' is the fixed capital per production-line worker in the firm. The total fixed capital of the firm is re-scaled by the number of production-line workers hired by the firm in the same period. This variable reflects the capital intensity of the firm's technical structure, which is hypothesized by the model simulations as an important factor featuring the attributes of the firm and thus has crucial influence on the contractual form determination. More fixed capital per worker implies that the production of the firm is more specialized and relatively harder to adapt to the distortion in the external environment. Hence, the firm is exposed to more operational risks and demands more assistance to acquire scarce resources, such as financial and human capital. A higher degree of capital intensity therefore has a negative effect on the decision of the local leader in the movement toward profit-sharing and fixed-payment contractual forms.

I use 'fixed capital per production-line worker' instead of 'total capital per employee' to indicate the capital intensity of the firm's technology, because this will, I believe, be better in reflecting the true technical structure of the firm. Due to the underdeveloped nature of the financial institutions and the frequent administrative intervention in the financial system in transitional China, the firm's operating or working capital (or 'circulating fund' [Liudong Zijin], the term used by Chinese business units) might fluctuate significantly from period to period. This fluctuation can take place without reference to its truly required amount to support its operation. 'Total capital' was defined in the field investigation as the sum of the fixed capital and the operating capital. Incidentally, using fixed capital rather than total capital as the explanatory variable will help to eliminate some possible distortions that outside factors might exert on the technical structure of the firm.

'Labor intensity' is the ratio of production-line workers to staff in sales and procurement in the firm. It represents the relative importance of labor to external management in the business of a firm. Hence, it also represents the technical structure of the firm. The number of the sales and procurement staff hired by a firm is determined by two factors. One is the level of difficulty in dealing with output marketing and input purchasing affairs. Another is the production scale of the firm. What is hypothesized to be relevant to the determination of the firm's contractual form is the first one -- the difficulty level to accomplish sales and procurement tasks. The firm will rely more on the community government leaders in the provision of external management if it faces more barriers to the markets or to the suppliers. This is because its operation is highly specialized with narrowed marketing channels and input sources. Therefore, intensive demand for external management in a firm's operation will affect the firm's contractual form choice in favor of fixed-wage contracts at one end and against fixed-payment contract at the other end. However, since the sample TVEs are not homogenous in size, the number of sales and procurement staff of the firm is thus not comparable across firms to reflect the level of difficulty of each firm's sales and procurement. The measurement is adjusted by calculating the ratio of production-line workers to staff in sales and procurement, 'labor intensity'. Lower 'labor intensity' means more sales and procurement staff is demanded by the firm for a given production scale, the external management is more important relative to internal management in the firm's technical structure, and *vice versa*. Therefore, a higher 'labor intensity' is expected to support the local leader's decision to move toward fixed-payment scheme.

The importance of a firm's profit remittance in township government's total revenue from TVEs is represented by 'profit remittance'. As hypothesized by the model, when a community government can collect more financial revenues from its TVEs, any single firm's profit delivery will count for a declining share in the total revenue of the government. The local leader's opportunity cost of personally managing an individual firm is increased. The community government will consider an alternative contractual form when such increase reaches a certain level. The absolute amount of the profit remittance made by the firm varies greatly across firms, as well as across regions in the research sample. In order to reflect the actual importance a firm's remittance to the community government and the relative opportunity cost for the local leaders to manage each of their enterprises in person, the firm's profit remittance is expressed as a share or percentage in the total revenue the township government acquires from its TVEs. Village enterprises do not deliver their profit directly to the township government but, rather, to the villagers' committee,[4] and the contractual form of a village enterprise is determined by the villagers' committee leader instead of the township government. The profit remittance of a sample village enterprise is also calculated as a share of the township government's total revenue in the regression. This is because the data regarding the total revenue of the villagers' committee is not available. However, the purpose of including 'profit remittance' as an explanatory variable is to illustrate the general idea of the relative management opportunity cost of the community government rather than actually measure such cost. Hence, 'profit remittance' might be good enough to approximate the real situation, especially when this treatment is consistent across sample firms and across sample regions. A higher 'profit remittance' is expected to have a negative effect on the adoption of profit-sharing and fixed-payment contractual forms, particularly for the latter.

The variable 'input market' is the market availability of the major input(s) of a firm. It is designed to show the development of specified firm inputs markets. If the major input of a firm is entirely distributed through markets, and it is easy for the firm to gain access to it, the firm's operation will be more independent of local leader's involvement. When it is necessary for a firm to gain access to its major input through specially arranged channels, the bridging function of the community government is indispensable to a successful business operation. This is what hypothesized by the model as to how the development of the market system affects the determination of the firm contractual form. To quantify the 'market availability', 'input market' is designed as an index variable. A value of '1' is assigned to it when a firm indicated its input was entirely purchased through free market transactions. When a firm indicated its major input was supplied via specially arranged channel(s), and it was extremely difficult to replace such channel(s) by other supply sources, a value of '0' is applied.

---

[4] As observed in the author's field investigation, in some cases village enterprises had to pay 'management fee' to the township government directly from firms' revenues. In other cases, villagers' committee paid the management fees to the township government for each of its enterprises after collecting profit remittance from the village enterprises.

However, if a firm reported that its major input was supplied through special channels, but it was easy to replace such channels by other suppliers or simply by purchasing on the markets, then, 'input market' will be assigned a value of '0.5'.

Vector Z_{t-1} contains two variables: 'product market' and 'number of firms'. They are locality specified variables characterizing the sample township in period t-1, within which the firm in concern is operating in period t. The variable in this vector is thus identical across firms within the same township and operating in the same period. However, it will differ across sample townships for the same t, and vary over time for the same firm.

'Product market' in this model is the per capita free market transaction value of the province to which the sample township belongs. This explanatory variable is selected to trace the general influence of the development of local markets. The expansion of local markets is expected to support the adoption of fixed-payment contractual arrangement and a move away from fixed-wage form.

'Number of firms' is defined as the number of TVEs in the sample township. The increase of 'number of firms' is hypothesized to increase the opportunity cost for the local leader when personally managing an individual firm. Therefore, it will have a positive effect on motivating the local leader to withdraw himself from direct management services and grant the firm manager a profit-sharing or fixed-payment contract.

Vector V consists of non-periodical dummy variables. 'Year' is the time dummy varying from 1990 to 1994, the time span for the dependent variable Y_t in the regressions. The time dummy is used to illustrate the dynamics that may feature a period and the evolutionary movement in the environment. The most important role it will play in the model is to approximate the time trend of market development in the whole economy (remember, 'product market' is a region specified variable presenting the market development in a certain locality).

Jiangsu, Zhejiang, Jiangxi, and Hubei are region dummies, representing the sample townships in Jiangsu, Zhejiang, Jiangxi, and Hubei respectively. The regional dummies are included to demonstrate the residual effects of other factors that may have had influence on the contractual form selection but have not been included in the model, particularly non-economic factors such as regional government's policies, geographic locations, cultural legacy, etc., that distinguish an area from others.

C is assumed a constant and μ the error term that follows normal distribution.

Table 5.7 List of Variables Used in the Estimation

Variable	Variable Description
Firm specified variables	
Capital intensity	Fixed capital per production-line workers
Labor intensity	Ratio of production-line workers to staff in sales and procurement
Profit remittance	percentage of firm's profit remittance in township government's total revenue
Input market	Market availability of firm's major input
Locality specified variables	
Product market	Per capita free market transaction value of the sample province in real term
Number of firms	Number of TVEs in the sample township
Year	Time trend dummy
Zhejiang	Region dummy -- Zhejiang
Jiangsu	Region dummy -- Jiangsu
Hubei	Region dummy -- Hubei
Jiangxi	Region dummy -- Jiangxi

One point should be noted that there exists strong interrelationship between two variables, 'product market' and 'year'. As seen in Table 5.1, the per capita free market transaction values in all four sample provinces have been increasing over time, *i.e.*, they are positively correlated to the time trend. To avoid the multicollinearity problem in regressions, one of them must be dropped. However, as illustrated above, the two variables are used to explain different exogenous forces: 'year' is mimicking the general marketization trend in the whole economy, while 'product market' is the indicator of local market development. Therefore, two rounds of regressions have been run, each carries one of these two variables, 'product market' or 'year', to explore the effects of each of them.

The explanatory variables used in the regressions are summarized in Table 5.7. From which, 'capital intensity' and 'labor intensity' characterize the firm's technical structure, and they are firm specific variables. 'Number of firms', 'profit remittance', and region dummies feature a locality. Among which, 'number of firms' is a region specific variable, and 'profit remittance' is firm specific. The remaining variables, 'input market', 'product market', and 'year' represent the development of markets. Among which, 'year' defines the general trend over time, 'product market' traces regional markets, while 'input market' specifies market for a given firm using certain input supplied by the market in concern. The contractual form of the firm is specified as a function of these exogenous variables.

2.2 The Data

The data used in the estimation is collected in the field investigation conducted in rural China in 1994. During this field investigation, more than 100 TVEs were visited, hundreds of firm managers, local community government leaders, and TVE workers were interviewed. On the basis of the extensive visits and interviews, 64 TVEs were semi-randomly selected[5] to constitute the empirical research sample. These 64 TVEs are located in four eastern and central Chinese townships: Huazhuang Township of Jiangsu Province, Doumen Township of Zhejiang Province, Qingyunpu Township of Jiangxi Province, and Guohe Township of Hubei Province.

Each of these 64 TVEs was asked to accomplish two different investigation surveys, one regarding the firm, another regarding the manager. The firm survey was conducted by firm accounting staff in most cases. The manager's survey was completed by the firm manager as

---

[5] I asked the sample township government to provide their TVEs list and randomly selected sample firms from the list. However, some selected firms did not provide the required data due to various reasons, and were then dropped from the sample. The village enterprise list provided by the township governments were partial, did not exhaust all village enterprises in the township. Guohe township government did not provide the information regarding its village enterprises.

required.[6] About two thirds of the sample TVEs conducted their survey questionnaires under the personal direction of the author and the author's research assistant, while the remainder was done independently with written survey instructions provided by the author at pre-survey meetings.

The firm survey consists of three types of information. The firm was asked to provide information regarding its property rights and contractual form evolution. It included the date of establishment, the source(s) of the original investment, the contractual form applied in each year of the past ten years (from 1984 to 1993). Then it asked for a detailed description of its current (1994) organizational structure, such as contract negotiations and renewals, contract duration, contracted financial obligations, reward and punishment in contract fulfillment, etc. Five years' data (1990 to 1994) in firm contractual forms has been used to run the regressions.

Then the firm was asked to provide its five years' accounting records (from 1989 to 1993).[7] The required information covers the firm's output value, pre and after tax profit, tax payment, profit remittance to the community government (in variety of ways), firm's retained profit and its distribution, firm's capital and employment, firm's investment and its sources, and firm employees' income. The information acquired regarding the firm's capital includes firm's total capital, fixed capital, and operating capital. Information on employment distinguishes production-line workers from the managerial staff, while the managerial staff is differentiated among various management fields, such as production monitoring, technology, accounting, marketing and procurement, and services. Based on this original data, the 'fixed capital per production-line worker' and the 'ratio of production-line workers to staff in sales and procurement' are derived as explanatory factors to run the regressions.

In the third part of the firm survey, the firm was asked to indicate its major input(s) and output(s), and provide information concerning procurement and marketing channels through which the firm obtained its inputs and sold outputs. If the firm had more than one channel to complete its transaction, the share of each channel was reported.

---

[6] In a few cases, the deputy manager conducted the survey because the manager was away.

[7] Not all firms provided entire records when requested. A few firms provided less than five years' data for some reasons or other, e.g., some firms were established after 1989; some firms were leased or auctioned to new managers after 1989, they might be unable to provide pre-transition accounting records. The total number of observations used in the regressions is 296.

The firm manager's survey supplements the firm survey in that it asked the manager to indicate his contractual obligations, his responsibilities in contract fulfillment, his managerial autonomies, and so on. The firm manager was also required to provide personal information that was summarized in Chapter 2. In a specially designed part of the survey, the manager was required to state his attitude toward further property rights reform, full marketization, and his expectation regarding his next job, if he needed one. The information regarding the firm's marketing and procurement channels obtained from the firm manager's survey overlaps similar information provided by the firm survey, but in a more detailed style. The manager was asked to describe how the marketing and procurement channels were established, and how easy or difficult such channels could be replaced. The information obtained in two surveys is combined to generate the index variable 'input market', representing the 'market availability of major firm input'.

Each of the four sample townships was asked to complete a survey questionnaire for the purpose of obtaining the information regarding the economic setting of the localities. The most important information acquired was summarized in Table 5.6, and the data of township government's total revenue from TVEs was combined with the data of each sample firm's profit remittance to generate the 'share of firm's profit remittance in township government's total revenue from TVEs' ('profit remittance').

The number of total observation applied in the regression is about 300 ($\leq$ 64 x 5). The data used for the dependent variable, Y_t, covers the years 1990 to 1994, while the data for each of the explanatory variables in period t-1 covers the years 1989 to 1993. Since only four years' data of sample township government's revenue from TVEs is available, the regression is divided into two parts. In the first round of regressions, four years' data with township government's revenue and firm's profit remittance included is used. Then, after omitting 'profit remittance' and 'number of firms' from the model, another round of regressions with five years' data is performed.

This data set used to estimate the coefficient of each exogenous variable is unique, not only because it is microeconomic data at the level of firms, more importantly, it is first-hand information collected with the personal presence of the author at the research sites. Any vague information that might cause confusion or inconsistency was easily clarified during the investigation. Therefore, despite the small size of the sample, the data is perhaps relatively more reliable than that collected through mail surveys with larger samples.

2.3 The Results and the Explanations

The results of the estimation for the coefficients of the contractual form determination equation are reported in Table 5.8 (Panel A and B) and Table 5.9 (Panel A and B). In all exercised regressions, the fixed-wage contractual form is normalized to zero. The estimated coefficients for the profit-sharing form and for the fixed-payment form are reported in column 1 and column 2 correspondingly in both tables.

Table 5.8 reports the estimation results of the first round of regressions. This regression uses four years' data with 'number of firms' and 'profit remittance' included, and the region dummy 'Hubei' dropped. The first regression is run with 'year' representing the time trend of market development (Panel A). The second one, however, has 'year' replaced by 'product market' (Panel B) to capture the effects of regional market development.

Almost all of the estimated coefficients in the two tables have the sign as expected. The technical structure of the firm shows a strong explanatory power in the determination of firm's contractual form. The negative and significant coefficients on the 'capital intensity' variable in both regressions confirm the model hypothesis that it is less possible for the local leader to withdraw himself from the operation of a more capital-intensive firm. The greater absolute value of the coefficient on 'capital intensity' for fixed-payment contract than that for profit-sharing contract means that, other things equal, the least capital-intensive firms would be in the first group to adopt fixed-payment contractual arrangements. Less capital-intensive firms might prefer to be run under a profit-sharing contract, while the most capital-intensive firms would persist in fixed-wage managerial contractual form for a prolonged period.

The positive and significant coefficients on the variable 'labor intensity' (the ratio of production-line workers to staff in sales and procurement) are consistent with the third prediction of the model. That prediction suggests that if external management plays a less important role relative to internal management in the firm's operation, local leaders would lose their comparative advantage and take further steps to delegate the control rights to firm managers.

Table 5.8 The Determination of Sample TVEs' Contractual Form
(4 years' data, 'fixed-wage' is normalized to zero, Hubei
is dropped)

Panel A

	Profit-sharing	**Fixed-payment**
Constant	-52.663	-104.780
	(-0.004)	(-0.005)
Capital intensity	-0.358**	-0.451**
	(-2.557)	(-2.176)
Labor intensity	0.019*	0.019*
	(1.902)	(1.864)
Input market	1.039	3.174**
	(1.084)	(3.020)
Profit remittance	-0.027	-0.049
	(-1.397)	(-1.270)
Number of firms	-0.008	0.002
	(-0.788)	(0.204)
Year	0.798**	1.103**
	(2.059)	(2.536)
Zhejiang	-20.925	-0.007
	(-0.001)	(-0.000)
Jiangxi	-15.975	0.892
	(-0.001)	(0.000)
Jiangsu	-14.146	-15.817
	(-0.001)	(-0.001)

Table 5.8 Continued

Panel B

	Profit-sharing	**Fixed-payment**
Constant	-72.995	-99.275
	(-0.005)	(-0.005)
Capital intensity	-0.347**	-0.444**
	(-2.501)	(-2.142)
Labor intensity	0.019*	0.019*
	(1.834)	(1.847)
Input market	1.016	3.156**
	(1.049)	(3.004)
Profit remittance	-0.027	-0.053
	(-1.429)	(-1.350)
Number of firms	0.006	0.004
	(0.279)	(0.149)
Product market	0.006	0.024
	(0.834)	(1.097)
Zhejiang	-20.315	-0.053
	(-0.001)	(-0.000)
Jiangxi	-23.375	-0.077
	(-0.002)	(-0.000)
Jiangsu	-18.612	-16.227
	(-0.001)	(-0.001)

t-statistics in parenthesis.
** significant at 5 percent level.
* significant at 10 percent level.

Since a bigger 'labor intensity' means increasing the importance of internal management relative to external management, or similarly, diminishing the relative importance of external management, as the regressions show, the adoption of profit-sharing and fixed-payment contractual form have a significant positive relationship with 'labor intensity'. However, unlike the case of capital intensity variable, the estimated coefficients on 'labor intensity' are the same for profit-sharing form and for fixed-payment form in both regressions. This result might suggest that, the relative importance of external management played a significant role when the local leader moved away from a fixed-wage contract. Admittedly, its influence on whether or not to move from profit-sharing toward fixed-payment arrangement is not so obvious. There are alternative explanations. Since the 'other things equal' assumption does not hold in the real world, the influence of other relevant exogenous factors might outweigh the relative importance of external management to such an extent that it would be more profitable for the local leader to implement same contractual form (profit-sharing or fixed-payment) to two firms for which external management plays different roles. For example, if the market is so poor in an area that the external management services provided by the local community government leaders are necessary for all TVEs in the area, though to different degrees by each of them; or, in an area where the market is fully developed, thus no individual firm needs the leader's services in external management, even though external management plays a different role in each firm's operation; then we may observe unique profit-sharing or fixed-payment forms applied to all firms despite their technical structure. Or in another case, the community government has a very thin financial revenue source (as was the situation in Hubei site), the community government leader might prefer to run all TVEs under profit-sharing contracts, though certain firms demanded less or more external management services of the leader than other firms did.

The results of the estimated coefficients on variable 'capital intensity' and 'labor intensity' demonstrate that the technical structure of the firm does have decisive influence on the determination of TVEs' contractual structure. It also explains the coexistence of multi-contractual forms in a given region. However, the capital intensity seems to have a more crucial influence than the relative importance of external management in contractual form selection procedure.

The estimated coefficients on the time trend dummy 'year' in Table 5.8 (Panel A) are positive and significant. This confirms the model prediction regarding the positive effects of the market development in the whole economy on the innovation of TVEs' contractual structure. The absolute value of the coefficient on 'year' is smaller for profit-sharing than for fixed-payment, implying that the market development first leads to the move from the fixed-wage form to the profit-sharing form. The accelerated market development then results in a further move from profit-sharing to fixed-payment contracts.

Besides the general trend in market development, the development in firm input specific markets also has prominent influence on the contractual form choice. The estimated coefficients on the variable 'input market' (the market availability of firm's major inputs) in both regressions are positive as expected. This confirms that when it became easier for a TVE to acquire its major inputs through markets, the comparative advantage of the local leader in performing external management tasks decreased. It would then be more profitable for the local leader to take an action to move away from fixed-wage contract toward fixed-payment contract. However, only the fixed-payment contractual form of the two estimated coefficients is significant. The results are similar in the two regressions. This may imply that, whether or not the firm could acquire its major input through market transaction was a major concern when the community government leader intended to adopt the fixed-payment scheme. Under certain circumstances, however, the discrepancy in the market availability of major firm inputs was a negligible factor in the selection between fixed-wage and profit-sharing managerial contractual forms.

The estimated coefficients on regional market development ('product market') have correct positive signs (Panel B), showing the positive correlation between market development and the evolution from fixed-wage toward fixed-payment in TVEs' contractual structure. However, they are not significant in this regression, implying that the development of the whole market system (represented by the time trend 'year') and the firm input specified market development might have had stronger influences on the contractual structure innovation than the general situation in local markets development.

The regressions result in negative but insignificant estimated coefficients on the variable 'profit remittance' (the share of firm's profit remittance in township government's total revenue). This result partially confirms the model hypothesis that when the community government has more financial revenue sources, a single firm's share becomes insignificant, and the community government leader is more likely to adopt non-fixed-wage contractual form. It may also explain the observation that community government treats its TVEs in a discriminating way -- keeping close control over 'key' revenue generating firms while letting others operate with more autonomies. However, this concern may play less significant role in the determination of the contractual structure than other exogenous factors do. The estimated coefficients on the 'number of firms' in the sample township are not significantly different from zero, indicating that this factor may not affect TVEs' contractual form choice as much as expected.

Model prediction 4 can not be accepted based upon the regression results, because all estimated coefficients are not significant. Such results suggest that either the economic setting of a locality has played a negligible role in firm's contractual form determination and innovation, or the two variables do not precisely measure the difference in economic setting, and thus fail to explain the influence such a setting has had on the contractual structure. Considering that all the estimated coefficients on 'profit remittance' and on 'number of firms' have correct signs, we may expect better estimation after re-specifying the variable(s) to more rigorously reflect the attributes of a locality. However, since alternative data at the same level is not available, it is difficult to substitute the two variables by other measurements.

All estimated coefficients on region dummies are insignificant in both regressions, indicating that very few residual effects could be explained by cross-regional variations that are not explicitly specified by the model explanatory variables.

Another round of regressions has been operated after the variables 'number of firms' and 'profit remittance' were eliminated from the model. It consists of two regressions, one with the variable 'year' included, another with 'product market'. Both regressions use 5 years' data and with the region dummy 'Jiangsu' dropped. The estimated results are reported in Table 5.9 (Panel A and Panel B). The omission of 'number of firms' and 'profit remittance' has improved the estimation results. All of the estimated coefficients shown in the table have correct signs and are significant in their effects.

Table 5.9 The Contractual Form Determination of Sample TVEs Without the Variables of Local Economic Setting
(5 years' data, Fixed-wage is normalized to zero, Jiangsu is dropped)

Panel A

	Profit-sharing	Fixed-payment
Constant	-45.298	-141.647
	(-2.885)	(-0.019)
Capital intensity	-0.402**	-0.582**
	(-3.490)	(-3.010)
Labor intensity	0.012*	0.017**
	(1.688)	(2.133)
Input market	1.444**	3.663**
	(2.205)	(3.815)
Year	0.518**	1.318**
	(3.003)	(5.384)
Zhejiang	-2.252**	17.671
	(-2.726)	(0.002)
Hubei	-0.693	16.075
	(-1.154)	(0.002)
Jiangxi	-1.986**	18.491
	(-2.566)	(0.002)

Table 5.9 Continued

Panel B

	Profit-sharing	Fixed-payment
Constant	1.834	-23.283
	(1.879)	(-0.003)
Capital intensity	-0.280**	-0.388**
	(-2.808)	(-2.032)
Labor intensity	0.011*	0.016**
	(1.704)	(2.003)
Input market	1.255*	3.468**
	(1.952)	(3.806)
Product market	0.0004	0.011**
	(0.167)	(3.676)
Zhejiang	-2.129**	17.671
	(-2.173)	(0.002)
Hubei	-0.690	16.075
	(-0.870)	(0.002)
Jiangxi	-1.677**	18.491
	(-2.320)	(0.002)

t-statistics in parentheses.
** significant at 5 percent level.
* significant at 10 percent level.

Similar to the estimation results of the first round regressions, the technical structure of the firm shows its decisive influence on the firm's contractual form choice. The estimated coefficients on 'capital intensity', as expected, are negative and significant, with the absolute value for the fixed-payment contract bigger than that for the profit-sharing contract in both regressions. Likewise, the estimated coefficients on 'labor intensity' have positive signs, and are significantly different from zero. Moreover, the estimated coefficients for profit-sharing and for fixed-payment are not identical as that found in four years' data regression (Table 5.8). They differ from each other. The absolute value of the coefficient for fixed-payment is greater than that for profit-sharing in both regressions, demonstrating that when the external management is less important in the firm's operation, *ceteris paribus*, the community government leader would choose to adopt the fixed-payment contract instead of the profit-sharing form for the enterprise. This result confirms the model prediction that with the increasing importance of internal management relative to external management, we will observe a consistent movement from fixed-wage to profit-sharing then to fixed-payment managerial contracts.

The estimated coefficients on the time trend variable 'year' are not only positive but also significant, with greater absolute value for the fixed-payment contractual choice than for the profit-sharing arrangement (1.318 vs. 0.518). This means the dynamic trend is more influential for the fixed-payment form than for the profit-sharing form, and proves again that the development of whole market system does play a crucial role in directing the evolution in TVEs contractual structure.

The development of local markets seems to have an undoubted effect on the adoption of fixed-payment contractual form. The estimated coefficient on 'product market' is positive and significant for the fixed-payment form (Panel B). The estimated coefficient for the profit-sharing form, however, is not significantly different from zero, demonstrating that local market development has very weak impact in the movement from a fixed-wage arrangement toward a profit-sharing partnership relation.

The development of firm input specified market has shown even more notable effects in this round of regressions. As expected, the signs of the estimated coefficients are positive; all of the estimated coefficients are significantly different from zero for either fixed-payment or profit-sharing contracts (the estimated coefficients are insignificant for profit-sharing in the first round of regression). The absolute value of the estimated coefficients is greater for fixed-payment than that for profit-sharing in both cases, indicating that the market availability of firm's major inputs does make a difference when the local leader made a choice among the three contractual forms.

The elimination of 'number of firms' and 'profit remittance', the variables characterizing a locality, has resulted in a notable difference in the coefficients of region dummies. The estimated coefficients on Zhejiang and Jiangxi become significantly negative for profit-sharing contract. This result might have captured a kind of cross-regional variation that is not included in the model specification, but has impact on firm's contractual structure determination, for example, local government policies. In fact, the sample township government in the Zhejiang site and in the Jiangxi site had more actively encouraged leasing and auction of TVEs (moving away from profit-sharing form) than sample township government in the Jiangsu site as observed in the author's field investigation.

2.4 Conclusions

The econometric analysis demonstrated in this section shows that the model prediction 1, 2, and 3 should be accepted as sound. Market development in transitional China has proved to be the determinant factor in TVEs contractual structure determination and innovation. The development of the whole market system in the economy is obviously the most influential catalyst that stimulates the community government leaders to search for more profitable managerial contractual forms in a relatively short time span. This search led to an evolution in TVEs contractual structure moving first from fixed-wage to profit-sharing, and then to fixed-payment.

Other things equal, the development in the firm specific input market might be a powerful explanatory factor to interpret the variation in local community government leader's decisions with respect to TVEs' contractual organizations. The markets for different goods and inputs can not be expected to develop simultaneously. Some markets might have lagged markedly behind in liberalization or development while others had become fully liberalized and developed. Depending on which type of markets for its major inputs determined the extent to which a firm had to rely on community government leaders to gain access to its suppliers. These facts affected the local leader's contractual form selection.

Local market development might also have had influence on the contractual structure determination. However, this factor is revealed to play a less important role than the whole market system development and industry specified market development. In the early stage of the TVE movement, most rural enterprises were regional market oriented. With the gradual process of establishing nationwide markets and their further development, TVEs became basically nationwide market oriented and undertook transactions over the entire country. It is not surprising to find that the development of whole market system to be relatively a more crucial factor than local market development in introducing institutional innovation to the TVE sector.

The technical structure of the firm showed another critical factor affecting the firm's contractual structure. A firm with capital-intensive technology would support the fixed-wage arrangement; in contrast, a labor-intensive firm would favor fixed-payment contract. Similarly, the fixed-payment contractual form would mostly be applied to those firms where internal management is valued more than external management to maintain a successful business. However, firms in demand of external management services would hesitate to change its fixed-wage or profit-sharing contractual structure.

On the basis of the empirical analysis, however, the fourth model prediction is not acceptable, for all of the estimated coefficients are not significant, though have correct signs. The descriptive statistical analysis conducted in Section 1 does reveal the correlation between TVEs' contractual structure and the economic setting of a locality. Therefore, the rejection of the prediction may be explained in two ways. One is that the economic setting does play a role in a greater or lesser degree in the local` community government leader's decisions in selecting the optimal solution among alternative managerial contracts. However, such an influence is not as significant as we had expected. The second is that, there does exist a significant correlation between firm's contractual form and the attributes of a locality, but the two explanatory variables in the model are not appropriately specified to represent such attributes. In comparing the first round regression results with the second round regression results, we note that, when 'profit remittance' and 'number of firms' have been included in the regression, all the estimated coefficients on the region dummies are not significantly different from zero (Table 5.8). This means that the effects of the cross-regional variation have been captured by other explanatory variables. When the variables 'profit remittance' and 'number of firms' are omitted from the model, however, the estimated coefficients on regional dummies become significant (Table 5.9). This means the region dummies have pinpointed some effects that might be derived from economic or non-economic peculiarities of each area. Therefore, the rejection of the fourth model prediction could be the result of a wrong specification of explanatory variables rather than a rejection of the predicted correlation. Due to restriction on data availability, it is impossible to formulate a new model to improve the estimation results. This is a pity for this research, however, it may also be a starting point for some follow-up studies.

6 Endogenous Reform and Induced Privatization: Concluding Remarks

1. Introduction

In this book, I have provided a rich set of descriptions on relations between rural community government leaders and firm managers in China's TVE sector. Far from moribund as some authors have suggested, the form of the managerial contract has evolved rapidly during the past ten years. Descriptive data and the theoretical model developed in this research predict that these changes are occurring in response to the rapid development of markets in rural China. The mechanism behind the move from local leader-run firms to fixed-payment firms is subtle, and involves a change in relative value of non-marketed inputs owned by local community government leaders and firm managers. Without good markets, local leaders have a comparative advantage in operating a firm. Their external management inputs more than offset any inefficiency due to the fact that a busy bureaucrat is managing a firm. As markets develop, however, this advantage disappears. In response to increasingly competitive pressure in the economy, local leaders find that they can make their firm more profitable by providing firm managers with more incentives to work harder, *i.e.,* providing them with more autonomy, and giving them even larger shares of the residual profit. It has been proved by the studies demonstrated in this book that the development of an effectively competitive market system in a transitional economy naturally leads to the evolution towards firms' managerial contractual structure. The ultimate implication of such organizational evolution may be a bottom-up spontaneous privatization in the economy, in spite of a lack of explicit policy support and encouragement of the central government. However, due to the heterogeneity in the firms' technical structure and the diversification in regional economic settings, such evolution or privatization is not instantaneous. Any sweeping implementation of a specific organizational

208

form directly commanded by the central government or other 'outside' forces may very well be resisted by local community government leaders or firm managers, if it is inconsistent with their benefit maximization objectives.

If this dynamic is what is really happening in rural China, a number of interesting observations are found which do not exist in other transitional economies. Instead of beginning with privatization, and relying on entrepreneurs to set up markets (as is the reform strategy followed in Eastern Europe and the former republics of the Soviet Union), China's experience shows that the process may also work in reverse. While the sample is too small to make any definitive conclusion, in the sample townships it shows that market development leads to privatization (or at least a contractual form with more of the characteristics of private enterprises). This process is actually quite similar to that noted by McMillan and Naughton (1991). They show that one of the unique features of China's gradual reform strategy lies in its slow development brining about the creation of institutions (including markets); and these institutions (with proper incentives) lead to greater competitive pressures. As augured by Jefferson and Rawski (1994a), many small changes induced by the competition may cumulate to result in an 'endogenous reform' in the economy. When fiscal constraints are hard, actors in China's economy have an incentive to innovate. One important way in which they have innovated is by changing the property rights of the firm.

The co-existence of various organizational forms and property rights in a prolonged period during the reform era in fact serves as a kind of lubricant to reduce the friction caused by replacing one economic system for another. As illustrated in this book, when local community government leaders and firm managers make their decision to select a more appropriate contractual form for a given firm in the various stages of the reform, they are actually making rational response to a changing economic environment with unambiguous objective of efficiency improvement and transaction cost reduction. Such rational behavior may effectively prevent production from decline. As a result, it eases possible tensions and social chaos caused by any decline in production. One of the most important implications of such findings may be for the economics of transition literature, especially when comparing the case of China with Eastern Europe and the former republics of the Soviet Union. The difference in the economic performance of China versus the rest of the reforming world is in some part related to this fundamental difference in reform strategy.

The development of china's TVE sector has provided a vivid example that besides the 'ideal' reform and development strategy, there can exist alternative path that will lead to the same outcome in economic reform. Though some researchers think China is so different from the other reforming countries that its reform experiences are unique and that there can be no lessons drawn (Sachs and Woo, 1994). Others argue that China's success is not unique to China but has elementary lessons valuable to the rest of the reforming world (McMillan, 1994). China's experiences are unique in two ways. The first is that the legacy of the socialist economic system inherited by the reformers does not exist in other developing economies. For example, after two decades of collective production under the commune system, communities in rural China had accumulated community collectively owned properties and wealth in a greater or lesser degree. The community governments have direct access to these collective properties and the administrative capacity to control the use of them. This effectively counteracted the weakness of private entrepreneurship in rural China and enabled the quick entry of rural enterprises into the liberalized commodity markets when such entry was allowed in the early stage of the reform era. As reported by the author's 64 sample TVEs, 83 percent of them had their initial capital investments either solely from community governments, or from community government's investment plus government guaranteed bank loans. Only 17 percent of the sample TVEs said their initial investment was from non-government sources (including private entrepreneurs' investment, fund raised from firm employees or local residents, and personal bank loans). The ability of community governments in controlling collectively owned properties and wealth to launch rural enterprises at a tremendous speed and scale is a unique Chinese phenomenon. In other developing countries, such sizable community collectively owned properties and wealth either did not exist, or were not at community governments' disposal.

The second is, unlike other reforming former socialist economies, the reformers in the Chinese government do not have a definitive reform objective or a clear strategy to approach such an objective. Rather, they follow the so-called strategy 'groping for stones to cross the river', meaning China's reform consists of expediency, one experiment after another. The reforming Chinese leaders have neither a clear vision of what a restructured economy should look like, nor a consensus of the policy mix or institutional arrangements best suited to meet their twin objectives: political continuity and accelerated economic growth (Jefferson and Rawski, 1994a). After each of the 'piece meal' innovations, the government adjusts its policies based upon the assessment of the results of the previous reform experiment, not only in reform measures but also frequently in the reform objectives themselves.

Chinese leaders initiated economic reform after the ten years of 'Cultural Revolution', which had resulted in sharp production decline and utter social chaos. This is because they were dissatisfied with their nation's economic performance, and feared that the inferior economic performance and the poor living conditions of the Chinese people might threaten the Chinese Communist Party's ascendant domestic position and its influence on world affairs. The general objective of the reform was to increase national productivity and to promote economic growth, so that China's economy matches the achievements of its Eastern Asian neighbors. Commodity market liberalization and the removal of market entry barriers to non-state owned enterprises unleashed the forces of competition. The replacement of plan targets with 'responsibility contracts' gave economic agents the incentive to improve economic efficiency. All of these reform experiments were designed to achieve the economic objectives. No essential institutional change was initiated by the reforming Chinese leaders. Privatization or other fundamental property rights reform has never been the core reform objective of the Chinese leaders. On the contrary, they were resisted by the central government, at least explicitly. To safeguard the authority of the communist government and political stabilization, the central government affirmed on the dominance of public ownership (state ownership and collective ownership) against private ownership. They declared that markets must function within the socialist framework. Therefore, the substantial rapid growth of the collective ownership dominated TVE sector is a unique experience of China, since *'in no other transitional economy has public ownership played such a dynamic role'* (Naughton, 1994b).

Furthermore, in Eastern Europe and the former republics of the Soviet Union, property rights privatization is a reform strategy pursued by the governments, and in many cases opposed by economic agents at the ground level. This is because the 'insiders' fear the loss of income, power, or benefit during such institutional innovation (Brada, 1996). Whereas in China's reform practice, as demonstrated in this book, the property rights innovation in rural collective enterprises is in fact initiated at the ground level by rural community government leaders and firm managers. Unlike some authors who view the property rights structure of TVEs as the solution of the central government's design problem (Chang and Wang, 1994), this book views the property rights structure of TVEs as the rationale of local communities in response to the institutional environment with imperfections both in market and in government. During this process, it was the central government which played a passive role. Hence, China's reform has a substantially different experience from that of other reforming ex-socialist economies. The central government's original reform pursuit of letting market forces play a role in stimulating production increase while defending the fundamental features of the socialist system (*i.e.*, keeping the public ownership dominance) was forced to gradually give way to permitting non-publicly owned economic entities compete with publicly owned ones. In the meantime, the government had to reluctantly accept the fact of an evolving organizational form in the direction of privatization in the collective ownership dominated TVE sector.

In comparison with the reform practice of other reforming economies, are there any elementary lessons we can learn from China's reform experiences? Or, are these experiences utterly unique and limited to China's situation? Are they thus useless for reference to other transitional economies? A brief discussion of such questions in this chapter will serve as concluding remarks in this book. The remainder of this chapter is organized as follows: Section 2 describes the 'endogenous reform' model of Jefferson and Rawski, and attempts to consummate the model by introducing the endogenous evolution of the firm's contractual form as the crucial link in completing the chain of 'induced privatization'. In Section 3, the feedback effects of the TVEs' contractual form innovation are demonstrated with a brief discussion of how such feedback effects may shape the general process of the economic reform in China. Section 4 turns to the issues of reform strategy comparison and further reform policy suggestions. An appendix to this chapter demonstrates the survey results from my follow-up investigation conducted in December 1998. This follow-up investigation confirmed the model predictions in Chapter 4 and 5. It also traces an interesting dynamic movement in firm contractual form transition after 1994.

2. The Endogenous Model of Economic Reform: 'Induced Privatization'

'Getting property rights right' is considered the crucial task to the development of transitional and developing economies. In transition and development economics, no single issue has received more attention by economists and policy-makers than the one of property rights and ownership. In mainstream economics, it is believed that markets require a clear assignment of initial entitlement to most productive resources and well-enforced rules of contract. Governments with an intention to foster a market economy should thus make sure an effective legal system is in place, one in which property rights are unambiguously defined, secure, and freely alienable. Due to such a belief, some economists and international agencies have asserted that privatization and a rapid replacement of market for the plan are the only sure path for transition away from a centrally planning system in Eastern Europe (Blanchard et al. 1991; Sachs, 1992). According to many western advisors to reformist governments in Eastern Europe and the former republics of the Soviet Union, quickly freeing up prices and creating a financial market, privatizing state-owned firms, and establishing laws of commerce are among the prerequisites for successful market activities. Among all these conditions, privatization occupies the center of the stage in such reform advice. Understandably so since *'the difference between socialism and capitalism lies in the ownership of property; the former is a system where nonhuman productive resources are primarily socially or state owned, while in the latter they are mainly owned by individuals. Thus, only if transition economies are able to make large and lasting changes in the ownership of productive assets away from the state and toward individual owners will they make the transition from socialism to capitalism'*. Though *'how to bring about such a change in ownership is bound to be a difficult and contentious issue'* (Brada, 1996, p.67) (it is easy to understand why the Chinese communist government who insists on the socialist political doctrine has rejected western advisors' suggestions for sweeping privatization as its fundamental reform strategy).

As pointed out by Jefferson and Rawski (1994a):

> *Most researchers view the reform of former socialist economies as a process driven by* exogenous *policy changes (abolition of planning, privatization, removal of price controls, etc.). Reform is seen as a process of creative institutional destruction that is imposed by central planners in a top-down fashion. In this linear view of reform, the self-interested response of agents within the economy is expected to stimulate profit-seeking behavior and market activities. If progress is inadequate, the center can impose further rounds of reform* (p.1).

The reforming Eastern Europe and the former republics of the Soviet Union have basically followed such an exogenous reform strategy, hoping that such instantaneous reform may curtail the painful transitional process, and the economy becomes well restructured after a short 'shock'. In this kind of 'exogenous reform' model, reform is a top-down process forced by a powerful central government or 'outsiders'. The property rights innovation is thus characterized by an 'imposed privatization'. Specialists from several international organizations who prefer such top-down exogenous reform strategy assert that *'Ideally, a path of gradual reform could be laid out which would minimize economic disturbance and lead to an early harvesting of the fruits of increased economic efficiency. But we know of no such path'* (IMF, 1990, p.2).

However, it was perhaps too early to make such assertions, because the fact is such a path may exist. At least one of the reforming socialist countries -- China -- has followed a different reform strategy,[1] an 'endogenous reform' model as formulated by Jefferson and Rawski. Jefferson and Rawski view China's reform as a partial and gradual cumulative process induced by endogenous forces.

> *Interactions among different groups of agents within the economy exert a significant impact on economic outcomes. Policy decisions respond to the circumstances of agents and to the impact of decentralized responses on the government's political and financial interests. The importance of* endogenous *influences in explaining the behavior of government is not limited to the routine decisions of lower-level functionaries. China's recent formal endorsement of a decentralized market system, an arrangement that stood far beyond the bounds of legitimate policy discussion at the start of reform, reflects the impact of endogenous forces even on the value and objectives of national political elite (Decisions, 1993)* (Jefferson and Rawski, 1994a, p.2).

Jefferson and Rawski described the 'endogenous reform' model as a *'cumulative and mutually reinforcing process of interaction among market leaning institutional change, technical innovation, and economizing*

---

[1] China's reform experience has been ignored by many economic researchers, because its economic success is overshadowed by its lack of progress in its political system reform and property ownership reform. However, as argued by McMillan (1994), even given such criticism, raising the living standards of a billion poor people to two-and-one-half times in less than two decades is a notable achievement, and its experiences deserve more careful studies.

behavior.[2] According to them, such interactions took place when the government launched a partial reform pursuit. Due to the hierarchy existing in China's domestic industrial sector, enterprises are heterogeneous and exhibit systematic difference in technological capabilities, cost structures, and institutional arrangements. State-owned enterprises enjoying favorable treatment under the centrally planning system have superior technical capacities, but are subject to greater restriction from institutional constraints; at the same time, collective enterprises as TVEs are generally at a disadvantage in technology, but are least affected by institutional limitations. When the Chinese government implements partial reform measures that reduce entry barriers and lower the cost of many types of transactions as observed in China's reform practice, these initiatives have a differential impact on the opportunity sets available to different groups of firms. The state-owned enterprises, on the one hand, were allowed to keep a portion of their profit to augment their efforts in taking full advantage of available resources. Meanwhile collective urban enterprises or TVEs, on the other hand, were enabled to obtain inputs and other resources to adopt new technologies and to produce substitutes that could compete with state-owned enterprises' products on the markets. This is due to the relaxation of restrictions on resources allocation throughout the enterprise hierarchy.

The differential impact of reform efforts destabilizes the existing divisions of industrial resources and product markets among different types of firms. Competition in industrial product markets intensifies. Stronger competition diminishes the firms' profitability at the micro-level, with some firms ending financial loss. Whereas at the macro-level, erosion of profits limits the growth of revenues accruing to local and provincial authorities, as well as to the central government.

Enterprises operating in competitive markets with declining profit margins react to market pressure by choosing strategies to improve their financial status. They may restructure their operation within existing institutional limits through economizing behavior in innovating technologies or cost-lowering measures. They also have the option to pursue institutional changes to ensure more financial gains, *e.g.*, through rent-seeking behavior, lobbying for direct subsidies or soft loans to offset losses (especially state-owned enterprises that enjoyed favorable treatment under the centrally planning system, seeking to restore their initial financial

---

[2] Barry Naughton (1994) and John McMillan (1994) have similar description, though not summarized as an 'endogenous reform' model.

position through official intervention). They can also pressure the government to expand its grant of autonomy to the firm to facilitate profit-seeking initiatives (state firm managers demand a 'level playing field' with their non-state competitors including relaxation of operating restrictions, lightening financial burdens, etc.). They can choose one or a combination of these measures in response to market competition pressure.

Governments also react to financial pressures that reduce their share of total output and destabilize the distribution of fiscal revenue across regions and administrative levels. Officials face conflicting enterprise lobbying efforts, some demanding further autonomy and deregulation in their operations, meanwhile others seeking protection from the outcome of earlier partial reforms. In response to the firms' reactions and to their own financial pressure, government policies tend to extend business autonomy, increase market exposure, and harden budget constraints.

These induced responses of firm and government further erode entry barriers and reduce transaction costs. These feedback effects reinforce the momentum of beneficial changes in that they intensify market competition, further diminish quasi-rent, and motivate additional reform effort on the part of enterprises and government. In other words, they can motivate further rounds of technical development, economizing efforts, and reform increments. More importantly, this entire process affects the attitudes of enterprise personnel and government officials toward the direction and outcome of reform. Changing attitudes affect the objectives and strategies of all the reform participants. This remarkable change in values and attitudes may cumulate to result in a policy of 'endogenous or induced privatization'.

As summarized by Jefferson and Rawski, China's reform has followed a bottom-up process driven by endogenous forces.

> This interaction (among endogenous forces) takes place in an environment of intense competition involving several types of firms, each with its own distinct technical capabilities and institutional constraints. Partial reform expands entry into product markets. Greater competition erodes enterprise profits and undermines the revenue base at every level of government. This financial strait generates pressures that promote innovation and cost reduction. Government efforts to ease the revenue constraint as well as enterprises' efforts to innovate and reduce costs lead to fresh rounds of market-directed institutional change. In the Chinese case, successive rounds of partial reform have cumulated into significant changes in

> *institutional structure, conduct, and performance affecting every types of firm, including old-line state firms* (Jefferson and Rawski, 1994a, p.3).

I completely agree with the description of the bottom-up endogenous reform model of Jefferson and Rawski. However, I would like to argue that, this model could be consummated by introducing the endogenous innovation of firm's contractual structure as a critical link to complete the chain of 'induced privatization'. A crucial difference between the 'exogenous reform' model and the 'endogenous reform' model resides not in the top-down or bottom-up reform process, but rather in the fundamental difference of how property rights institutions have been changed, in other words, 'imposed privatization' versus 'induced privatization'. In order to understand the underlying difference between 'imposed privatization' and 'induced privatization', the focal point is to understand the mechanism through which property rights institutions have been reformed. It is relatively easy to understand 'imposed privatization', since it is a simple problem of policy design, *i.e.*, privatizing previously publicly owned properties by artificial devices designed by reformers or specialists (surely I am not saying the design of each concrete measure is a simple task). In contrast, 'induced privatization' is a much more complicated process. It is not designed or forced by exogenous forces, but rather gradually it takes form through interaction of endogenous forces. Then we must explore under what kind of exogenous conditions or environment, through what kind of endogenous interaction the new property rights institutions take shape to replace the old institutions, thus accomplishing endogenous institutional reform.

The weakness of the Jefferson and Rawski model is that they stop at the argument that firms in reacting to market competition pressure seek institutional innovation by demanding more autonomy and incentives. The cumulative effects of such innovation may affect reform participants' attitude and thus result in property rights reform of privatization. However, they did not provide a systematic analysis of how those changes in attitude were actually translated into institutional innovations that gradually led to privatization of public properties. They emphasized the effects of non-state enterprises' entry on the reform incentives of state-owned enterprises, but did not pay enough attention to the fundamental evolution in organizational form of the firms in both sectors. Jefferson and Rawski's 'endogenous reform' model provided a comprehensive explanation of how the partial reform pursuit of the Chinese government effectively improved the overall performance of the economy through the firms' economizing behavior and technical innovation. However, what was not clearly explained is the institutional innovation at the firms' level. Expansion of business autonomy, strengthening of profit-seeking incentives, and changing attitude toward ownership reform constituted a quantitative movement. What was missing from the model is the critical link in the chain of 'induced privatization' -- how this quantitative movement cumulated into a qualitative innovation.

Combining the endogenous innovation of firm contractual forms demonstrated in this research work with the Jefferson-Rawski model[3] will reinforce the model and make it a more inherently consistent explanation of the endogenous reform characterized by the 'induced privatization'. The restructured model framework is summarized as follows:

A. The central government implements partial reform measures that reduce entry barriers and lower transaction costs for the purpose of increasing output and improving efficiency.

B. Partial reform leads to intensified market competition, which diminishes profitability of firms and erodes government's financial revenues.

C. The differential impact of partial reforms on different groups of firms induces responses of firms based upon the comparative advantage of each group. Firms react to changing exogenous environment by choosing strategies involving economic innovation and institutional innovation. They take action to restructure their operations through technical innovation and cost reduction. They also pursue institutional innovation by demanding more business freedom and operation autonomy.

D. The government at various administrative levels reacts to the changing exogenous environment by granting firms in their jurisdiction extended autonomy to strengthen their profit-seeking incentives and to motivate them to improve efficiency, for the purpose of maximizing financial revenues.

E. The interaction between the government authorities and the firm managers result in firm contractual form innovation, one in which the government reduces its administrative intervention and direct managerial

---

[3] Although this research work focuses on the institutional innovation in the TVE sector, such innovation may not be limited only to the TVE sector. As mentioned by Jefferson and Rawski (1994a), similar organizational innovations took place in the state-owned sectors too. Other researchers also confirmed that lease and auction have been diffused into small and medium state-owned factories in recent years (Zhou and Zhou, 1996). Hence, the endogenous firm contractual form innovation may be appropriately treated as a general factor in the model.

supervision. More control rights are delegated to the firm managers, at the same time residual claim rights are granted to the firm managers in an increasing scale.

F. The contractual form innovation motivated reformed firms to take further steps in economizing efforts and technical innovations. Meanwhile as market competition intensifies again, other firms are forced to seek similar institutional as well as economic innovations. Eventually, institutional innovation diffuses across firms and sectors, spreading across the economy and at a certain point the institutional structure of the entire economy experiences a qualitative change.

G. In conjunction with improved efficiency and economic performance as the feedback effects of institutional innovation, markets develop. A fresh round of reform is launched since further deregulation movement and incentives are in demand by firms in response to new market conditions. More partial reform measures are put into practice by the government in response to such demand. New dimensions of reform induce another round of firm contractual structure innovation.

H. The pervasive contractual form innovation cumulates into an evolution in firm property rights structure, and affects the attitude of reform participants toward ownership reform. As a consequence, the ideological obstacle towards privatization is removed, and 'induced privatization' in a former socialist economy can be realized. The change is effected solely through interaction of endogenous forces, without exogenous orders.

This book illustrates the induced contractual form innovation in detail. The following section is devoted to a discussion of the feedback effect of such innovation.

3. The Feedback Effects of Contractual Form Innovation

As described in previous chapters, the development of the market system enhances the ability of firm managers and erodes community government leaders' comparative advantage in external management. New contractual form is attained through such endogenous interaction, and the resultant evolution of the contractual form develops towards privatization in firm property rights. Institutional economists believe that fundamental and pervasive innovation in firm governance institutions will conceivably have impact on the institutional environment, such as the legal system or political constitutions. This is because governance innovations change the relationship of various interest groups and their relative influences and bargaining power. My research sample is probably too small and covers too short a period to make any comprehensive and ascertained conclusions or predictions with respect to the feedback effects of the contractual form innovation on the whole process of the reform. However, a brief description of the feedback effects in several dimensions will provide clarification to the mechanism of 'induced privatization'.

TVE managers are the group of individuals who have been influenced the most by the contractual form innovation. Recall that at the early stage of the TVE movement, most of the collective rural enterprises were run by local leaders. There did not exist a class of 'professional firm managers'. Most of the firm leaders would like to call themselves 'party cadres' or 'government officials' rather than 'factory managers'. Not only because they viewed 'manager' as an inferior title than 'cadre' or 'official', but also because they were in fact cadres appointed by community governments, and relied mainly on political reputation and promotion to attain their self-confidence and satisfaction. At that stage, their income was independent of the financial performance of the firms, and with only a marginal difference from firm employee compensations. They were strongly risk-averse, mentally and financially, because they had little business experience and personal wealth to take on any substantial risk. Insofar as administrative intervention and plan continued to be the effective means of business operations, they were satisfied in their role as followers instead of initiators in management. Local party cadres and government staff constituted the only pool of TVE managers.

When the number and the size of TVEs in a given area grew to a certain level, the community government leaders, particularly the primary leaders, found themselves unable to deal with the operation of the firms personally. Then a group of individuals, either from the local government cadre pool, or from experienced or talented personnel of the firms, were appointed as managers to run the daily operations of the firms. By this time, the 'professional firm managers' as a class started to take shape. As described above, they were granted more business autonomies and managerial control rights. At the same time, they established a partnership-kind of relationship with the community governments through profit-sharing contractual arrangements. Due to the change in markets and in their own status in firm business operations, firm managers had to deal with internal managerial tasks independently, as well as with market transactions to a greater or lesser extent. The shared firm profit motivated them to take on more responsibilities in firm financial performance. Consequently, they became more sensitive to market conditions (supply, demand, prices, etc.), transaction opportunities, technological information, and so on. They acquired more and more managerial knowledge, experiences, and skills through practice (and training in some cases). Many of them preferred identifying themselves as 'rural entrepreneurs' rather than 'rural cadres'. Some even viewed the 'firm manager' a better position than that of a community government staff,[4] though few of the firm managers would actually give up their positions at collective enterprises to become private entrepreneurs. The more they learnt in managerial practice, the better they knew the business, and the less risk-averse they became. Besides self-confidence, another reason they became less risk-averse was that the profit-sharing arrangement enabled a portion of the firm managers to have increased ability to take business risks. For example, when the sample community governments adopted the personal mortgage responsibility contractual form in the early 1990s, most of the firm managers were able to deposit the required amount of cash (plus personal properties like residential houses in some cases). However, during this stage, firm manager selection remained basically an administrative affair of the community governments, no fundamental changes had been observed in this field. Firm managers formed and maintained their partnership kind relationship with the community governments through administrative rather than market mechanisms. No manager market was functioning.

Profit-sharing contractual arrangement fostered entrepreneurship in the TVE sector after nearly one decade (1984 -1993) of practice. A proportion of the TVE managers, talented firm personnel, and even skilled workers, motivated by wealth-seeking incentives were ready to undertake more responsibilities and risks as independent managers or owners of firms. Hence, when the sample community governments began the fixed-payment (leasing or auction) contractual experiments, they were able to attract competitive bidders. The individuals who had established solid personal transaction connections, had superior ability in management, or possessed special technological knowledge or skills, became the first group granted fixed-payment contracts. At the same time, former managers who lacked entrepreneurship or the needed ability to manage their firms were eliminated in the contract competition (as observed in the Case Study 8 of Chapter 3). Their positions were taken over by more capable and risk-

---

[4] See Chapter 4.

tolerant individuals. The success of the 'early birds' in the fixed-payment contractual experiment encouraged not only community governments to extend the experiment to more firms, but also other potential candidates for participation in the managerial contract competition. Fixed-payment contractual form first diffused from one firm to another in a given area, then to neighbor areas, and finally it became a prevailing organizational form in most areas.[5] Then, the interaction between the community governments, who were willing to depend on more capable individuals to improve firm efficiency and generate more financial revenues,[6] and the potential firm managers or owners, who were willing to take more business risks in exchange for the opportunity to inflate personal incomes, would help to form a competitive manager market in rural China. Firm manager selection would gradually become a market behavior rather than an administrative affair, and the 'firm managers' as a class would be restructured. The real entrepreneurs and professional managers would replace the government cadres or officials to constitute a large section of this class. The restructured firm manager constitution and the development of rural management market would undoubtedly benefit the further reform in TVEs' property rights and economic growth.

The responses of sample TVE managers to the question of what method they intended to use to get their next job if they had to leave their then positions confirmed this management marketization trend (Table 6.1). From the 64 responses of managers, only 8 percent indicated they would wait for the government to appoint them to new positions. As contrast, a surprisingly high percentage (64 percent) intended to become private firm owners if they left their current positions. The remainder was divided into two groups, one would depend on their personal connections in future job-search, and the other viewed the market as the normal channel of job access. This observation implies that, with the contractual form evolution, firm managers as a class has separated from the government administrative hierarchy to constitute an independent class. In recognizing their market value, they had become active market competition participants. Given a certain period of

---

[5] See Appendix.

[6] Remember, though the community government only obtains the fixed rent from the firm under a fixed-payment contract, which is independent of firm's financial performance, however, it may receive increased share of tax return if the improved firm efficiency of local TVEs increases total tax payment to the government. The township government may also benefit from increased firm 'management fee' payment, that is related to firm's output and sales.

wealth accumulation under the fixed-rent leasing contract, many would become qualified private entrepreneurs (some of them already had, as the firm buyers in Case Study 8). They will be the catalyst of the rural development in the next decade.

Table 6.1 The Intended Method of Sample Managers to Get Next Job, 1994 (%)*

	Sample	Zhejiang	Hubei	Jiangxi	Jiangsu
Government appointment	7.9	0	44.4	5.6	0
Friend recommendation	15.9	22.7	0	11.1	20.0
Bidding competition	5.6	4.5	11.1	5.6	6.7
Response to advertisement	7.1	4.5	22.2	5.6	6.7
Private owner	63.5	68.2	22.2	72.2	66.7

* Each column adds up to 100 percent.

Source: Author's Survey, 1994.

However, the cross-regional disparity is prominent. The managers' responses in Zhejiang and Jiangsu sites are very much the same -- none were looking to the government for job access, and about two thirds wanted to be private firm owners. This is perhaps because TVEs in these two research sites were at a similar level of development. TVE managers in these two sites had the same amount of experience and expertise in business management. The Zhejiang site adopted fixed-payment contracts in 1993, firm managers there were directly affected by the innovation. Though lagging behind in fixed-payment contractual experiment at the time, firm managers in the Jiangsu site were well informed about the new contractual form implemented in Zhejiang because of the geographical closeness of the sites and the vast transaction relations between the two regions. They expressed dissatisfaction over their profit-sharing or fixed-wage contractual arrangements during the investigation, and were demanding a move toward the fixed-payment contractual form.[7]

The Hubei site, on the other hand, is in an area where the TVE sector was not as developed as in the coastal regions. Not only did the community government refuse to withdraw its administrative intervention from TVE operations, the firm managers themselves with regard to their job-searching behavior seemed relatively more conservative than their counterparts in the coastal areas. Compared with the over two thirds in the other three sites, less than one fourth of sample managers in the Hubei site indicated that they wanted to become private owners, while over 40 percent still preferred appointment from the government in their future careers. However, since one third of the sample managers in the Hubei site chose market as their next job-searching channel, added to those who intended to be private firm owners, the sample managers who preferred non-government institutions came to over one half. We may expect more market or private oriented managers after 1994.

Firm managers are possibly not the only group of individuals who have been affected by the contractual form evolution. The competitive fixed-payment contract bidding has, at least nominally, opened the door to many individuals who would otherwise be excluded from the firm manager pool under other contractual arrangements. TVEs' ordinary staff, workers, or non-firm-employee residents who considered themselves qualified candidates and motivated by observable opportunities may participate in the contract competition. This will have a significant impact on the formation of the manager market since it breaks the monopolistic restriction on the firm manager pool set by the government. Given such opportunities, the rural Chinese who have been involved in TVE operations are becoming more market-oriented and risk-tolerant. For example, among 94 sample TVE workers who responded to the investigation survey, 52 (55 percent) said they yearned to have their own firms. 'Lack of investment financial sources' was ranked number one among the obstacles to prevent them from

---

[7] This may be among other reasons that gave impetus to the community governments in Jiangsu site to start the fixed-payment experiment after 1994. See appendix to this chapter.

realizing their dreams stated these 'potential' firm owners (84 percent of these 52 people selected this answer). Eighty percent of them said they would use bank loans to start their business venture if such loans were available to private entrepreneurs. Considering the long-standing tradition in rural China to hoard one's money and avoid borrowing, this observation reflected a significant change in rural culture and ideology.

The feedback effect on rural labor market induced by firm contractual form innovation echoed that on the manager market. Moving from fixed-wage to profit-sharing then to fixed-payment contracts extended firm managers' autonomy in labor decisions (Chapter 3). Under a fixed-wage contract, a firm manager usually had no power to determine worker hiring or dismissal. Whereas under a profit-sharing arrangement, the manager could hire workers but could not dismiss them. When the firm manager became an independent entrepreneur under the fixed-payment contract, he could dismiss workers for various reasons. As discussed in the above chapters, provision of employment opportunities to local residents was a major objective of community government leaders in the TVE movement. Therefore, local residents were protected against dismissal even when such protection undermined the productive efficiency of firms. Firm managers under fixed-wage or profit-sharing contracts were subject to such constraints, and forced to discriminate in favor of local residents in their labor decisions. However, things changed when the fixed-payment contract replaced other contractual arrangements. Driven by profit incentives, firm managers searched for means to reduce production costs. Dismissal of redundant employees and replacing higher cost local workers by lower cost but same quality non-resident workers were the common methods used as observed in the author's investigation.

As mentioned in Case Study 8 of Chapter 3, the new owners of the firm dismissed about half of the existing employees after the auction (total employees of the firm were reduced from 220 to 118). At the same time, part of the local employees was replaced by workers from other provinces. (Among 118 employees, 35 were non-resident workers who were hired after the auction to replace local workers. Hence, the firm actually dismissed more than 60 percent of its local employees.) As explained by the new owner,[8] 'local workers are lazy, do not want to take on heavy or dirty tasks, because they have the "iron-bowl". Most outside workers are hard working and do not complain about their working conditions. Moreover, local

---

[8] Informant M9.

workers are paid higher wages plus benefits, such as medical subsidy and retirement pension,[9] while outside workers enjoyed none of such benefits and they are willing to accept lower wage rates'. He emphasized: 'the former manager could not do this (dismissing local workers), because he is a party cadre, and had to be concerned about his political image. But I can. I don't care what people say.' In the restructured firm labor force, the remaining local employees were skilled or technically proficient, while the outside workers mainly took on manual tasks. When asked what the dismissed workers were doing, the township government official who accompanied me in the investigation said some of them got jobs in other local factories, some went to other regions looking for new jobs, some had their own business, and some others resumed household agricultural production. This is a good example of how the change in TVE contractual forms helped to restructure the rural labor force and promote cross-regional labor mobility, which are preconditions for an effectively functioning labor market.

Furthermore, as reported by the same township government official, local residents not only tolerated but also understood such changes. They agreed that the new owners of the firm had no obligation to support 'useless' redundant workers since this was *their* firm. If it is reasonable to 'eat' the government ('Chi Zhengfu' -- meaning relying on the government for easy money) in a collective enterprise, there is no reason to 'eat' a private firm owner.

However, it is still open to question which factor -- the changing contractual form or the local employment situation -- has a greater influence on firm labor decisions to hire non-resident workers. The reason that the residents in the Zhejiang site tolerated the dismissal and replacement of local employees is possibly because the sample township had reached full employment and was in labor supply shortage. It was quite easy for the dismissed local workers to find other jobs if they had certain skills or knowledge. The sample TVE labor constitution data (proportion of non-resident workers among employees) analysis reveals no systematic difference across contractual forms (Table 6.2). However, it does confirm a significant difference across research sites. The Zhejiang and Jiangsu sites hired more outside workers because they had a larger TVE sector and were

---

[9] As reported by the new owner, he continued to provide all the beneficial treatment enjoyed by local employees. However, whether or not this was required by the township government at the auction is unclear. Local workers were paid more than outside workers due to the differential working positions assigned.

in local labor supply shortage. It seems that, change in firm contractual form basically affects managerial decisions in redundant worker dismissal, some times in replacement of lower cost outside workers for expensive local workers. Incidentally, an expansion of outside worker employment is generally the result of local labor supply shortage. Based upon these observations, it is safe to argue that development of local TVEs will reduce local unemployment, thus encouraging the community government to adopt the fixed-payment organizational form. Also, the extent to which the community tolerates local labor dismissal is inversely related to local unemployment rate. Firms under a fixed-payment contract have more incentives and freedom to re-organize their labor force to minimize production costs. Such labor force reorganization has positive effects in promoting the development of a rural labor market.

Table 6.2 The Proportion of Non-resident Workers in Sample TVEs, 1993

	Proportion of Non-resident Worker in Employees (%)
By Contractual Form	
Fixed-wage	30
Profit-sharing	18
Fixed-payment	33
By Region	
Doumen Township, Zhejiang	31
Guohe Township, Hubei	5
Qingyunpu Township, Jiangxi	15
Huazhuang Township, Jiangsu	27

Source: Author's Survey, 1994.

According to the endogenous reform model, China's reform is a gradual process, one in which partial reform measures initiate a learning process that expands the horizon of all participants. Firms organized under heterogeneous institutional arrangements compete for more favorable organizational forms to strengthen market competitive power. This leads to a dynamic endogenous reform in institutional structure. As argued by Jefferson and Rawski (1994a, p.39):

> ....*competition forces participants to compare the merit of alternative institutional arrangements in exactly the same way that managers analyze the profit consequences of different product designs, machines, or compensation arrangements. Heterogeneity encourages a culture of envy in which firms and managers demand access to more attractive institutional possibilities to 'level the playing field' for their competition with rivals operating under different institutional arrangements.*

Although Jefferson and Rawski emphasize this kind of institutional arrangement 'envy' mainly existing between state-owned and non-state-owned enterprises, such 'envy' also exists across firms under different contractual forms and plays an important role in the diffusion of the more attractive contractual forms. As reported by the sample township government leader in the Zhejiang research site,[10] after several months of fixed rent leasing contractual experiment, many township or village enterprise managers, whose firms were not among the experimental group, complained about the 'unfair' treatment. They asked the community governments to grant them similar contractual arrangements, which resulted in the diffusion of leasing contract in the township. Before long, community government officials and firm managers from neighbor areas came to visit to learn the experience of the leasing contract implementation. The TVE managers in those areas had been informed of such innovation and demanded access to the same arrangement.

Therefore, an important feedback effect of the contractual form evolution is that, the institutional innovation benefits the 'early birds' and cause 'envy' in other firms afterwards. Inspired by such 'envy', the 'followers' will raise a strong voice to demand access to similar favorable institutional arrangements. The institutional innovation will thus diffuse from firm to firm, then from region to region, and cumulate into a significant reform in the institutional structure of the whole economy.[11]

---

[10] Informant L11.

[11] See Appendix.

TVE managers' attitudes towards ownership privatization in their firms and full marketization in the economy could be a convincing demonstration of how changing organizational forms affect the direction of further reform in this sector. The TVE managers' survey asked the firm manager to predict whether the firm's managerial situation would become 'better', 'the same', or 'worse' if (1) the firm is privatized; and (2) the economy is fully marketized. The responses of the 64 sample managers are summarized in Table 6.3 (Panel A and Panel B).[12] The first portion of the table demonstrates the cross-regional variation, while the second portion the cross-contractual-form variation.

Generally speaking, TVE managers are solid supporters of privatization and marketization. The majority of the sample managers expected improved or at least the same managerial situation after privatization or marketization. Among them, those currently under the profit-sharing arrangement most strongly supported privatization (78.8 percent predicted 'better', 18.2 percent predicted 'the same', while none expected 'worse'), reflecting the 'envy' toward a more attractive *i.e.*, fixed-payment, treatment. It is interesting to find that firm managers with a fixed-wage arrangement were least in favor of privatization and marketization (only one third of them predicted a better managerial situation after privatization or marketization). One explanation is that the few sample TVEs under fixed-wage managerial form in 1994 were either highly capital intensive firms with sizable fixed capital, or firms dependent on community governments in access to government controlled resources (say, soil for construction materials factory). Managing the operation of such firms might be beyond the ability of the managers acting as private owners or completely market-oriented independent agents.

---

[12] Sample managers' attitude toward full marketization might be a little biased against marketization. Because the sharp price fluctuation in input material markets severely affected many TVEs' operation during 1993 to 1994. Quite a number of firm managers and local officials attributed such negative effects to market liberalization.

Table 6.3 The Attitude of Sample TVE Managers toward Privatization and Marketization, 1994 (%)

Panel A Privatization

	Better	**The Same**	**Worse**
Sample	66.7	23.8	9.5
By Region			
Zhejiang	45.5	31.8	22.7
Hubei	88.9	11.1	0
Jiangxi	82.4	11.8	5.8
Jiangsu	66.7	33.3	0
By Contractual Form			
Fixed-wage	33.3	55.6	11.1
Profit-sharing	78.8	18.2	0
Fixed-payment	52.2	26.1	21.7

Panel B Marketization

	Better	**The Same**	**Worse**
Sample	52.4	36.5	11.1
By Region			
Zhejiang	27.3	45.5	27.3
Hubei	55.6	44.4	0
Jiangxi	76.5	23.5	0
Jiangsu	60.0	33.3	6.7
By Contractual Form			
Fixed-wage	33.3	44.4	22.2
Profit-sharing	57.6	36.3	3.0
Fixed-payment	56.5	26.1	17.4

Source: Author's Survey, 1994.

Sample TVE managers under fixed-payment contracts, especially private firm owners, complained about the discrimination against them in political and economic dimensions. Those who were then 'becoming' private owners felt the most pressure after the withdrawal of government assistance and exposure to severe market competition and discrimination. This might be the reason why a considerable portion of managers (around 20 percent) in this group thought privatization or marketization had a negative effect on their managerial situations. However, even those who selected the answer 'worse' to privatization or marketization in this group argued they would have chosen 'better' if the discrimination had been eliminated and they were treated as fairly as their rivals in non-private enterprises. This is an example of institutional 'envy' in another direction -- the demand for a 'level playing field' in the legal system, the taxation system, the political system, and so on for all firms no matter their ownership structure. This is extremely important because private enterprises as a sector in China's economy are still not strong enough to make their demand in the institutional reform sufficiently recognized by the government. These 'transferred' private firms have more influence on the reform decisions of local governments because of their pervious relations with the community government leaders and their role in governments' fiscal revenues.

This explanation might well be applicable to the response of firm managers in the Zhejiang site. The Zhejiang site was advanced in the adoption of the fixed-payment contractual form, but a high percentage of sample TVE managers responded negatively to privatization and marketization. Firm managers in the other three investigation sites all favored privatization and marketization. The firm managers in the Hubei site of all the others were the most enthusiastic supporters of privatization. This situation could be due to the fact that this site was lagging behind in the movement toward the fixed-payment contractual form.

As Jefferson and Rawski noted, the most profound feedback effect of the partial reform was the cumulated change in reform participants' attitude toward the reform objectives and strategies. As described above, the contractual form innovation had gradually changed rural Chinese people's behavior in job-searching, risk-tolerance, as well as the attitude toward private ownership. Unlike conditions in Eastern Europe and the former republics of the Soviet Union where ground level 'insiders' resisted the top-down privatization reform strategy, China's rural ground level reform participants -- the emerging class of professional firm managers and the community government leaders -- had become solid supporters of privatization. Almost every local community government official I interviewed in the investigation, -- from villagers' committee executive to secretary of county Communist Party Committee, -- asserted that privatization was the final destination of property rights reform in the TVE sector and the only way to accelerate further growth in TVEs. Despite the negative attitude of the central government, the ideological obstacle in privatization could be removed with the evolving institutions of firm organizations. This will become the most important foundation supporting the 'induced privatization'.

These observations on the feedback effects of TVE contractual form innovation help to depict the entire perspective of the mechanism of endogenous institutional reform in this sector. As illustrated in the last section, the partial reform of the central government intensifies market competition. The competition stimulates community governments and firm managers to search for more effective institutional arrangements in firm operation. Through institutional 'envy' among firms under heterogeneous contractual forms, more private and market-oriented institutional arrangements diffuse from firm to firm, region to region. When more and more firms are organized under more private and market oriented contractual forms, rural labor market and manager market develop, economic activity participants become more risk-tolerant and market supportive. Ideological obstacles that prevent a former socialist economy from privatizing its public properties are then be removed or reduced. The expanding class of rural private entrepreneurs may voice their demand for a more effective legal and political system that will provide a fair competition environment for firms under all kinds of institutional arrangements. This will push the central government ahead to take action to launch a fresh round of reforms, hopefully in legal and/or political fields. Through such endogenous interaction, the cumulative effect will gradually consolidate the foundation of the reform, and the economy will be restructured in a direction advocated by many western economists and specialists. This direction, however, will be reached via a path completely different from the one they suggested.

4. What Can We Learn?

This is a big question. Before we can answer this question, we must ask: is there anything to be learnt from China's experiences?

Despite the fact that China under reform has achieved spectacular economic growth and sustained the growth over a long period, many authors have ignored China, representing studies of 'transitional economics' that focus exclusively on Eastern Europe and the former republics of the Soviet Union. It is true that China has taken a unique path of economic reform that is entirely different from what was recommended by western economists and followed by the rest of the reforming world. Admittedly, China's economic achievements are overshadowed by her lack of progress in political reforms. However, as argued by Rawski (1995): '*since production, productivity, incomes, employment, and exports have increased under Chinese reform but, at least at the initial stages, decreased in other reforming economies, studies restricted to the latter are unlikely to produce viable generalizations about the transition process*' (p.1).

Many researchers in the field of China's economic reform agree that one of the most distinctive features of China's transition to a market economy has been the role played by TVEs. However, the success of TVEs is due greatly to a set of external conditions that are unique to China's reform practice, *i.e.*, China's transition as a whole is characterized by an early creation of product markets. The product market had existed for a prolonged period without well-developed markets for factors of production or assets (Naughton, 1994b). Given imperfections both in market and in government, the community public ownership of collective TVEs turned out to be a fairly robust ownership form that made collective TVEs thrive better in competition with state-owned enterprises and to private enterprises. As demonstrated in this book, TVEs are an effective adaptation to such an 'imperfect' external environment. Through this special institutional arrangement, TVEs gave full play to the comparative advantages of community government leaders and firm managers, hence effectively promoted rural economic development and prevented national production from decline. Moreover, a continuous though gradual innovation in TVEs contractual forms in response to the development in the market system reduced social conflicts that are generally associated with instantaneous institutional reforms. As a result, obstruction in property rights privatization can be removed to a great extent without severe shock to social stability.

Insofar as the whole market system achieves considerable development, however, the special external conditions will be eliminated, the robustness of TVE community public ownership will open to question. As pointed out by Naughton (1994b, p.270):

> *Given the existence of these preconditions, local government ownership of firms operating in a predominantly market environment was an alternative to early privatization. It is conceivable that such an option was administratively less costly than early privatization, permitting avoidance of difficult and complex problems at an early stage of reform, thus allowing time and managerial energy to be concentrated on move directly productive activities. If this analysis is correct, TVEs will be less important in the future. As markets for assets and factors of production become more complete, the advantage of TVEs will fade.*

In other words, community public ownership of TVEs is an alternative option to early privatization. It is effective only under certain special external conditions, thus not a general lesson that can be learned by every reforming or developing economy.

However, the success of collective TVEs does provide a general lesson to reform designers: imposing a top-down privatization in the early stage of the reform is possibly not the 'only sure strategy' that may lead to success, and *'economists' insistence on clear enforcement of property rights and contracts as a pre-requisite to a functioning market may be putting the cart before the horse'* (Rapaczynski, 1996, p.95-96).

A number of authors have noted the different roles the Chinese central government and the local community governments have played in property rights reform (McMillan, 1994; Jefferson and Rawski, 1994a). The commitment of property rights reform came not from any inherent strength of the government, but from the early and cumulative reform success and the initiative of grass roots economic agents. The central government's role often was to permit happening changes passively rather than to initiate such changes. This is not a surprising observation, however. According to institutional economics, economic agents belonging to different interest groups differ significantly in their attitude toward a given institutional innovation, because the cost-benefit calculation correlated to the innovation for one group may not be identical to that for the another.

In China's case, community governments benefit directly from a privatization-oriented contractual form innovation through improved firm efficiency and transaction cost reduction. At the same time, rapid local economic growth and substantial income increase wins high political reputation for the community government leaders too. As described in Chapter 2, government leaders at the ground level are less subject to constraints in political stabilization and ideological control, and are not responsible for social problems such as rural unemployment outside of their jurisdiction. Therefore, if the privatization-oriented contractual form innovation brings about some 'negative' effects in the political or ideological dimensions, it is unlikely that a community government leader will be forced to change his decision to adopt the innovations. If the social problem caused by the innovation (say, labor dismissal) does not severely affect economic activities and residents' lives in the community, the community government leaders will mostly view such problems a negligible cost in pursuing the innovation.

On the other hand, however, the central government stands on a diametrical standpoint. In order to preserve with the 'basic socialist principles', the central government will view any possible derogation in public ownership and socialist ideology associated with the privatization-oriented firm contractual form innovation as a more severe threat to the political stabilization and the rule of the communist government. A vast labor dismissal is not a situation the central government prefers to see either. It will hesitate to support a fixed-payment innovation should it be unavoidably related to sizable labor dismissal. Compared with this kind of cost, the economic benefit brought about by privatization-oriented contractual form innovation would be too weak and indirect for the central government to enthusiastically support the innovation.

Bardhan pointed out (1989b), in any economy,

> it is sometimes important to distinguish between the top political leadership, which takes general political decisions, and the hierarchy of agents, the bureaucracy, which is supposed to implement those decisions. The process of implementation often generates various kinds of rental income which, to a significant extent, accrues to the bureaucracy (and sometimes to the lower functionaries of the ruling party), and the latter may form a pressure group to secure this income flow, with goals that are much narrower than those set by the state elite (top political leadership) (p.15).

In China's case, the deviation and the pressures from the lower functionaries propelled the reform process in a direction that the central government did not intend to go. This is perhaps the most fundamental difference between an 'exogenous reform' and an 'endogenous reform'. In the case of privatization imposed in a top-down fashion, the reformers in the central government have to design a series of policy measures to overcome resistance from the lower functionaries and the millions of grassroots agents. However, when privatization is 'induced' through a bottom-up endogenous interaction, instead of being obstacles, the lower functionaries and grass roots agents become the catalysts to form strong pressure groups to determine the reform objectives and strategies.

If we agree that in the long run privatization is the only way to ensure that firms are fully subject to market disciplines, and that is the only way to prevent politicians and bureaucrats from intervention in the firm decisions in politically tempting but economically unproductive ways (McMillan, 1994), we do not have to agree that the instantaneous top-down privatization is the 'only sure' path to reach the destination.

> *China's gradual and partial path of industrial reform was not determined by a few top officials. Industrial reform evolved from sequences of decisions made by tens of thousands of enterprises and millions of administrators, managers, and workers. The large number of participants and the extended duration of the reform process, which gave people ample time to evaluate alternatives and reconsider their initial views, eventually built a constituency for market-directed change that was far stronger than any official announcement could have produced. This process is very different from western parliamentary democracy, but it has produced a durable reform constituency that easily rebuffed high-level efforts to roll back reform in the wake of the inflation scare and political repression in 1989* (Jefferson and Rawski, 1994, p.42).

China's reform, as believed by many observers, can never be reversed to restore its original system. No one pursuing an essential reform should ever forget this lesson from China's experiences.

Despite the assertions made by many western economists, China's experiences have provided an obvious lesson that partial and gradual reform of public sectors *can* produce substantial results and improvement in financial performance in an economy. However, it does not mean that other reforming economies should rush to embrace Chinese strategies. Just as early privatization may be useful in some circumstances, it is not essential to the reform enterprises in every country. The superiority of China's recent economic performance over that of its counterparts in Eastern Europe and the former republics of the Soviet Union does not mean that Chinese-style reform strategy would necessarily do better in these countries (Naughton, 1994b).

If privatization and the restructure of the economic system are the final destination of the reform in ex-socialist economies, the top-down sweeping privatization could be described as a short path, and the reformers who take this path must climb directly to pass over the peak of the mountain. In contrast, the bottom-up spontaneous privatization seems a winding road to lead to the same destination. This path is much longer and sometimes heads in a direction seemingly opposite to the final destination. It is really difficult to judge which path is better.

The reformers who take the short path have to prepare to overcome many difficulties and remove numerous obstacles. They must be strong enough to bear the exhausting, perhaps painful, process of a climb, (sometimes even to take the risk of falling headlong half way). If the climber is capable and lucky enough to overcome all these obstacles without too much trouble, then he will reach the destination in a shorter period. In contrast, those who take the winding road can avoid severe obstructions on the way and reduce the painful efforts of quick climbing. However, patience and willingness to take a prolonged period to accomplish the proposed objectives will be necessary to success. Which path the reformer should choose solely depends on the existing conditions of the economy, and to what extent the economy is able to bear reform disturbance. No unique solution exists which is optimal to every reforming economy, though some authors think China's gradual reform model is less radical but more viable (Oi, 1992).

In the reforming practice, the problem in many transitional and developing economies is perhaps that much faith was put on the pursuit of *ideal* market and government institutions, but not much attention was paid to the reality of the given *existing* institutional environment (Che and Qian, 1998). Experiences from China's TVEs demonstrate that the reforming countries need to fully consider the environments, in which alternative organizational forms differing from those found in matured market economies may actually function better. In other words, '*The transition cannot be planned, because what will work cannot be anticipated. Reformers can design new institutions for the transition economy, ... but the reformers must be willing to accept novel solutions that do not conform to preconceived views*' (Mcmillan, 1994, p.12). This is possibly the most important lesson we can learn from the reform experiences of China's rural enterprises. Governments committed to reforming their former socialist economies may have to pay more attention in their policies to create a more market-friendly and fairly competitive economic environment before pursuing a sweeping property rights privatization.

The last part of the book addresses an important issue, which is closely related to the privatization-oriented contractual form innovation and may deserve discussions in depth, *i.e.*, the private embezzlement of community public properties. This is a problem of the 'induced privatization' that may incur much criticism from the instantaneous privatization advocates.

As described in Chapter 3, in some cases the (competitive) bidding for leasing contract or in firm auction was only a nominal procedure. Many transactions were in fact completed through personal negotiation between community government leaders and potential buyer(s) or lease-holder(s). During such procedures, the publicly owned community properties of the collective TVEs could be channeled into private pockets in a variety of ways. As the *de facto* owner of the firm, the community government leaders had the power to select the buyer or leaseholder in a discriminating way, sometimes even neglecting economic rules. Under such circumstances, firm buyers or leaseholders were most likely 'insiders', such as current managers, local officials,[13] or their relatives and friends (Putterman, 1994). As I learned in the investigation, a township (a township in the neighborhood of the Zhejiang research site) government turned down a combined bid of four firm employees in an auction, but sold the firm to its current manager. The accepted bid was only three-quarters of the combined bid (around 0.6 million yuan vs. 0.8 million yuan).[14]

Another problem arises in that assessing enterprise properties is a difficult task. In some cases the value of firm properties was determined in an arbitrary way. The buyer(s) thus experience a large windfall at the expense of the communities. The rent determination in leasing sometimes causes problems too. A township official in the Zhejiang site complained that certain village leaders set the rent for a firm's fixed capital at the prevailing bank interest rate without charging an appropriate depreciation fund. Firm leaseholders were thus encouraged to maximize personal income by abusing firm equipment.[15]

A lack of monitors to represent the interests of all the community residents, not merely the 'insiders', has made the problem even more

---

[13] After 1993, in some areas local government officials were prohibited to become firm buyers, leaseholders, or responsibility contractors unless he/she gave up his/her position in the government.

[14] I was unable to confirm this information, especially the exact bids the two sides offered. However, I believe such a thing did happen in the procedure of fixed-payment contract implementation. Similar stories were reported in various areas during my investigation.

[15] Informant L12. However, he admitted that increasing the rent to include depreciation would drive away potential leaseholders, because many of leasing firms were small and not very profitable as indicated in Chapter 3.

severe. If such private embezzlement of community public property intensifies the already existing friction between firm managers and ordinary firm employees, or between community residents and members of local political *elite*, it may become a critical obstacle to firm contractual form innovation and property rights privatization in the TVE sector. Problems in measurement and assessment are easy to solve for they are technical problems. However, administrative disturbance caused by unsupervised political power is a problem beyond the reach of economics.

We are facing the crucial problem of political reform, just as China is.

5. Appendix

When revising this book, I conducted a follow-up investigation in December 1998 on the contractual form transition of TVEs between 1994 (when I conducted my original field investigation) and 1998. I sent survey forms to four of my original field investigation sample townships and 64 sample firms. Three sample townships (Doumen Township of Zhejiang Province, Huazhuang Township of Jiangsu province, and Qingyunpu Township of Jiangxi Province) and 57 sample firms responded to this investigation and returned the survey forms. The survey results are summarized in Table 6.A1, Table 6.A2, and Table 6.A3.[16] Based upon the information acquired in this follow-up investigation, we have some interesting findings.

5.1 Diffusion of Fixed-payment Contractual Form

From Table 6.A1 and Table 6.A2 we may observe a significant diffusion of the fixed-payment contractual form in sample firms and sample townships after 1994. Table 6.A1 summarizes the survey results from 50 sample firms. The proportion of firms under fixed-payment contracts in this sample increased from 37 percent in 1994 to 58 percent in 1998. The Huazhuang Township of Jiangsu Province moved the fastest among others in this transition. In 1994, none of sample firms in this township was under a leasing contract or auctioned to private owners. In 1998, however, 60 percent of its sample firms now belonged to the fixed-payment category. In

---

[16] Among 57 responded sample firms, 7 closed down during the period of 1994 to 1998. Therefore, the number of firms in this follow-up investigation sample is 50 rather than 57 after dropping these 7 firms.

the Qingyunpu Township of Jiangxi province, seven of my original sample firms closed down after 1994. Of the remaining thirteen firms, seven (54 percent) were under fixed-payment contracts in 1998, increased from four firms (31 percent) in 1994.

Table 6.A1 Contractual Structure Transition in Sample Firms, 1994-1998

	Fixed-wage (%)	Profit-sharing (%)	Fixed-payment (%)
Sample (50 firms)			
1994	26	38	36
1998	24	18	58
Doumen of Zhejiang (22 firms)			
1994	23	14	64
1998	27	14	60
Huazhuang of Jiangsu (15 firms)			
1994	20	80	0
1998	33	7	60
Qingyunpu of Jiangxi (13 firms)			
1994	38	31	31
1998	8	38	54

Source: Author's survey, 1998

Table 6.A2 summarizes survey results from sample townships. In this survey, sample townships reported the contractual structure of all township and village enterprises in their jurisdiction. Similar survey reports from several sample villages are also included. In Huazhuang Township, we observe the same fast movement toward a fixed-payment contract. In 1994, only 25 percent of its 389 TVEs were under fixed-payment contracts. By 1998, this ratio had increased to 90 percent. In two sample villages of this township, Friendship Village and Jiahe Village, we observe similar contractual form transition between 1994 and 1998. In 1998, the fixed-payment contract became the dominant form (100 percent and 82 percent of the total firms in the two villages respectively), though none of the firms in these two villages was under such contract only four years ago. In the

Qingyunpu Township of Jiangxi Province, we note a similar phenomenon.[17]
A sample village, Huangxi Village in this township demonstrated the same
movement. Fixed-payment firms accounted for 44 percent of the total firms
in that village in 1998, which was 17 percent higher than that in 1994.

**Table 6.A2 Contractual Structure Transition in Sample Townships,
1994-1998**

	Fixed-wage (%)	Profit-sharing (%)	Fixed-payment (%)
Doumen of Zhejiang			
1994	10	23	68
1998	9	23	68
Paogu Village			
1994	0	0	100
1998	0	20	80
Huazhuang of Jiangsu			
1994	9	66	25
1998	6	4	90
Friendship Village			
1994	0	100	0
1998	0	0	100
Jiahe Village			
1994	9	91	0
1998	18	0	82
Qingyunpu of Jiangxi			
1994	15	55	30
1998	8	38	54
Huangxi Village			
1994	64	9	27
1998	56	0	44

Source: Author's survey, 1998.

---

[17] The data may be not as reliable as that of Huazhuang Township, because
Qingyunpu Township government only reported contractual status of township
enterprises while village enterprises were excluded from their returned survey
report.

5.2 Stagnation in the Zhejiang Investigation Site

From Table 6.A1 and Table 6.A2, we observe an interesting phenomenon: the stagnation in firm contractual form transition in the Zhejiang investigation site. As demonstrated in this book, the Doumen Township of Zhejiang Province was the first one among other sample townships to move toward the fixed-payment contractual form before 1994. However, after four years, we do not observe any further transition in this direction. From Table 6.A2 we can see that the percentage of TVEs under three contractual forms were exactly the same in 1998 as they were in 1994. From its 22 sample firms, one firm terminated its leasing contract and resumed township government direct management in 1995.[18] This resulted in a declined share of fixed-payment firms (from 64 percent to 60 percent) and increased share of fixed-wage firms (from 23 percent to 27 percent) in Table 6.A1.

5.3 Trend of Privatization

As predicted by the endogenous reform model illustrated in Section 2 of Chapter 6, contractual form innovation may finally lead to an 'induced privatization' in the TVE sector. The survey results of the follow-up investigation have confirmed such a prediction.

In Table 6.A3, we find privatization to be the definite trend after 1994 whether with the entire fifty firms sample or in each sub-sample of the three townships. From the fifty sample firms, only six were private firms in 1994 (either initiated by private owners or collective firms auctioned to private owners before 1994). However, thirteen sample firms were auctioned off and became private firms between 1994 and 1998. This resulted in 38 percent of the sample firms belonging to the 'private firm' category. Among other sample townships, the Huazhuang Township of Jiangsu Province once again had the most remarkable movement. In 1994, no sample firm in that township was privately owned. By 1998, 53 percent of its sample firms had changed status into 'private firms'. We observe similar transitions in the Zhejiang and the Jiangxi samples, though not as manifest as in the Huazhuang Township.

---

[18] See section 4 of this appendix for details.

Table 6.A3 The Privatization Trend in Sample TVEs, 1994-1998

	1994 Number of private firm (as % of total firms)	1998 Number of private firm (as % of total firms)
Sample (50 firms)	6 (12%)	19 (38%)
Doumen of Zhejiang (22 firm)	4 (18%)	6 (27%)
Huazhuang of Jiangsu (15 firms)	0 (0%)	8 (53%)
Qingyunpu of Jiangxi (13 firms)	2 (15%)	5 (38%)

Source: Author's survey, 1998.

If we take the whole Huazhuang Township as a sample, we find an even more fundamental transition toward privatization in its TVEs. In 1994, only 24 percent (94 out of 389 firms in total) of its TVEs were privately owned firms. Whereas in 1998, however, this ratio increased to 83 percent (401 out of 484 firms in total). Two sample villages in this township had the very same remarkable transition too. Both Friendship Village and Jiahe Village had no private firm in 1994. Between 1994 and 1998, Friendship Village auctioned 9 of its 12 village enterprises, while Jiahe Village auctioned 9 of its 11 firms. Therefore, private firms accounted for 75 percent and 81 percent respectively in these two villages in 1998.

5.4 Persistence of the Fixed-wage Managerial Form

Another interesting finding in the investigation is the persistent existence of the fixed-wage managerial form.[19] Far from disappearing as one might expect, fixed-wage firms remained nearly constant between 1994 and 1998 as we see from Table 6.A1 and Table 6.A2. In some cases, this share was

---

[19] Throughout the whole book, I classify firms under community government's direct management (no responsibility contract signed) and share-cooperation firms into this category.

even higher in 1998 than in 1994. A closer look reveals firms that were still under the fixed-wage managerial form in 1998 generally belonged to two categories. One category consisted of large and very profitable firms with an enormous fixed capital investment. In most cases, such firms were re-organized into share-cooperation enterprises. Community government controlled the majority of firm shares and had a dominant influence in firm manager appointment and firm operation decisions. Community government also claimed the biggest share of firm profits.

Another category of fixed-wage firms were made up of either resources-intensive firms (such as construction materials factory that uses land/soil to produce bricks) or firms with excessive debts. A special example is observed in the Doumen Township of Zhejiang Province. A previously leasing township firm realized that the projected highway construction in that region would take half of the land occupied by the factory. The township government then approved the leaseholder's request to terminate his leasing contract in 1995. Since the factory was not very profitable, the township government had no incentive to relocate the factory but maintained its operation under government's direct management. They expected to close it down when the highway construction reached the factory site.

5.5 Conclusions

The observations revealed in this follow-up investigation strongly support the model predictions demonstrated in this book. With the development of the whole market system, firm contractual structure will converge to the fixed-payment form. Such transition will then lead to 'induced privatization' in TVE sector.

In the late 1990s, product markets and most production factor markets have sufficiently developed. Community government has lost its comparative advantage in external management in most TVEs' daily operation. For this reason, the profit-sharing contractual form became a much less important managerial form after 1994, while fixed-payment took the dominant position in TVE contractual structure. However, the absence or underdevelopment of markets for certain kinds of production inputs, such as natural resources and financial capital, may have been the major obstacle to transition toward privatization. Public ownership of natural resources, land in particular, made the community government a monopolist with regard to access to those resources. Due to lack of market prices for such resources, it is difficult for a community government to set an appropriate rent scale to lease out or auction off resources-intensive firms. On the other hand, lack of capital market is probably the crucial reason why community governments have been unable to get rid of firms with excessive debts through lease or auction but, rather, bear such burdens by themselves. When all firms that are not subject to market development constraint in its jurisdiction have been transferred into fixed-payment firms, a community government will have no way to pursue contractual form innovation for other firms that are still subject to such constraint under current circumstances. Instead, they will have to wait for a new round of development in production factor markets, so that they may take further action in such a transition. This seems to be the reason why do we observe fast transition in the Jiangsu site with stagnation in further transition in the Zhejiang site.

However, when market development reaches a certain level, other factors may outperform market development as the dominant force in determining firm contractual structure. The re-organization of large and very profitable TVEs into share-cooperative enterprises and the direct control of community government over such enterprises are a typical example of such a situation. In such cases, the revenue consideration of the community government becomes the determinant factor in firm managerial form selection.

Bibliography

Alchian, A.A., and Demsetz, H. 1972. 'Production, Information costs, and Economic Organization', *American Economic Review*, 62: pp. 777-795.

-------- 1973. 'The Property Rights Paradigm', *The Journal of Economic History*, 33: pp. 16-27.

Amemiya, T. 1985. *Advanced Econometrics*, Harvard University Press: Cambridge, MA.

Ash, R. 1991. 'The Peasant and the State', *The China Quarterly*, 127(September): pp. 493-526.

Bardhan, P. ed. 1989a. *The Economic Theory of Agrarian Institutions*, Oxford University Press, Oxford.

-------- 1989b. 'Alternative Approaches to the Theory of Institutions in Economic Development', in Bardhan, P. ed. *The Economic Theory of Agrarian Institutions*, Oxford University Press, Oxford.

Barzel, Y. 1989. *Economic Analysis of Property Rights*, Cambridge University Press: New York.

Basu, K. 1984. *The Less Developed Economy*, Basil Blackwell.

Berle, A. and Means, G. 1968. *The Modern Corporation and Private Property*, New York: Harcourt, Brace and World.

Binswanger, H.P. and Ruttan, V. 1978. *Induced Innovation: Technology, Institutions and Development*, The Johns Hopkins University Press, Baltimore.

Blanchard, O. J., Dornbusch, R., Krugman, P., Layard, R., Summers, L. 1992. *Reform in Eastern Europe*, MIT press, Cambridge, MA.

Bolton, P. 1995. 'Privatization and the Separation of Ownership and Control: Lessons from Chinese Enterprises Reform', *Economics of Transition*, 3(1): pp. 1-12.

Brada, J. 1996. 'Privatization Is Transition -- Or Is It?' *Journal of Economic Perspectives*, 10(2): pp. 67-86.

Bromley, D. 1989. *Economic Interests and Institutions*, Basil Blackwell: New York.

Brus, W. 1989. 'Evolution of the Communist Economic System: Scope and Limits', in Nee, V. and Stark, D. eds., 1989. *Remaking the Economic*

Institutions of Socialism: China and Eastern Europe, Stanford University, Stanford, CA.

Brus, W. and Laski, K. 1989. *From Marx to the Market: Socialism in Search of an Economic System*, Oxford University Press, Oxford.

Buchanan, J.M., Tollison, R.D., and Tullock, G. eds. 1980. *Toward A Theory of the Rent-Seeking Society*, Texas A & M University Press, TX.

Byrd, W. 1989. 'Plan and Market in the Chinese Economy: A Simple General Equilibrium Model', *Journal of Comparative Economics*, 13(2): pp. 177-204.

-------- 1990. 'Entrepreneurship, Capital, and Ownership', in Byrd, W. and Lin, Q. eds. *China's Rural Industry*.

-------- 1991. *The Market Mechanism and Economic Reform in China*, M.E.Sharpe, New York.

-------- ed. 1992. *Chinese Industrial Firms Under Reform*, Oxford University Press, New York.

Byrd, W. and Gelb, A. 1990. 'Why Industrialize? The Incentives for Rural Community Governments', in Byrd, W. and Lin, Q. eds. *China's Rural Industry: Structure, development, and Reform*, Oxford University Press: London

Byrd, W. and Lin, Q. eds. 1990. *China's Rural Industry: Structure, Development, and Reform*, Oxford University Press: London.

Chang, C. and Wang, Y. 1994. 'The Nature of the Township-Village Enterprises', *Journal of Comparative Economics*, 19 (3 December), pp. 434-452

Chang, P. K. 1949. *Agriculture and Industrialization: The Adjustments that Take Place as an Agricultural Country is Industrialized*, Harvard University Press, Cambridge, MA.

-------- 1991. *Industrialization of Agricultural Countries*, [Nongyeguo Gongyehua Wenti -- in Chinese], Hunan Press, China.

-------- 1992. ed. *New Development Economics*, [Xin Fazhan Jingjixue -- in Chinese], Henan Press, China.

Che, J. 1995. 'How does the Governance Structure Emerge: Conglomerate Effect and Credible Commitment', Working Paper, Department of Economics, Stanford University, Stanford, CA.

Che, J. and Qian, Y. 1998. 'Institutional Environment, Community Government, and Corporate Governance: Understanding China's Township-Village Enterprises', *Journal of Law, Economics, and Organization*, 14 (1 April), pp. 1-23.

Chen, K. et al. 1988. 'Productivity Change in Chinese Industry: 1953-1985', *Journal of Comparative Economics,* 12: pp. 570-591.

Chen, J., Deng, Y., Xue, Y., and Liu, J. 1992. *The Transformation and Development in Rural China,* [Zhongguo Nongcun de Biange yu Fazhan -- in Chinese], Guangdong Higher Education Publisher, China.

Chen, J. and Han, J. eds. 1993. *Rural China's Path of Industrialization,* [Zhongguo Nongcun Gongyehua Daolu -- in Chinese]. China Social Science Press, China.

Chen, P. 1994. 'China's challenge to Economic Orthodoxy: Asian Reform as an Evolutionary, Self-organized Process', *China Economic Review,* 4(2): pp. 137-142.

Chen, W. 1993. 'Rebuild the Development Advantage of TVEs in Pearl Delta in the Reliant upon Technical Progress', [Yikao Keji JinBu, Zaizao Zhujiang Sanjiaozhou Xiangzhen Qiye Gongye Fazhan Xinyoushi -- in Chinese], *Linnan Academic Journal,* 93-2. China.

Chow, G. 1987. *The Chinese Economy,* 2nd ed. World Scientific Publishing Co. Singapore.

-------- 1994. *Understanding China's Economy,* World Scientific Publishing Co. Singapore.

Clague, C. and Rausser, G. eds. 1992. *The Emergence of Market Economies in Eastern Europe,* Basil Blackwell: Cambridge, MA.

Coase, R.H. 1937. 'The Nature of the Firm', *Economica,* 4: pp. 386-405.

-------- 1960. 'The Problem of Social Cost', *Journal of Law and Economics,* 3: pp. 1-44.

-------- 1988. *The Firm, The Market, and the Law.* Chicago University Press: Chicago.

-------- 1992. 'The Institutional Structure of Production', *American Economic Review,* 82(4): pp. 713-720.

Committee of Economic System Reform, Taizhou Prefecture of ZhejiangProvince, 1994, *Property Rights Reform: Policies, Practice, and Searching,* [Chanquan Gaige: Zhengce, Shijian, Tansuo -- in Chinese], Zhejiang, China.

Cook, L. 1996. 'Trade Finance, Capital-market Imperfections, and Corporate Investment: the Case of Russia', Working Paper, Department of Economics, University of California, Berkeley, CA.

Cui, Z. 1994. 'Can Privatization Solve the Problem of Soft Budget Constraints?' in Milor, V. and Boulder, C. eds. *Changing Political Economies: Privatization in Post- Communist and Reforming Communist States,* Lynne Rienner: pp. 213-227.

Dahlman, C.J. 1979. 'The Problem of Externality', *Journal of Law and Economics,* 22: pp. 141-162.

Davis, L. E. and North, D. 1971. *Institutional Change and American Economic Growth,* Cambridge University Press: Cambridge.

Dealessi, L. 1980. 'The Economics of Property Rights: A Review of the Evidence', *Research in Law and Economics,* 2: pp. 1-47.

de Janvry, A. 1973. 'A Socioeconomic Model of Induced Innovations for Argentine Agricultural Development', *Quarterly Journal of Economics* 87: pp. 410-435.

Demsetz, H. 1967. 'Towards A theory of Property Rights', *American Economic Review,* 57(2), May: pp. 347-359.

-------- 1983. 'The Structure of Ownership and the Theory of the Firm', *Journal of Law and Economics,* 26(June): pp. 375-390.

-------- 1988. *Ownership, Control, and the Firm,* Vol.1, Blackwell. Oxford.

Dernberger, R. 1993. 'The Drive for Economic Modernization and Growth: Performance and Trends', in Kau, M. and Marsh, S. eds. *China in the Era of Deng Xiaoping: A Decade of Reform,* M. E. Sharpe, New York.

Decisions (1993). 'China's Central Government Decisions on Resolving Several Problems Concerning the Establishment of A Socialist Market System', *Renmin Ribao* [People's Daily], November 17, p.1.

Dollar, D. 1990. 'Economic Reform and Allocative Efficiency in China's State-owned Industry', *Economic Development and Cultural Change,* 34: pp. 89-105.

Dong, X. and Putterman, L. 1995. 'China's Rural Industry and monoposony: An Exploration', Working Paper, University of Winnipeg, Canada.

Du, H. 1990. 'Causes of Rapid Rural Industrial Development', in Byrd, W. and Lin, Q. eds. *China's Rural Industry.*

-------- 1992. *Research on Rural China's Industrialization,* China Price Press, China.

Eswaran, M. and Kotwal, A 1985. 'A Theory of Contractual Structure in Agriculture', *American Economic Review,* 75(3), June: pp. 352-367

Eugene, F. and Jensen, M. 1983. 'Separation of Ownership and Control', *Journal of Law and Economics,* 26(June): pp. 301-326.

Experiment Office, Agricultural Research Center of the State Council, 1989, *Property Rights, Circulation, Scale: An Research on China's Rural Land System,* [Chanquan, Liuzhuan, Guimo: Zhongguo Nongcun Tudi Zhidu Yanjiu -- in Chinese], China.

Fan, G. 1994. 'Dual-track Transition in China', *Economic Policy,* December: pp. 99-122.

-------- 1995. 'On the New Norm in Public Revenue and Expenditure: Studies on some Cases regarding the 'Non-standard Revenue' in China's Townships' [Lun Gonggong Shouzhi de Xinguifan -- in Chinese], *Jingji Yanjiu, 1995-6.*

Fei, X. 1989. *Rural Development in China: Prospects and Retrospect,* University of Chicago Press: Chicago.

Findlay, C., Watson, A., and Wu, H.X. eds. 1994. *Rural Enterprises in China,* St. Martin's Press, New York.

Fischer, S., Sahay, R., and Vegh, C. 1996. 'Stabilization and Growth in Transition Economies: the Early Experience', *Journal of Economic Perspectives,* 10(2): pp. 45-66.

Friedman, E., Pickowicz, P., and Selden, M. 1991. *Chinese Village, Socialist State,* Yale University Press, New Haven.

Furubotn, E. and Pejovich, S. 1972. 'Property Rights and Economic Theory: A Survey of Recent Literature', *Journal of Economic Literature,* 10(4), December: pp. 1137-1162.

-------- eds. 1974. *The Economics of Property Rights,* Ballinger Publishing Co., Cambridge, MA.

Furubotn, E. and Richter, R. eds. 1991. *The New Institutional Economics,* Texas A & M University Press: College Station, TX.

-------- 1991. 'The New Institutional Economics: An Assessment', Chapter 1 of Furubotn, E. and Richter, R. eds. *The New Institutional Economics,* Texas A & M University Press: College Station, TX.

Goldman, M. I. 1994. *Lost Opportunity: Why Economic Reforms in Russia Have not Worked,* Norton, New York.

Granick, D. 1990. *Chinese State Enterprises: A Regional Property Rights Analysis,* Chicago University Press, Chicago.

Greene, W. 1990. *Econometric Analysis,* Macmillan Publishing Company: New York, NY.

Griffin, K. ed. 1984. *Institutional Reform and Economic Development in the Chinese Countryside,* Macmillan: London.

Grossman, S. and Hart, O. 1986. 'The Costs and Benefits of Ownership: A Theory of Vertical and Lateral Integration', *Journal of Political Economy,* 94(4): pp. 691-719.

Groves, T., Hong, Y., McMillan, J., and Naughton, B. 1994. 'Autonomy and Incentives in Chinese State Enterprises', *Quarterly Journal of Economics,* 109(1): pp. 1-27.

Gu, Y. 1994. 'An theoretical Thinking on the Practice of Property Rights Reform in Collective TVEs' [Dui Xiangzhen Jiti Qiye Chanquan Zhidu Gaige Shijian de Lilun Sikao -- in Chinese], Paper presented at the *International Conference on the Property Rights Reform in China's TVEs,* Hangzhou, China.

Guangdong Province Labor Bureau, 1993. 'An Analysis on the Labor System Reform in Pearl Delta' [Zhujiang Shajiaozhou Laodong Zhidu Gaige Tantao -- in Chinese], *Linnan Academic Journal,* 1993-3, China.

Han, J. 1994, *An Over-century Difficult Problem: The Transfer of Chinese Agricultural Labor Force* [Kuashiji de Nanti -- Zhongguo Nongye Laodongli Zhuanyi -- in Chinese], Shanxi Jingji Press, China.

Han, J. and Zhang, Q. eds. 1993. *China's Rural Share-cooperative Economy: Theories, Practice, and Policies* [Zhongguo Nongcun Gufen Hezuo Jingji: Lilun, Shijian, Zhengce -- in Chinese], Economic Management Press, China.

Hare, D. and West, L. 1995. 'The Role of Township and Village Enterprises in China's Rural Economic Development', Working Paper, Contemporary China Center, Reed College, Portland, OR.

Hart, O. 1988. 'Incomplete Contracts and the Theory of the Firm', *Journal of Law, Economics, and Organization,* 4 (Spring).

Hart, O., and Moore, J. 1990. 'Property Rights and the Nature of the Firm', *Journal of Political Economy,* 98(6): pp. 1119-1158.

Hayami, Y. and Otsuka, K. 1993. *The Economics of Contract Choice: An Agrarian Perspective,* Oxford University Press: Oxford.

Hayami, Y. and Ruttan, V. 1971. *Agricultural Development: An International Perspective,* The John Hopkins University Press, Baltimore.

-------- 1993. 'Induced Technical and Institutional Change Evaluation and Reassessment: Two Chapters', Economic Development Center, Department of Economics and Department of Agricultural and Applied Economics, University of Minnesota.

Hayek, F. 1945. 'The Use of Knowledge in Society', *American Economic Review,* 35(September): pp. 519-530.

-------- 1967. *Studies in Philosophy, Politics, and Economics,* Routledge and Kegan: London.

He, R. 1994. 'The Development and the Property Rights Reform in Zhejiang TVEs' [Zhejiang Sheng Xiangzhen Qiye Fazhan yu Chanquan Zhidu de Gaige -- in Chinese], Paper Presented at the *International*

Conference on the Property Rights Reform in China's TVEs, Hangzhou, China.

Hsiao, C., Nugent, J., Perrigne, I., and Qiu, J.C. 1998. 'Shares versus Residual Claimant Contracts: The Case of Chinese TVEs', *Journal of Comparative Economics,* 26 (2 June), pp. 317-337

Hu, T. 1989. 'Factors Determining the Ownership Structure of Township and Village Enterprises and Its Tendency', in Cheng, J. and Xia, D. eds. *Studying Models of Township and Village Enterprises* [Xiangzhen Qiye Moshi Yanjiu -- in Chinese], China Social Science Press, Beijing, China.

Huang, M. 1993. 'The Transition of the Dual Economy and the Transform of Rural Labor: Examples from Suzhou, Wuxi, and Changzhou Districts'[Eryuan Jingji Zhuanbian yu Nongcun Laodongli Zhuanhua -- Yi Su-Xi-Chang Diqu Weili de Yanjiu -- in Chinese], *East China Normal University Journal,* Shanghai, China.

Huang, P. C. C. 1990. *The Peasant Family and Rural Development in the Yangzi Delta: 1350-1988,* Stanford University Press, Stanford, CA.

Huang, Y. 1990. 'Web of Interests and Patterns of Behavior of Chinese Local Economic Bureaucracies and Enterprises during Reforms', *The China Quarterly,* 123, September: pp. 431-458.

IMF 1990. IMF, IBRD, OECD, and EBRD. *The Economy of the USSR Summary and Recommendations.* Washington, DC.

Institute of Development, Agricultural Research Center of the State Council, 1987. *Making Choice for Modernization* [Zouxiang Xiandaihua de Jueze -- in Chinese], Economic Science Press, China.

Institute of Development, *Reform Is Facing Institutional Innovation,* Shanghai Sanlian Press, Shanghai, China.

Institute of Economic Research, China Academy of Social Science, 1987. *The Economic Development and Economic System of China's TVEs* [Zhongguo Xiangzhen Qiye de Jingji Fazhan yu Jingji Tizhi -- in Chinese], China Economic Press, Beijing, China.

Jefferson, G. and Rawski, T. 1994a. 'A Model of Endogenous Innovation, Competition and Property Rights Reform in Chinese Industry', Working Paper #289, Department of Economics, University of Pittsburgh, Pittsburgh, PA.

-------- 1994b. 'Enterprise Reform in Chinese Industry', *Journal of Economic Perspectives,* 8(2): pp. 47-70.

Jefferson, G. Rawski, T. and Zheng, Y. 1992a. 'Innovation and Reform in Chinese Industry: A preliminary Analysis of Survey Data', Working Paper, Department of Economics, Brandeis University, Waltham, MA.

-------- 1992b. 'Growth, Efficiency, and Convergence in China's State and Collective Industry', *Economic Development and Cultural Change*, 40(2): pp. 239-266.

Jefferson, G. and Xu, W. 1991. 'The Impact of Reform on Socialist Enterprises in Transition: Structure, Conduct, and Performance in Chinese Industry', *Journal of Comparative Economics*, 15: pp. 45-64.

Jiang, J. and Zhou, Y. 1990. 'An Assessment on TVEs' Efficiency inJiangsu Province' [Wosheng Xiangzhen Qiye Xiaoyi Pingjia -- in Chinese], *Nanjing University Journal: Social Science Edition*, 1990-4: pp. 124-129.

Jin, H. and Du, Z. 'The productivity of China's Rural Industry: Growth Rate and Regional Divergence', *Research on Rural Industrialization, Report #2* [in Chinese], China Academy of Social Science: Beijing, China.

Jin, H. and Qian, Y. 1998. 'Public vs. Private Ownership: Evidence from Rural China', *Quarterly Journal of Economics*, 113 (3 August), pp. 773-808

Joskow, P. 1987. 'Contract Duration and Relationship-Specific Investments', *American Economic Review*, 77(March): pp. 168-185.

-------- 1988. 'Assets Specificity and the Structure of Vertical Relationships: Empirical Evidence', *Journal of Law, Economics, and Organization*, 4(Spring).

Judge, G., Hill, R.C., Griffiths, W., Lutkepohl, H. and Lee, T. 1988. *Introduction to the Theory and Practice of Econometrics*, 2nd ed. John Wiley and Sons, Inc.

Kirsch, O., Worz, J., and Engel, J. 1994. *Agrarian Reform in China: Back to the Family Responsibility System*, Verlag fur Entwicklungspolitik Breitenbach GmbH: Saarbrucken, Germany.

Klein, P. and Shelanski, H. 1994. 'Empirical Research in Transaction Cost Economics: A Survey and Assessment', Working Paper, Department of Economics, University of California, Berkeley, CA.

Kornai, J. 1980. *Economics of Shortage*, North-Holand Publishing Co.

-------- 1990. *The Road to a Free Economy*, Norton, New York.

-------- 1992. *The Socialist System: The Political Economy of Communism*, Princeton University Press, Princeton.

Kung, J. and Liu, S. 1996. 'Contractual Change in 6 Wuxi Villages', Working Paper, Social Science Division, Hong Kong University of Science and Technology, Hong Kong.

Lardy, N. 1983. *Agriculture in China's Modern Economic Development*, Cambridge University Press, New York.

Larner, R. 1966. 'The 200 Largest Non-financial Corporations', *American Economic Review,* 56(September): pp. 777-787.

Li, D. 1995. 'A Theory of Ambiguous Property Rights in Transitional Economies', Working Paper, Department of Economics, University of Michigan, Ann Arbor, MI.

Li, K. 1992. *The Development of Chinese Rural Communities in A Transitional Society* [Shehui Bianqian Zhong de Zhongguo Nongcun Shequ Fazhan -- in Chinese], China Science and Technology Press, China.

Li, W. 1990. 'An Analysis on the Industrial Technical Progress of TVEs in Fujian Province' [Fujiansheng Xiangzhen Gongye Jishu Jinbu Zhuangkuang Fenxi -- in Chinese], *Fujian Jingji,* 1990-4: pp. 10-12.

Lin, J. 1993. 'Several Questions Regarding the Rural Industrialization of Large Developing Countries', [Guanyu Fazhan Zhong Daguo Nongcun Gongyehua Zhong de Jige Wenti -- in Chinese], *Academic Quarterly,* 1993-2. China.

Lin, J. Y. 1996, 'China's and the East Asian Miracles: An Analytical Interpretation', Working Paper, China Center for Economic Research, Beijing University, Beijing, China.

Lin, J.Y., Cai, F., and Li. Z. 1996. *The China Miracle: Development Strategy and Economic Reform,* The Chinese University of Hong Kong Press, Hong Kong.

-------- 1995. 'Creating a Fairly Competitive Environment is the Core of Enterprise Reform' [Qiye Gaige de Hexin Shi Chuangzao Gongping Jingzheng de Huanjing -- in Chinese], Working Paper Series #1995001, China Center for Economic Research, Beijing University, Beijing, China.

-------- 1995. 'Why China's Economic Reforms Have been Successful: Implications for Other Reforming Economies', Working Paper Series #E1995002, China Center for Economic Research, Beijing University, Beijing, China.

Lin, Q. 1990. 'Private Enterprises: Their Emergence, Rapid Growth, and Problems', in Byrd, W. and Lin, Q. eds. *China's Rural Industry: Structure, Development, and Reform,* Oxford University Press: London.

Liu, Y. 1992. 'Reform from Below: The Private Economy and Local Politics in the Rural Industrialization of Wenzhou', *The China Quarterly,* 130 (June): pp. 293-316.

Liu, Z. et al. 1995. *Property Rights, Markets, and Development*[Chanquan, Shichang, yu Fazhan -- in Chinese], Jiangsu People's Press, China.

Luo, X. 1990. 'Ownership and Status Stratification', in Byrd, W. and Lin, Q. eds. *China's Rural Industry: Structure, Development, and Reform,* Oxford University Press: London.

Lyons, T. 1991. 'Interprovincal Disparities in China: Output and Consumption, 1952-1987', *Economic Development and Cultural Change,* 39(3): pp. 471-506.

Ma, R., Huang, C., Wang, H., and Yang, M. eds. 1994. *Investigations on China's TVEs in 1990s* [Jiushi Niandai Xiangzhen Qiye Diaocha -- in Chinese], Oxford University Press: Hong Kong.

McKinnon, R.I. 1992. 'Spontaneous Order on the Road Back from Socialism: an Asian Perspective', *American Economic Review,* 82(May): pp. 31-36.

-------- 1994. 'Financial Growth and Macroeconomic Stability in China, 1978-1992: Implications for Russia and Other Transitional Economies',*Journal of Comparative Economics,* 18(June): pp. 438-469.

McMillan, J. 1994. 'China's Nonconformist Reform', Policy Paper #11,Institute on Global Conflict and Cooperation, University of California, San Diego, La Jolla, CA.

McMillan, J. and Naughton, B. 1991. 'How to Reform a Planned Economy: Lessons from China', *Oxford Review of Economics,* 8(1): pp. 130-144.

-------- eds. 1994. *Reforming Asian Socialism: The Growth of MarketInstitutions,* University of Michigan Press, Ann Arbor, MI.

Meng, X. 1990. 'The Structure of Labor Markets in Rural China's TVE Sector', in Byrd, W. and Lin, Q. eds. *China's Rural Industry: Structure, Development, and Reform,* Oxford University Press: London.

Milgrom, P. and Roberts, J. 1992. *Economics, Organization, and Management,* Prentice Hall.

Mo, Y. ed. 1987. *The Development History of Rural Industry in Jiangsu,* [Jiangsu Xiangzhen Gongye Fazhanshi -- in Chinese], Nanjing University of Industry Press, Nanjing, China.

Murrell, P. 1996. 'How Far Has the Transition Progressed?' *Journal of Economic Perspectives,* 10(2): pp. 25-44.

Murrell, P. and Wang, Y. 1993. 'When Privatization Should Be Delayed: The Effect of Communist Legacies on Organizational and Institutional Reform', *Journal of Comparative Economics,* 17(June): pp. 385-406.

Naughton, B. 1987. 'Macroeconomic Policy and Response in the Chinese Economy: the Impact of the Reform Process', *Journal of Comparative Economics,* 11(3): pp. 334-353.

-------- 1992. 'Hierarchy and the Bargaining Economy: Government and Enterprises in the Reform Process', in Lieberthal, K. and Lampton, D. eds. *Bureaucracy, Politics, Decision Making in Post-Mao China*, 245-279. University of California Press, Berkeley and Los Angeles, CA.

-------- 1994a. 'What is distinctive about China's Economic Transition? State Enterprises Reform and Overall System Transformation', *Journal of Comparative Economics*, 18(3), June: pp. 470-490.

------------ 1994b. 'Chinese Institutional Innovation and Privatization from Below', *China's Reforms: Structural and Welfare Aspects*, AEA Papers and Proceedings, *American Economic Review*, 84(2), May: pp. 266-270.

----------- 1995. *Growing Out of the Plan: Chinese Economic Reform: 1978-1993*, Cambridge University Press, New York.

----------- 1996. 'Why are [Some of] China's Rural Industries Publicly Owned', Working Paper, Graduate School of International Relations and Pacific Studies, University of California, San Diego, La Jolla, CA.

------------ 1997. *The China Circle*, Brookings Institution Press, Washington, DC.

Nee, V. 1989a. 'Toward an Institutional Analysis of State Socialism', in Nee, V. and Stark, D. eds. 1989. *Remaking the Economic Institutions of Socialism: China and Eastern Europe*, Stanford University Press, Stanford, CA.

----------- 1989b. 'Peasant Entrepreneurship and the Politics of Regulation in China', in Nee, V. and Stark. D. eds. 1989.

----------- 1992. 'Organizational Dynamics of Market Transition: Hybrid Forms, Property Rights, and Mixed Economy in China', *Administrative Science Quarterly*, 37 (March): pp. 1-27.

Nee, V. and Stark, D. eds. 1989. *Remaking the Economic Institutions of Socialism: China and East Europe*, Stanford University Press: Stanford, CA.

Nee, V. and Su, S. 1990. 'Institutional Change and Economic Growth in China: The View From the Villages', *Journal of Asian Studies*, 49 (February): pp. 3-25.

Nee, V. and Young, F.W. 1991. 'Peasant Entrepreneurs in China's 'Second Economy': An Institutional Analysis', *Economic Development and Cultural Change*, 39(2), January: pp. 293-308.

North, D. 1981. *Structure and Change In Economic History*, Norton, New York.

----------- 1983. 'A Theory of Economic Change', *Science*, 219: pp. 163-164.

----------- 1984a. 'Transaction Costs, Institutions, and Economic History', *Journal of Institutional and Theoretical Economics,* 140(March): pp. 7-17.

------------ 1984b. 'Three Approaches to the Study of Institutions', in Colander, D. ed. *Neoclassical Political Economy: The Analysis of Rent-seeking and DUP Activities:* pp. 33-40. Harper and Row, Ballinger.

------------ 1990. *Institutions, Institutional Changes, and Economic Performance,* Cambridge University Press, Cambridge.

------------ 1991. 'Institutions', *Journal of Economic Perspectives,* 5(1), Winter: pp. 97-112.

North, D. and Thomas, R.P. 1970. 'An Economic Theory of the Growth of the Western World', *The Economic History Review,* 22: pp. 1-17.

North, D. and Weingast, B. 1989. 'Constitutions and Credit Commitments: The Evolution of the Institutions of Public Choice in 17th Century England', *Journal of Economic History.*

Ody, A. J. 1992. 'Rural Enterprises Development in China, 1986-90', The World Bank Discussion Paper, No.162. The World Bank, Washington, DC.

OECD, 1996. *China in the 21st Century: Long-term Global Implications,* OECD, France.

Oi, J.C. 1989. *State and Peasant in Contemporary China: The PoliticalEconomy of Village Government,* University of California Press, CA.

----------- 1992. 'Fiscal Reform and the Economic Foundations of Local State Corporation in China', *World Politics,* 45 (October): pp. 99-126.

----------- 1995. 'The role of Local States In China's Transitional Economy', *The China Quarterly,* 144(December): pp. 1132-1149.

----------- 1996. *Rural China Takes Off: Incentives for Industrialization,* University of California Press, Berkeley, CA.

Otsuka, K., Chuma, H., and Hayami, Y. 1992. 'Land and Labor Contracts In Agrarian Economies: Theories and Facts', *Journal of Economic Literature,* 30(December): pp. 1965-2018.

Pan, W. 1996. *Politics of Marketization in Rural China: The Coalition Between Grassroots Authorities and Rural Industries.* Unpublished Ph. D. Dissertation, Department of Political Science, University of California, Berkeley, CA.

Parish, W. ed. 1985. *Chinese Rural Development: The Great Transformation,* M.E. Sharpe, New York.

Parris, K. 1993. 'Local Initiative and National Reform: the Wenzhou Model of Development', *The China Quarterly:* pp. 242-263.

Peng, Y. 1992. 'Wage Determination in Rural and Urban China: a Comparison of Public and Private Industrial Sectors', *American Sociology Review*, 57: pp. 198-213.

Perkins, D. 1994. 'Completing China's Move to the Market', *Journal of Economic Perspectives*, 8(2), Spring: pp. 23-46.

---------- 1996. 'China's Future: Economic and social Development Scenarios for the Twenty-first Century', in OECD: *China in the 21st Century: Long-term Global Implications*, OECD, France.

Perkins, D. et al. 1977. *Rural Small-Scale Industry in the People's Republic of China*, University of California Press, Berkeley, CA.

Perkins, D. and Yusuf, S. 1984. *Rural Development in China*, The World Bank, Washington, DC.

Pitt, M. and Putterman, L. 1995. 'Employment and Wages In Township, Village, and Other Rural Enterprises', Working Paper, Department of Economics, Brown University, Providence, RI.

Posner, R. 1993. 'The New Institutional Economics Meets Law and Economics', *Journal of Institutional and Theoretical Economics*, 149(1): pp. 73-87.

Poznanski, K. Z. 1993. 'Restructuring of Property Rights in Poland: A Study in Evolutionary Economics', *East European Politics and Societies*, 7: pp. 395-421.

Putterman, L. 1992. 'Dualism and Reform in China', *Economic Development and Cultural Change*, 40(April): pp. 467-493.

------------ 1993a. *Continuity and Change in China's Rural Development*, Oxford University Press: New York.

------------ 1993b. 'Ownership and the Nature of the Firm', *Journal of Comparative Economics*, 17: pp. 243-263.

------------ 1994. 'On the Past and Future of China's Township and Village Owned Enterprises', Working Paper, Department of Economics, Brown University, Providence, RI.

Ranis, G. and Stewart, F. 1993. 'Rural Nonagricultural Activities in Development: Theory and Applications', *Journal of Development Economics*, 40(1), February: pp. 75-101.

Rapaczynski, A. 1996. 'The role of the State and the Market in Establishing Property Rights', *Journal of Economic Perspectives*, 10(2), Spring: pp. 87-103.

Rausser, G. 1992. 'Lessons for Emerging Market Economies in Eastern Europe', in Clague, C. and Rausser, G. eds. *The Emergence of Market Economies in Eastern Europe*, pp. 311-332. Basil Blackwell: Cambridge, MA.

Rausser, G. and Simon, L. 1992. 'The Political Economy of Transition in Eastern Europe', in Clague, C. and Rausser, G. eds. Basil Blackwell: Cambridge, MA.

Rawski, T. 1994. 'Chinese Industrial Reform: Accomplishments, Prospects,and Implications', *China's Reforms: Structural and Welfare Aspects*, AEA Papers and Proceedings, *American Economic Review*, 84(2), May: pp. 271-275.

----------- 1995a. 'Institutional Aspects of China's Emergence As a Market Economy', Working Paper, Department of Economics, University of Pittsburgh, Pittsburgh, PA.

----------- 1995b. 'Who Has Soft Budget Constraints?' Working Paper, Department of Economics, University of Pittsburgh, Pittsburgh, PA.

----------- 1995c. 'Implications of China's Reform Experience', Working Paper, Department of Economics, University of Pittsburgh, Pittsburgh,PA.

Reynolds, B. ed. 1987. *Reform in China: Challenges and Choices*, M.E. Sharpe, New York.

----------- ed. 1988. *Chinese Economic Reform: How Far? How Fast?* Academic Press.

Riordan, M. and Williamson, O. 1985. 'Asset Specificity and Economic Organization', *International Journal of Industrial Organization*, 3: pp. 365-378. North-Holland.

Riskin, C. 1994. 'Chinese Rural Poverty: Marginalized or Dispersed?' *China's Reforms: Structural and Welfare Aspects*, AEA Papers and Proceedings, *American Economic Review*, 84(2): pp. 281-284.

Rozelle, S. 1994. 'Decision-making in China's Rural Economy: the Linkage Between Village Leaders and Farm Households', *The China Quarterly*, March: pp. 99-122.

Rozelle, S. and Boisvert, R. 1994. 'Quantifying Chinese Village Leaders' Multiple Objectives', *Journal of Comparative Economics*, 18(1), February: pp. 25-45.

Rural Development Institute of China Social Science Academy, 1988. *Research Report on China's Rural Industrial Structure* [Zhongguo Nongcun Chanye Jiegou Yanjiu Baogao -- in Chinese], China Social Science Academy, China.

Ruttan, V. 1991. 'What Happened to Political Development?' *Economic Development and Cultural Change,* 39(2), January: pp. 265-292.

Ruttan, V. and Hayami, Y. 1984. 'Toward a Theory of Induced Institutional Innovation', *Journal of Development Studies,* 20(4), July: pp. 203-223.

Sachs, J. D. 1992. 'Privatization in Russia: Some Lessons From Eastern Europe', *American Economic Review,* 80(May): pp. 43-48.

Sachs, J. D. and Woo, W. T. 1994. 'Structural Factors in the Economic Reform of China, Eastern Europe, and Former Soviet Union', *Economic Policy,* 18(1): pp. 102-145.

Samuelson, P. 1966. *Economics,* 7th edition, New York: Mcgraw Hill.

Schmid, A. 1972. 'Analytical Institutional Economics', *America Journal of Agricultural Economics,* 54: pp. 893-901.

Schultz, T.W. 1975. 'The Value of the Ability to Deal with Disequilibria', *Journal of Economic Literature,* 13: pp. 822-846.

Sen, A. 1966. 'Peasants and Dualism with or without Surplus Labor', *Journal of Political Economy,* 74(5): pp. 425-450.

Shirk, S. L. 1993. *The Political Logic of Economic Reform in China,* University of California Press, Berkeley, CA.

Simon, H. 1957. *Models of Man,* Wiley: New York.

---------- 1961. *Administrative Behavior,* 2nd ed. Macmillan: New York.

Smith, S. 1995. 'Employee Participation in China's TVEs', *China Economic Review,* 6(1): pp. 157-167.

Singh, I., Ratha, D., and Xiao, G. 1993. 'Non-state Enterprises as an Engine of Growth: An Analysis of Provincial Industrial Growth in Post-Reform China', World Bank Research Paper Series, China, CH-RPS No.20, Washington, DC.

Song, L. and Du, N. 1990. 'The Role of Township Governments in Rural Industrialization', in Byrd, W. and Lin, Q. eds. *China's Rural Industry: Structure, Development, and Reform,* Oxford University Press: London.

Stark, D. 1989. 'Coexisting Organizational Forms in Hungary's Emerging Mixed Economy', in Nee, V. and Stark, D. eds. 1989. *Remaking the Economic Institutions of Socialism: China and Eastern Europe,* Stanford University, Stanford, CA.

Stigler, G. 1992. 'Law and Economics', *Journal of Law and Economics,* 35(October): pp. 455- 468.

Stiglitz, J. 1974. 'Incentives and Risk Sharing in Sharecropping', *Review of Economic Studies,* 41: pp. 219-257.

---------- 1989. 'Markets, Market Failures, and Development', *American Economic Review,* 79: pp. 197-203.

Svejnar, J. 1990a. 'Productive Efficiency and Employment', in Byrd, W. and Lin, Q. eds. *China's Rural Industry.*

---------- 1990b. 'Productive Efficiency and Employment', in Byrd, W. and Lin, Q. eds. *China's Rural Industry.*

Tian, G. 1994. 'A Theory of Endogenous Ownership Arrangements in Imperfect Market and Transitional Economies', Working Paper, Texas A & M University.

---------- 1995. 'State-owned Enterprise Reform and Smooth Institutional Transition in China -- A Three-stage economic Reform Method', Working Paper, Department of Economics, Texas A & M University, TX.

Tsai, L. 1995. 'Report on Field Trip', Memo, Stanford University, Stanford, CA.

Walder, A. 1989. 'Factory and Manager in an Era of Reform', *The China Quarterly,* 118: pp. 242-264.

---------- 1991. 'Workers, Managers, and the State: The Reform Era and the Political Crisis of 1989', *The China Quarterly,* 127: pp. 467-492.

---------- 1992. 'Property Rights and Stratification in Socialist Redistributive Economy', *American Sociology Review,* 57: pp. 524-539.

---------- 1994. 'Corporate Organization and Local Property Rights in China', in Milor, V. ed. *Changing Political Economies: Privatization in Post-communist and Reforming Communist States,* pp. 53-66. Lynne Rienner: Boulder, Colo.

---------- 1995a. 'Local Government as Industrial Firm: An Organizational Analysis of China's Transitional Economy', *American Journal of Sociology,* 101(2), September: pp. 263-301.

---------- 1995b. 'China's Transitional Economy: Interpreting its Significance', *The China Quarterly,* 144(December).

---------- 1996 ed. *China's Transitional Economy,* Oxford University Press.

Wang, G. and Yu, D. et al. 1991. *On the Industrial Structure of Rural China* [Zhongguo Nongcun Chanye Jiegou Run -- in Chinese], People's Press, China.

Wang, W. et al. ed. 1988. *An Introduction to China's TVEs* [Zhongguo Xiangzhen Qiye GaiRun -- in Chinese], Shanghai Social Science Press,Shanghai, China.

Wang, X. 1990. 'Capital Formation and Utilization', in Byrd, W. and Lin,Q. eds. *China's Rural Industry.*

Weingast, B. 1993. 'Constitutions as Governance Structures: the Political Foundations of Secure Markets', *Journal of Institutional and Theoretical Economics,* 149(1): pp. 286-311.

----------- 1995. 'The Economic Role of Political Institutions: Market-preserving Federalism and Economic Growth', *Journal of Law, Economics, and Organization,* Spring.

Weitzman, M. and Xu, C. 1994. 'Chinese Township Village Enterprises as Vaguely Defined Cooperatives', *Journal of Comparative Economics,* 18(2), April: pp. 121-145.

Wen, G. J. and Xu, D. 1996. *The Reformability of China's State Sector,* World Scientific Publishing Co. Singapore.

Whiting, S. 1993. 'Contract Incentives and Market Discipline in China's Rural Industrial Sector', mimeo, University of Michigan, Ann Arbor.

----------- 1995. *The Micro-foundation of Institutional Change in Reform China: Property Rights and Revenue Extraction in the Rural Industrial Sector.* Unpublished Ph.D. Dissertation. Department of Political Science, University of Michigan, Ann Arbor, MI.

Williamson, O. 1975. *Markets and Hierarchies,* Free Press, New York.

----------- 1979. 'Transaction-cost Economics: the Governance of Contractual Relations', *Journal of Law and Economics,* 22(October): pp. 233-261.

------------ 1981. 'The Modern Corporation: Origins, Evolution, Attributes', *Journal of Economic Literature,* 19(December): pp. 1537-1568.

------------ 1985. *The Economic Institutions of Capitalism,* The Free Press, New York.

------------ 1987. 'Transaction Cost Economics: The Comparative Contracting Perspective', *Journal of Economic Behavior and Organization.*

------------ 1996. *The Mechanism of Governance,* Oxford University Press.

Williamson, O. and Winter, S. eds. 1991. *The Nature of the Firm, Origins, Evolution, and Development,* Oxford University press: Oxford.

Winiecki, J. 1990. 'Why Economic Reform Fail in the Soviet System', *Economic Inquiry,* 28(April): pp. 195-221.

Wong, C. 1987. 'Between Plan and Market: the Role of the Local Sector in Post-Mao China', *Journal of Comparative Economics,* 11: pp. 385-398.

------------ 1991. 'Central-local Relations in an Era of Fiscal Decline: the Paradox of Fiscal Decentralization in Post-Mao China', *The China Quarterly,* 128(December): pp. 691-715.

------------ 1992. 'Fiscal Reform and Local Industrialization: the Problematic Sequencing of Reform in Post-Mao China', *Modern China*, 18: pp. 197-227.

Woo, W. T., Fan, G., Hai, W., and Jin, Y. 1993. 'The Efficiency and Macroeconomic Consequences of Chinese Enterprises Reform', *China Economic Review*, 4: pp. 153-168.

Woo, W. T., Hai, W., Jin, Y., and Fan, G. 1993. 'How Successful Has Chinese Enterprises Reform Been? Pitfalls In Opposite Biases and Focus', *Journal of Comparative Economics*, 18: pp. 410-437.

Wu, J. 1993. 'An Empirical Study on the Stagnation in China TVEs' Employment Growth and the Policy Suggestions', [Woguo Xiangzhen Qiye Giuye Zengzhang Paihuai de Shizheng Fenxi Yu Duice Yanjiu -- in Chinese], *Study and Exploration*, 1993-5. China.

Xie, Z. and Lin, Y. eds. 1994. *A Research On the Operation Mechanism of TVEs* [Xiangzhen Qiye Yunxing Jizhi Yanjiu -- in Chinese], Shanghai Social Science Academy Press, Shanghai, China.

Xu, D., Lui, F. and Chang, H. eds. 1991, *China's Economic Reform: Analysis, Reflections, and Prospects* [Zhongguo Jingji Gaige: Fenxi, Fanying Qianzhan in Chinese], The Chinese University of Hong Kong, Hong Kong.

Yan, C. 1994. 'The Technical Measures in the Property Rights Clarification of China's TVEs', [Zhongguo Xiangzhen Qiye Chanquan Mingxihua de Jishu Chuli -- in Chinese], Paper Presented at the *International Conference on the Property Rights Reform in China's TVEs*, Hangzhou, China.

Yang, D. 1990. 'Patterns of China's Regional Development Strategy', *The China Quarterly*, 122(June): pp. 230-257.

Yang, D. 1995. 'Economic Institutions and Labor Market Efficiency', Paper Prepared for the Symposium on *Transformation of the Chinese State Enterprises*, Shanghai, China.

Yang, M. 1994. 'Discussion: How the 'TVE miracle' emerged in China'[TaoRun: Zhongguo Xiangzhen Qiye de Qiji Shi Zenyang Chuxian de – in Chinese], in Ma et al. eds.

Yu, C. 1994. 'The Investigation on C Township X Technical School Training Factory' [C Zhen X Jigong Xuexiao Disan Shixi Fenchan -- in Chinese], in Ma et al. eds.

Yu, C. and Huang, H. eds. 1991. *TVEs in Modern China* [Dangdai Zhongguo de Xiangzhen Qiye -- in Chinese], Modern China Press, Beijing, China.

Yu, D. ed. 1992. *The Investigation Data on Rural Household Economic Behavior and the Labor Time Utilization* [Nonghu Jingji Xinwei Ji Laodong Shijian Liyong Diaocha Ziliaoji -- in Chinese], China Statistics Press, China.

Yu, J., Zhan, Y., and Sun, W. eds. 1995. *Rural Cooperative Economy and Its Management* [Nongcun Hezuo Jingji Yu Guanli -- in Chinese], People's Press, China.

Yu, Y. ed. 1991. *TVEs Research* [Xiangzhen Qiye Yanjiu -- in Chinese], China Economic, Press, Beijing, China.

Zhang, W. 1995. 'Decision Rights, Residual Claim and Performance: A Theory of How the Chinese State Enterprises Reform Works', Working Paper Series #E1995004, China Center for Economic Research, Beijing University, Beijing, China.

Zhang, W. and Yi, G. 1995. 'China's Gradual Reform: A Historical Perspective', Working Paper Series #E1995001, China Center for Economic Research, Beijing University, Beijing, China.

Zhang, Y. 1993. *China's TVEs toward 21st Century* [Benxiang 21 Shiji de Zhongguo Xiangzhen Qiye -- in Chinese], Beijing Press, Beijing, China.

Zhou, H. and Zhou, D. eds. 1996. *Research on the Development Characteristics of Suzhou-Wuxi-Changzhou Regions* [Suxichang FaZhan Tese Yanjiu -- in Chinese], People's Daily Press, China.

Zhou, K. 1993. 'Recent Inter-regional Economic Conflict in China and the Means to Solve It' [Dangqian Woguo Quji Jingji Guanxi de Maodun Yu Duice -- in Chinese], *East China Normal University Journal,* Shanghai, China.

Zhou, Q. and Hu, Z. 1987. 'Assets Formation, Operational Features, and Macro -economic Impact of TVEs: an Analysis of a Sample Survey of Large Township Enterprises in Ten Provinces' [Zhongguo Xiangzhen Gongye Qiye de Zichan Xingcheng, Yingyun Tezheng, Jiqi Hongguan Xiaoying -- dui 10 Sheng Daxing Xiangzhen Gongye Qiye Chouyang Diaocha de Fenxi -- in Chinese], *China Social Science,* 1987-6.

Zhou, S. and Liu, J. 1993. *China's Township and Village Enterprises* [Xiangzhen Qiye Xue -- in Chinese], Shanghai People's Press, Shanghai China.

Zweig, D. 1991. 'Internationalizing China's Countryside: The Political Economy of Exports from Rural Industry', *The China Quarterly,* 128 (December): pp. 716-741.

ZGNYNJ. China Agricultural Yearbook, 1990; 1991; 1994 [ZhongguoNongye Nianjian -- in Chinese]. State Statistical Bureau: Beijing, China.

ZGTJNJ. China Statistical Yearbook, Various Volumes [Zhongguo Tongji Nianjian -- in Chinese]. State Statistical Bureau: Beijing, China.

ZGWJNJ. China Price Yearbook, Various volumes [Zhongguo Wujia Nianjian -- in Chinese]

ZGXZQYNJ. China TVE Yearbook, Various Volumes [Zhongguo Xiangzhen Qiye Nianjian -- in Chinese]. China Agricultural Press, Beijing, China.

ZGXZQYTJ. China TVE Statistics, Various Volumes [Zhongguo Xiangzhen Qiye Tongji -- in Chinese]. China Statistics Press, Beijing, China.

Index